Champions for Life

By John B. Scott and James S. Ward
Edited by Bob Allen and Joe Wojcik
Foreword by Chuck Cobb
2004

FIRST EDITION

Copyright © 2004 by John B. Scott and James S. Ward

Printed in the United States of America

Printed on acid-free paper

Library of Congress Cataloging-in-Publication Data has been applied for.

ISBN # 0-9760447-3-0

Publisher:
     Nicholas Ward Publishing LLC
     3095 Scioto Trace Road
     Columbus, Ohio 43221

     SAN number 256-2669

In memory of David Barrett Scott, U.S. Navy SEAL officer (nine years) and older son of co-author John B. Scott. David died in an accident while deployed overseas with his SEAL team.

Foreword

This is a thoughtful book on the life of Payton Jordan who created and instilled "champions for life." Payton Jordan is not only individually a "champion for life," he also succeeded in bringing out the "champions for life" in all whom he coached and mentored.

It is an honor for me to write the Foreword for this definitive book on the life of Payton Jordan, as he is the teacher, coach and role model that most influenced my life. As you read this book, you will learn that there were many hundreds of us that attribute our life successes to his motivation and discipline. He inspired us to perform like champions, act like champions, dress like champions, groom like champions and to speak like champions.

Payton Jordan was a legendary athlete and coach whose lasting legacy is that of a teacher of character and a teacher of team building. The Payton Jordan lessons have been invaluable to me as a business leader, as a civic leader, as a university chairman, as a government official, as an Ambassador and as a parent. *Champions for Life* explains how Payton Jordan taught so many of us these valuable lessons.

The setting for this book is the middle of the 20th Century when track and field in the United States was one of our major sports and when Payton Jordan frequently had 60,000 spectators a day in Stanford Stadium (the 1960 U.S. Olympic Trials and the 1962 USA/USSR meet). This is the story of how Payton Jordan helped make track and field one of America's most popular pastimes.

Some teachers exhibit their genius in the classroom and some in the laboratory. Payton Jordan articulated his genius everyday on Angell Field where the Stanford track team and local Olympic athletes trained. I am honored that this facility now is called Cobb Track and Angell Field, a majestic setting on the beautiful Stanford campus at the foot of Hoover Tower. The authors do a superb job of describing this setting and its context during a period of great social upheaval in America.

I had the pleasure of spending eight years of my life on the Stanford campus - four years as an undergraduate, two years stationed at the Stanford Navy ROTC unit while training under Coach Jordan for the Olympics, and two years gaining my MBA at the Stanford Business School. All who came in contact with Payton Jordan during their time at Stanford were richly rewarded. With my eight years, I was fortunate to benefit from the Jordan magic more than most. The authors of this book explain how the Jordan magic works and how so many of us were blessed to become one of his "champions for life."

There have been many "beloved coaches books" written over the years. This is not just another beloved coaches book. This is a book about how one individual dramatically changed the lives of his disciples. This also is not a 12-step guide to character improvement, but the reader instead will experience Payton Jordan's philosophy first hand, read of his team building lessons, and read teammate testimonials written with the benefit of four decades of hindsight and reflection. When was the last book or article you read or television coverage you saw laud real character much less character development? I know the reader will find that in this book as you "experience Payton Jordan."

I am sure you are going to enjoy this read.

Chuck Cobb
September 2004

Authors' Note
During the mid-1950s Chuck Cobb was a Stanford hurdler, team captain, holder of several school records, and an All-American. After completing his Stanford undergraduate work, Chuck was the alternate for the 110-meter high hurdles on the 1960 USA Olympic team. His official winning times of 13.7 for the 110-meter high hurdles and 22.8 for the 200-meter low hurdles still remain the best times by a Stanford athlete or graduate 45 years later. Chuck made the lead financial gift that enabled Stanford to recreate Cobb Track and Angell Field in the 1990s. He has been a successful corporate CEO of several companies, a board member of seven public companies including The Walt Disney Company, Chairman of the Board of Trustees of the University of Miami, an Under Secretary of Commerce for President Reagan, and U.S. Ambassador for President George H. W. Bush. Chuck credits Payton Jordan with being the teacher, coach and role model that most influenced his life. Coach Jordan also has had a profound impact on the life of Chuck's wife of 45 years, Ambassador Sue Cobb, the U.S. Ambassador to Jamaica. Ambassador Sue also is a Stanford graduate, a lawyer and the author of *The Edge of Everest*, where she chronicles her attempt to be the first American woman to summit Mt. Everest.

John B. Scott
James S. Ward

Preface

As a star athlete at the University of Southern California, Payton Jordan may have been California's first "golden boy." In 1938, he ran on the 440-yard relay team that set a world record. In 1939, he played on the Trojan football team that beat previously un-scored upon Duke 7-3 in Rose Bowl. He also played rugby. He then captained the track team to a repeat NCAA championship. As a result of these achievements, he was featured on the cover of *LIFE* magazine with the caption, "Captain of Champions."

As an inspirational coach at Redlands High School, Occidental College, and finally Stanford University, Jordan produced 13 Olympians, 7 world records, and 11 national champions. In the 1964 Olympics he was first assistant coach of the USA men's track and field team. As head coach of the 1968 USA men's track & field team in Mexico City, he brought his team together in the face of turbulent social pressures and produced the most successful results of any Olympic men's track & field team: a record 24 medals, 12 of them gold. Jordan, subsequently, has been honored at the 2000 and 2004 USA Olympic Trials as the most successful and, now, senior living Olympic coach.

However, Payton Jordan is more than a successful competitor and coach. His former student-athletes, now with the benefit of four decades of hindsight, remember him foremost as a teacher of character. He exhorted all his athletes to stretch their limits of what is possible on the track, in the classroom, and in life overall. His lessons on "being a champion" on the track as well as in life are his lasting legacy. When asked what is his greatest memory as a competitor and coach, Jordan responded without hesitation, "Having eighteen young men I coached name their children after me."

Acknowledgements

- Payton Jordan for sharing his extensive files, insight, and wisdom.

- Marge Jordan for permitting Payton to devote such time to this effort.

- Cheryl and Marnie who shared their father with so many appreciative teammates.

- Julie Ward and sons Travis, Nick, Zack, and Grayson, who consistently encouraged and supported Jim's undertaking such a major project.

- Maggie Scott and son Michael, who encouraged Jack to take on writing the book, assisted with proofreading, and were understanding of the time commitment it involved.

- Ellen Lyons Santiago, great Stanford distance runner of the 80s, who wrote the chapter on Post-Jordan Era: Stanford Women's Athletics.

- Editors Bob Allen and Joe Wojcik. Bob, Stanford graduate and professional editor, provided a valuable inside perspective. Joe, West Point graduate and long-time marathoner, provided a valuable non-Stanford perspective.

- David Lee and Ed Locker, Jim Ward's business partners, who demonstrated understanding and support with their company facilities and resources, as well as providing thoughts and ideas in the early formation of the book.

- Aurelia Figueroa, full-time student at San Jose State University, who helped Jim Ward launch the project.

- Stacy Geiken, former teammate and now noted photographer, who took the authors' vision and made it a vivid reality in the cover photo; Eunice Ockerman who provided the professional jacket design.

- Chuck Cobb, Stanford All-American, business leader, and U.S. Ambassador, who wrote the Foreword; Pitch Johnson, long-time friend of Stanford track and field, who wrote the Concluding Comment.

- Craig Barrett, Laura Hillenbrand, Jack Kemp, Bob Mathias, and John Wooden who provided supportive testimonials included on the jacket.

- Bob Murphy, former Stanford Sports Information Director and now broadcaster affectionately known as "the Voice of the Cardinal," who wrote the inside-jacket testimonial.

- Gordon Forbes, Sports Writer at USA TODAY, for valuable guidance and direction.

- Rich Karlgaard, publisher of Forbes magazine and former teammate, for professional advice and encouragement.

- Dave Milliman and Steve Simmons, who reviewed and commented on the text.

- Jim Mauro for his valuable assistance with organizational and production matters.

- Brook Thomas, professor of English & Comparative Literature at the University of California, Irving and former Stanford All-American, who prepared the write-up on Marshall Clark.

- Phil Conley, Olympian, Stanford volunteer coach and friend, for his enthusiastic support throughout.

- John Kates, recently retired from the Stanford Department of Athletics, who helped with research and direction.

- Keith Peters, long-time Bay Area sports writer, who provided numerous ideas and research material.

- Kristin Fowle and Samrath Chem, full-time students at Ohio State University, who helped research and edit teammate write-ups.

- Earleen Chapman and Wendy Symes of Technigraphics, Inc. of Wilmington, DE for their professional service preparing the printer proof including the photo layout.

- Andrew Grant of Ocean Gate, NJ for his professional service preparing the index.

- Over 200 former Stanford, Occidental, and Redlands teammates, faculty, coaches, Olympians, and track and field enthusiasts, who responded enthusiastically to our request for their input.

Table of Contents

Foreword iv
Preface vi
Acknowledgements vii

1. The Greatest Track and Field Meet of All Times 1
2. Payton Jordan: Youth through High School 7
3. On to USC and Captain of Champions 10
4. Jamaican Olympiad 15
5. WWII Military Service 17
6. In Redlands They Still Call Him Coach 19
7. At "Oxy" They Call Him the "Coach of Champions" 23
8. Greece: A Timeless Friendship 29
9. 1960 USA Olympic Trials 33
10. 1968 Olympics: Trying Times - Greatest Team 35
11. Stanford Jordan-Era: Facts and Stats 43
12. Stanford Years: 1957 through 1961 45
13. Stanford Years: 1962 through 1967 52
14. Stanford Years: 1968 through 1973 63
15. Stanford Years: 1974 through 1979 70
16. Post-Jordan Era: Coach of the Coaches 78
17. Post-Jordan Era: Stanford Women's Athletics 85
18. A Masters Runner Enjoying the Quality of Life 87
19. Namesakes 92
20. Concluding Comment 94
21. Epilogue 95
    Index 98

Stanford Jordan-Era Track and Field Supplement 103
    I.   Payton Jordan: Awards and Positions Held as Sports Ambassador 105
    II. Assistant and Volunteer Coaches 107
    III. Team Captains 113
    IV. Top-10 Stanford Marks with Jordan-Era Marks Highlighted 115
    V.   Varsity Team Rosters 120
    VI. Teammate Write-ups 142

1. The Greatest Track and Field Meet of All Times

*"I have just seen the greatest sports spectacle of my life." - Badin Birukov,
reporter for the Soviet news agency, TASS*

It was July 1962 and the location was Stanford, California. It was USA versus the USSR. Quite simply, it was the greatest track and field meet of all times.

President John F. Kennedy wrote in a letter that appeared in the program for the track meet, "The love of youth for athletics is worldwide, and nothing can enhance international understanding more, or better, than the kind of game which will take place in Stanford."

But, this was the height of the Cold War Era. Just eleven months earlier, the two superpowers had locked horns over building of the Berlin Wall. And, little did anyone know at the time of the meet, the Soviets were preparing missile sites in Cuba. In just 90 days, the world would be on the verge of nuclear war.

Nevertheless, the two nations, as different as their political beliefs, came together on a playing field. It was East against West, the Reds against the Red, White and Blue, and the Hammer and Sickle against the Stars and Stripes. It was the ultimate rivalry. And, a two-day crowd of 153,500 was the largest ever to watch a track and field meet in the United States. It also was the first track meet to be televised nationally.

For a brief few days, the Cold War seemed to thaw a bit - at least for the athletes and spectators at Stanford. Enemies became close friends. People cheered. And, they cried. "It was a wonderful moment," according to Jordan, Stanford's head track coach who organized what many have called the greatest track and field meet in U.S. history. "It had more value in that respect than any Olympics I've ever been to. I constantly hear people say it was the best event they've been to in their lifetime. You'll never see it again. It was a one-time thing."

"It all seemed to go downhill after Stanford," said Jon Hendershott, associate editor of *Track & Field News* magazine and a former national track writer of the year. "In 1962, it was the Big Red Menace, it was us versus them. It was long gone by the 1970s. The desire and need for international dual meets just died."

While the Stanford meet was not the last between the two countries, its successors never matched the intensity, spectator enthusiasm, or camaraderie among athletes. Two years later, the U.S. hosted the event in Los Angeles and attendance was down to 40,000. In 1978 a Soviet team came to Berkeley for what was the last dual meet with the USA and fewer than 22,000 attended.

Hastening the demise of such a grand track & field event was the European circuit and start-up of the Grand Prix system that focused entirely on individual performance, not team competition. Significant prize money became available to top athletes. The call of one's country was replaced by the call of rich meet promoters.[1]

---

[1] Keith Peters, U.S. vs. U.S.S.R., *Peninsula Times Tribune.*

How the Meet Came to Stanford

Fortunately, the 1962 meet came about as a way to solve a budget deficit in the Stanford Athletic Department. The 1960 Stanford football team had compiled a 0-10 record and the department was $100,000 in the red. The late Al Masters, then the athletic director, approached Jordan and asked if a track meet could generate revenue. Jordan said, "Sure." Then, Masters asked, "Do you think we could get the Russians here?" Jordan, of course, made it happen.

As a premier world-class sprinter in the late 1930s and the early 1940s, Jordan had received a letter from a Soviet athlete asking for some training tips. Jordan responded. That athlete, Gavriel Korobkov, later became head coach of the Soviet track and field team. Jordan, one of three USA coaches selected to take a U.S. Team to compete in Moscow in 1958, finally met Korobkov - and a friendship developed. It was Korobkov whom Jordan contacted for the 1962 meet.

Following long planning sessions to make sure everything would run smoothly, Stanford put up $125,000 to cover the cost to bring the Soviet team to the West Coast for the first time. In those days there was a small but dedicated Athletic Department staff to help Jordan bring about this major event. In addition to Jordan there was Al Masters, Chuck Taylor, Bob Young, Mel Nelson, Eunice DuPrau, Don Liebendorfer, and a secretarial staff. And, after splitting the proceeds with the Russians and the U.S. Amateur Athletic Union, Stanford netted about $150,000. "That was the first big money we ever made," noted Bob Young.

Jordan: Master of Planning and Execution

"My aim is to make this the greatest track and field meet ever held in this country," said Jordan with respect to preparation leading up to the July meet. "This meet will have the flavor of the Olympics with flags, bands, and the teams marching into the stadium."

As meet director, Jordan had 121 people working directly under him to conduct the practice sessions and meet. "We tried not to miss even any small detail," said Jordan. "We tried some new things that never had been done before, like rotating scoreboards that could be turned so all the fans in the stadium could see. I had fellows on the field who would fill in divots made during the field events, fill them with sand and spray paint the sand green."

This was to be the very first nationally televised track meet in America. Since such coverage was a new undertaking for both the ABC network and Stanford, Jordan had become concerned that cameramen and technicians on the playing field could interfere with the athletes' performances and the spectators' views. So, Jordan called John Howard, ABC vice president in New York, and pointed out that on-field TV technicians could create a problem. After listening to the persuasive Jordan, Howard instructed his folks at Stanford Stadium to go along with Jordan's request, which was to restrict the on-field crew to just two roving cameramen.[2]

Not only did the details of the meet need attention, but arrangements also had to be made to house and feed both the USA and USSR teams on campus, visit private homes

---

[2] Walt Gamage, Sport Shots.

in the area, and take them on tours that included San Francisco. "It required a great deal of organization involving folks in many functions: dormitory and food service, grounds crew, university and athletic department staff, local residents who volunteered their time and services, and strong support both during and after the meet by local writers such as Walt Gamage, Keith Peters, and Harry Press. It was gratifying to see everyone take such pride in their work," said Jordan, who, along with his many colleagues, worked long hours during the weeks leading up to the meet. Because of the political situation, "there were government agencies involved, too, and that added to the complexities," Jordan noted.

The Meet

"This community went for it hook, line, and sinker," Jordan said. "They embraced the meet and the people." Soviet workouts attracted crowds of 5,000 to Angell Field and Stanford Stadium. After all, it was a chance to see the "Reds," as the media described them during their stay. Local residents, however, discovered that these strangers from behind the Iron Curtain were hardly cold-hearted individuals. "People sat there and saw the Soviet athletes were decent human beings," Jordan said, recalling the moment when Soviet woman discus and shot put winner Tamara Press, unable to bend down to receive her gold medal, picked up AAU official Harold Berlinger and gave him a big kiss as he placed the medal around her neck.

The USA men won with a score of 127 to 108. The Soviet women won with a score of 66 to 41. Memorable highlights included.

- Soviet high jumper Valeri Brumel broke his own world record with a leap of 7'5". "Nobody who was there will ever forget that moment," said Jordan, "The crowd exploded like a cannon going off."

- Olympic medallist Wilma Rudolph, who had overcome so much adversity including polio as a child, won the 100 meters and ran the anchor leg for the USA women's victorious 4x100 meter relay team.

- American hammer thrower, Hal Connolly, bettered his world record with a throw of 231'10".

- USA Team co-captain, Jim Beatty, won the 1500 meters in an American record time of 3:39.9, a time roughly equivalent to a 3:57 mile.

- American discus thrower, Al Oerter exceeded the listed world record in the event with a winning toss of 200'1". USA teammate, Rink Babka, came in second.

- New meet records were established by Willie Atterberry in the 400-meter hurdles (50.3), Jerry Siebert in the 800 meters (1:46.4), and the American quartet of Ray Saddler, Rex Cawley, Dave Archibald, and Ulis Williams in the 4x400 meter relay.

- George Young and Pat Traynor placed second and third in the 3000-meter steeplechase after Young fell during the race.

- Paul Drayton led the USA to victory in the 200 meters and future NFL star Bob Hayes, won the 100 meters.

- Soviet winners included Nikolai Sokolov in the steeplechase, Janis Lusis in the javelin, and Vasily Kuznetsov in the decathlon.

But the best was saved for last. The planned closing ceremony was to have been a line-up of the two teams, parallel across one end of the football field. Flag-bearers John Thomas of the USA and Viktor Tsibulenko of the USSR were to lead the teams off the field and exit at the open end of the stadium. With a band blaring a march and the teams leaving to a standing ovation, Tsibulenko turned to Thomas and said in broken English: "We go all the way around, yes?" Thomas nodded and the teams headed to a victory lap. Then something special happened. American and Russian men and women began slipping arm through arm, putting arms around each others shoulders and intertwining the white USA uniforms with the red and blue of the USSR. They no longer were in separate lines. Instead, they were two groups of great athletes, now, marching as one.

It was an emotional scene as the 81,000 spectators stood and applauded. Many were in tears. They had all witnessed something special, something historic, and something that never would happen, again.[3]

Post-Meet Comments
With his recognized international track prominence, infectious positive attitude, and attention to detail, Jordan proved to be the ideal meet promoter and press corps liaison.

Joseph M. Sheehan, of the New York Times reported, "A festive crowd of 81,000 at Stanford Stadium brought the two-day attendance to 153,500 for this greatest United States track and field spectacle since the 1932 Olympics. The spectators more than got their money's worth."[4]

Paul Zimmerman of the Los Angeles Times commented, "Time was when Southern California could claim the undisputed title of the track and field capital of the world, no more. The great outpouring of fans at Stanford Stadium these last two days for the meet between the United States and Russia, coming on top of the Olympic trials here two years ago, certainly should clinch the honor for Northern California."[5]

Badin Birukov, a reporter for the Soviet news agency, TASS, led off his story with these glowing words: "I have just seen the greatest sports spectacle of my life." It's safe to say that Birukov did. What happened in July 1962 at Stanford Stadium was a moment in history that likely never will be repeated.[6]

And, Soviet Coach Korobkov commented, "That was a magnificent meet at Stanford. It was one of the great memories of my life, especially the closing part where the athletes of both countries embraced one another. That Payton Jordan was a marvel. He organized that meet without a mistake. And, I mean to say, without a mistake. I must say frankly that we were quite disappointed in the [Soviet-American] track meet in Philadelphia in 1959. But now we understand that the capital of track and field in the United States is the West Coast."[7]

---

[3] Keith Peters, U.S. vs. U.S.S.R., *Peninsula Times Tribune*.

[4] Joseph M. Sheehan, *New York Times*, Jul 23, 62.

[5] Paul Zimmerman, Sports Editor, *Los Angeles Times*, Jul 23, 62.

[6] Walt Gamage, Sport Shots.

[7] Peter Grothe, interview by.

Record crowd attends the two-day event (153,500).

Jordan's hands-on organization and execution.

USA's Paul Drayton wins the 200 meters with teammate Roger Sayers taking second.

Athletes spontaneously circle the track "arm-in-arm" during closing ceremonies.

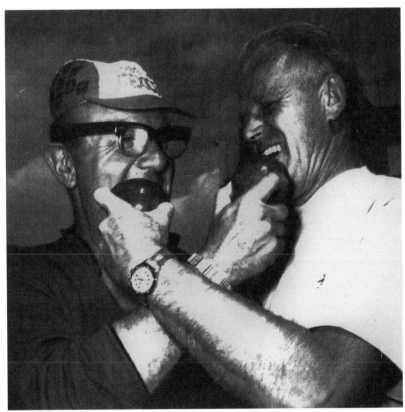

Soviet Coach "Gabe" Korobkov with his friend Payton Jordan.

2. Payton Jordan: Youth through High School

"Young man, I think someday you're going to be a 'real champion' if you keep working at it." - Charlie Paddock, 1920 Olympic sprint champion

George Payton Jordan, Jr. ("Payton Jordan") was born in Whittier, California in 1917. However, early in his youth he moved to Pasadena, where he remained through high school.

Jordan's ancestors migrated from England to Maine, then on to Iowa, and Southern California. Jordan's father, George Payton Jordan, Sr., was born in Southern California and attended Whittier High School. Here he was known as one of the foremost high school athletes in Los Angeles County, playing football, baseball, and starring in track. George Payton, Sr. was a spirited youth who struck out at a young age to make his mark. He started as an oil field roustabout in the early days of oil well drilling in California, then formed a company called Jordan Oil Tool Company. He also was a professional boxer in the days of bare-knuckle champions.

Payton Jordan's mother, Marjorie Bawden Jordan, also attended Whittier High School where she enjoyed music and was a talented pianist. Marjorie and George Payton, Sr. married in 1916 and initially lived in Whittier. Later, they separated and Marjorie and her son, Payton, moved to Pasadena. Marjorie worked as an Associate Director of Film Editing for M.G.M. Studios.

George Payton, Sr. remarried and had two more sons: Dale and Paul. Paul passed away at age 11. Although the two brothers, Payton and Dale, lived apart in their youth, they spent a good deal of time together. Over the years Payton and Dale and their wives, Marge and Bette, have remained close friends.

Payton Jordan's extraordinary potential as a runner first attracted attention in junior high school. After winning a junior high school 100-yard dash, Jordan was approached by a stranger. "Young man, I think someday you're going to be a 'real champion' if you keep working at it." It turned out this stranger was 1920 Olympic gold medal winner and world record holder, Charlie Paddock, also from Pasadena. At the time, Charlie Paddock wrote a sports column in a local newspaper. He followed up with an article about Jordan, a fifteen year old with outstanding promise as a sprinter. "He did inspire me at a very impressionable time in my life," said Jordan. "Both of us were Pasadena products, and to me, he was my idol as an Olympic champion and looked upon as the World's Fastest Human."

Two years later, Marjorie took her son, Payton, to the 1932 Olympic Games, held in the Los Angeles Coliseum. Young Payton was so inspired by seeing the world's best track and field athletes that he told his mother his dream was to realize the potential Charlie Paddock said he has. "Someday I will compete right here in the L.A. Coliseum and run against the very best in the Olympics, too." Little did Payton know at the time that, in fact, he would realize his dream. Through a lifetime of organized goal setting, discipline, commitment, and of course talent, he made the L.A. Coliseum his home field. As captain of the University of Southern California's track team and a member of its football team, he would become a leading contender to make the USA Olympic team in 1940 and 44, but the Olympics would be cancelled during World War II. Never to be deterred, Jordan would realize his Olympic dream by becoming head coach of the 1968 USA men's Olympic track and field team, the team track enthusiasts consider the most successful, ever.

At Pasadena High School, Jordan was a standout athlete in both track and football. He also was president of the men's student body. It is at Pasadena High School that he also met Marjorie Bettannier, who was president of the women's student body and also an outstanding athlete. Both would go on to attend the University of Southern California to study education. After graduating in 1939 they married and both began teaching in the Redlands California school system.

Mother and Father: Marjorie and George Payton, Sr.

Payton Jordan (age 8) with his dog, Babsy, and donkey, Sparky, in the wide-open spaces of Sierra Madre, CA.

Payton Jordan (age 4)

Pasadena Champions

□ By Charles W. Paddock □

Payton Jordan

This Boy Has Great Supply of Natural Speed

Woodrow Wilson Junior High School has an outstanding young sprinter in Payton Jordan. At 15 Payton stands 5 feet 8 inches and weighs 136 pounds. He has long, lithe muscles and a world of speed. The 220 yards has so far proven to be his best event. Young Jordan is not yet a good starter. This, however, happens to be the best kind of a fault in a young sprinter.

One may be able to improve form and the various parts of a race but little enough can be accomplished in developing speed. Payton has the speed and a faster start will undoubtedly come in time.

Payton is the son of Mr. and Mrs. G. P. Jordan, of 181 Vista Circle drive, Sierra Madre. When he finishes his work in the Pasadena school system he hopes to enter the University of Southern California. He would like very much to work under Coach Dean Cromwell and to follow in the footsteps of the long list of outstanding sprinters which this coach has developed.

HOBBY IS MUSIC

Payton's hobby is music and his ambition is to some day be a successful construction engineer. Will Rogers is his choice as the greatest American today while his favorite athletic hero is the diminutive Cotton Warburton. The latter as all football followers know is the dynamic little quarterback of the Southern California varsity who played such an important part in the success of the Trojan team last season.

BUILDS UP PHYSICALLY

Bill Sangster is the best athlete at Woodrow Wilson in Payton's opinion while he names Bert Lawrence as the finest sportsman in his school. Jordan went out for athletics at the age of 13. He felt that competition would build him up physically and give him a better sense of team spirit and school loyalty. Besides starring in the sprints Payton has also proven himself to be a good broad and high jumper.

Chas. W. Paddock

Payton Jordan (age 15) recognized for his natural speed by sports writer and Olympic Champion, Charlie Paddock.

Charlie Paddock, world record holder in the 220-yard dash equals the world record for 100-yard dash.

PADDOCK EQUALS WORLD'S RECORD FOR 100-YARDS

Charley Paddock, the Los Angeles speed marvel who has just broken the 220-yd. world's record, is seen leaping into the tape at the finish of his remarkable century dash clocked to 9 3-5 seconds. Kirksey of Stanford has his foot on the line as Paddock breasts the worsted.

3. On to USC and Captain of Champions

"You are a living legend and a class act. We are honored to have you as a member of the Trojan Family!" - Michael Garrett, USC Director of Athletics

Jordan attended the University of Southern California on a track scholarship. This was during the depression, and Coach Dean Cromwell made it possible for Jordan to attend the University of Southern California and to continue his academic and athletic careers. While Jordan excelled at various other events in track (e.g., the long jump, hurdles, and even the decathlon), he recognized his strongest talent was in the sprints. And, it was during those memorable years, with the exposure to the wonderful coaching of Dean Cromwell in track and field and Howard Jones in football, that Jordan realized coaching would become his life's work.

Mentors Remembered

USC Track and Field

According to Jordan, "Coach Dean Cromwell had a convincing way of always calling us fellows 'champs,' continually making us believe we could be champions if we worked hard enough. That's the key part of coaching which goes well beyond the teaching of technique - motivation - and he was an outstanding motivator." Nicknamed "Maker of Champions," Cromwell was the head coach at the University of Southern California for 39 years, establishing a renowned track and field heritage.

Cromwell participated in track and field and played baseball and football at Occidental College, from which he was graduated in 1902. After working for the telephone company for seven years, he became head track and field coach at USC in 1909. Over the next 39 years, his track teams won 12 NCAA championships, including 9 in a row from 1935 through 1943. They also won 9 IC4A titles. From 1939 through 1948, USC lost only three dual meets. During his tenure, USC athletes won 33 national college titles and 38 National AAU crowns. They also set 14 individual world records plus three more in the relays. He coached 10 Olympic gold medal winners, including at least one at every Olympics from 1912 through 1948, and had 36 USA Olympic team members. Among his athletes were such fellow USA Track & Field Hall of Famers as Charlie Paddock, Bud Houser, Mel Patton, Vern Wolfe, Frank Wykoff, and Payton Jordan. Cromwell retired in 1948 after coaching the USA Olympic team to 10 gold medals.[8]

USC Football

Referring to head football coach, Howard Jones, Jordan said, "Coach Jones could be addressing the whole team, but, somehow, he made it seem he was talking particularly to you. You knew he had confidence in you...that you were capable of performing at the highest level. Perhaps nothing illustrates that better than the Rose Bowl game of 1939. I was only a bench warmer that day, but I watched Coach Jones perform an inspirational miracle. Many old timers may recall that game, one of the most memorable in Rose Bowl history. Southern Cal was playing unbeaten, un-scored upon Duke. And, the Blue Devils managed to keep their goal line and goal posts defended without a score for 59 minutes of the game while they clung to a 3-0 lead."

---

[8] USA Track & Field Association Hall of Fame.

"The teams surged back and forth, neither side able to get anywhere. We were totally frustrated. Then, Jones called Doyle Nave off the bench. 'Get in there, Doyle, and throw the ball,' said Jones. Poor Nave hadn't even earned a letter up to game time, and there he was replacing our two All-American quarterbacks, Granny Lansdell and Amby Schindler. By golly, the team began to move as Nave connected on pass after pass to another second stringer named 'Antelope' Al Krueger. Then, with 40 seconds left, and the ball on Duke's 11-yard line, a true Hollywood finish happened. Krueger broke clear of Duke's great Eric "The Red" Tipton in the end zone and Nave tossed the ball into his outstretched hands for the upset of upsets and one of the most dramatic Rose Bowl finishes, ever. The final score was USC 7, Duke 3."

High School and Junior College
Jordan's Pasadena High School coach, Carl Metten, was not only a very fine technician of sports but also a caring and inspirational man that played a major role in shaping Jordan's career. He helped Jordan realize his potential and gave him the discipline needed. And, Jordan's Santa Monica Junior College coach, Larry Horn, helped refine Jordan's technique and bolster his confidence with his fatherly manner. In his one year at Santa Monica (1935) Jordan set a national junior-college 220-yard record with a time of 21.1 seconds. And, he lowered his 100-yard time to 9.6 seconds.

"These four great coaches shaped my philosophy and established my basic style as a coach. I remain forever grateful to all four of these wonderful men," said Jordan.[9]

Jordan's Varsity Years at USC
During Jordan's varsity years at USC from 1937 to1939, the Trojans won every dual meet, every conference title, the IC4A and NCAA championships as well as all major relays entered — quite a track and field powerhouse, to say the least. LIFE magazine featured Jordan on its June 19, 1939 cover with the title, "Captain of Champions." After graduating from USC Jordan captained an AAU team that won the 1941 National AAU Championship, where Jordan also won the 100-yard dash.

In 1937, during Jordan's first varsity season at USC, Mr. Abraham Lincoln Monteverde came to Jordan after watching the team practice and introduced himself. He asked, "Do you keep clippings of what you do?" To which Jordan replied, "No, I don't but my mother, dad, and brother do from time to time." With that Monteverde said, " I'm a retired bookbinder, need a hobby, and feel you are going to do things that should be recorded. So, I'd like to put together a book each year for you."

Montverde's interest in running was not entirely as a spectator. He was an amazing runner in his own right. In 1929, at the age of 56, he established an Amateur Athletic Union record by running from New York City to San Francisco, a distance of 3,415 miles, in 79 days, 10 hours, and 10 minutes-an incredible average of 43 miles per day!

---

[9] Joseph A. King, "Truly The Luckiest Man in Track and Field," *American Athletics*, Summer 1993.

From the day that he met Jordan until 1967 when he passed away at the age of 94, Montverde prepared a book for Jordan each year bound in either red or black leather with gold leaf titles and dates on each one. Words cannot describe the gratitude Payton Jordan feels towards this kind gentleman.

In 1938, Jordan joined with Mickey Anderson, Lee LaFond, and Adrian Talley to race the 440-relay in 40.5 seconds, a world record that survived for 18 years. Ironically, a Jordan-coached Stanford team would set a new 440-relay world record in 1965.

In 1939, Jordan was captain of the USC track team. In May the twenty members of the USC track team traveled by train to New York City to compete in the Intercollegiate Association of Amateur Athletes of America - the IC4A - Championships. There were 237 athletes representing 34 colleges. The young men from USC not only won the championship but their point total of 71-½ was more than triple that of second-place Pittsburgh. The men of Troy took six intercollegiate titles, tied for two more, broke three records, and tied another. In June they went on to win the NCAA title in track and field.

Expectations were high among the USC Trojans for the 1940 Olympic games, scheduled to be held in Helsinki but ultimately cancelled due to the war. USC had placed ten members on the 1936 team and prospects were good that even more could make the 1940 team. Standouts included Louis Zamperini,[10] a miler who held the intercollegiate record of 4:08.3; Bud Day, one of the few consistent 14'3" pole vaulters; Earl Vickery, who set a meet record of 22.8 in the low hurdles in New York; Jim Humphrey, whose best time in the high hurdles was 14.2 seconds; and Bob Peoples, a sophomore javelin thrower who held the American record of 234'1-⅞".[11]

After his successful athletic career, Jordan was graduated from USC in 1939 with a Bachelor of Science degree in Education. He was a member of the Skull and Dagger, an honorary service organization, Kappa Alpha fraternity, and Phi Epsilon Kappa a professional fraternity in physical education.

Early Insight to Jordan's Thoughts on Competing
As a class assignment for an English course at USC in 1939, Jordan wrote the following poem. He was a bit rushed because he had to submit it before catching the train with his teammates from Los Angeles to New York City for the IC4A Championships. You can imagine the ribbing he later took from teammates, when this poem was selected as a winner to be published in the USC literary magazine, *The Apolliad*.

---

[10] Louis Zamperini, Jordan's close friend, became a pilot in the Army Air Corps. He was shot down over the Pacific then endured 47 days on a raft followed by two and a half years in a Japanese prison camp. He had struggled from poverty to the Olympics (1936), endured a POW camp and a troubled readjustment, then finally found life's meaning through religion. His life's story is the subject of his book titled, *Devil at My Heels*.
[11] "Captain of Champions," *LIFE* magazine, Jun 19, 1939.

The Runner - by Payton Jordan

Crash, gun, crash and turn them free
These winged feet spiked for victory
Crash, gun, crash and loose a soul
That strains at fetters while the goal
Pulls like bands of tempered steel
Drawing heart and head and heel
Crash, gun, crash and lift the haze
That fogs these eyes and let them blaze
Crash, gun, crash and turn them free
These winged feet spiked for victory

Two Stanford Competitors Remember Jordan

Clyde Jeffrey is one of Stanford's all-time greats. He is a member of the Stanford Hall of Fame and was the 1939 NCAA champion in the 220-yard dash with a time of 21.1. Speaking recently of Jordan, Clyde said, "I am so glad that your extraordinary athletic and coaching accomplishments are going to be chronicled in a book. I know that many will be inspired as they read of your life, as I have always felt that your role model goes beyond sport and lies in your gifts as a person. Believe me, Payt, I always looked to you as an athlete who was a friend and fellow competitor. I look back on those days as the 'Age of Innocence' for track and field. All we sprinters and hurdlers did was to dig divots in the track as we tried to gain maximum speed in the shortest time possible."

John Fulton arguably is the most versatile runner in Stanford history. In high school, he won the Los Angeles City Cross Country Championship. At Stanford, he competed in every event from100 yards through the mile run, including relays. He was an All-American and won the 1946 AAU Championship in the 880. In a recent letter to Jordan a gracious John Fulton said, "Payton, I can never thank you enough for that wonderful mention of my track days at Stanford that you wrote in your 'Reflections of the Meet' column in 1995. It provides me with something I can readily provide friends to show what an aging old man did 57 years ago. Glory be for days of old!"

USC's world-record 440-yard relay team (40.5) set at
1938 Fresno Relays. (l-r) A. Talley, P. Jordan,
M. Anderson, L. LaFond.

13

Marjorie Jordan and son,
Payton Jordan, at his last race as
a Trojan and team captain,
LA Coliseum, 1939.

Life's cover: The sprinter is 21–year–old Payton Jordan, who lives in Pasadena and has a scholarship at the University of Southern California. Jordan is captain of America's Greatest Track Team, which won the Intercollegiate Association of Amateur Athletes of America in New York last month hands down. Jordan is photographed at top speed by Gjon Mili's fast action camera.

"Captain of Champions," LIFE magazine,
Jun 19, 1939.

Marge and Payton Jordan's
wedding photo (1940).

Jordan on USC football team.

4. Jamaican Olympiad

"These were the best of times. These were the worst of times." -
Charles Dickens' *Tale of Two Cities*

The Jamaican Amateur Athletic Association invited two American track stars to participate in the Jamaican Olympiad held in Kingston, Jamaica, July 1941. The two were Payton Jordan, then on the staff of Redlands High School, and Hubert Kerns, still at the University of Southern California and world record holder in the 400 meters. Jordan and Kerns were excited at the opportunity to travel to and compete in the Jamaican Olympiad. Perhaps they sensed that with the 1940 Olympics cancelled and war underway, this just might prove to be the only shot at international competition for them and their generation. This, of course, proved to be the case, as no Olympics were held between the 1936 Berlin Games and the 1948 Games in London.

But for the moment the American pair, accompanied by Jordan's wife, Marge, was off on a goodwill adventure. Arrangements were made for the young Americans to board a United Fruit Company Lines steamship in New York for the 5-day voyage to and from Kingston, Jamaica with a brief stop over in Santiago de Cuba. And, the real meaning of "amateur" was apparent back then. In a letter from the AAU Secretary-Treasurer to Jordan, the American athletes were advised they each would be provided $5 per day to cover "living expenses in New York" for the one day they would remain there before heading back to California by train.

The Americans were received with great hospitality in Jamaica. However, running conditions offered a new challenge to the pair. The track in Sabina Park near Kingston was grass, not cinder or clay. And, the shape was more of a circle than an oval. Nevertheless, Jordan and Kerns liked the conditions and looked forward to the competition.

In the competition Jordan won the 100-yard dash in a time of 9.5 seconds, the 100-meter dash in 10.3 seconds, and the 220-yard dash in 21.1, all world records on a grass surface. Kerns won the 440 yards the first day in a time of 49.3, despite suffering an attack of acute ptomaine poisoning. On the second day, Kerns had recovered a bit and was able to win in a time of 48.6.

As goodwill ambassadors, Jordan and Kerns had ample opportunity to mix with the local athletes, attend social gatherings, and get to know various officials such as Herbert MacDonald, President of the Jamaican Amateur Athletic Association. In fact, after the trip MacDonald sent Jordan a letter commending Jordan and Kerns on "doing their bit in cementing the friendship between your great democracy and this far-flung outpost of the British Empire."

Jordan wins 1941 U.S. National AAU Championships 100-yard dash, Franklin Field, Philadelphia, PA, which led to his invitation to compete in Jamaica.

Jordan and Hube Kerns receive awards at 1941 Jamaican Olympiad, Kingston, Jamaica, July 26, 1941.

Jordan wins the 100-yard dash, followed by "Coco" Brown and future great Herb McKenley.

Hube Kerns, Marge and Payton Jordan with Jamaican dignitaries.

5. WWII Military Service

In 1942, Jordan volunteered for service in the U.S. Navy. First, he was assigned to the U.S. Naval Academy for Officer Candidate School. After being commissioned an Ensign, he moved to St. Mary's Pre Flight School in Moraga California, where he served as a physical conditioning instructor. Here, pilot candidates were prepared physically, mentally, and emotionally to handle the rigors of pilot training and the combat conditions that lie ahead. In addition to physical conditioning Jordan and the other instructors were tasked to develop in these candidates a sense of discipline and teamwork.

Not surprisingly, St. Mary's also had some very competitive sports teams. Representing the Navy, Jordan ran his last official race in 1942 beating "Hurrying" Hal Davis, then the fastest man on American tracks in the 100 yards. Davis had not lost in twenty-five consecutive races. Jordan played football at St. Mary's with collegiate and pro players such as Frankie Albert.

After two years at St. Mary's, Jordan was transferred to a Primary Flight School at the Naval Air Station, Ottumwa, Iowa. Here student pilots learned actual flying skills; but, of course, teambuilding and conditioning continued and this was Jordan's primary responsibility. He also served on the base court-martial board and was the Officer in Charge of the base enlisted personnel. Here, Jordan participated on the Naval Air Station's football team and was selected by the Associated Press as an Armed Services All-American. The U.S. Track & Field Writers Association named Jordan to the "mythical 1940 and 1944 USA Olympic Teams." The writers felt they should honor the best track and field athletes who in their judgment would have represented the United States in the 1940 and 44 Olympics, had they not been cancelled due to the war.

According to Jordan, " These four years were a great learning experience working with outstanding young men. This taught me so much about people, organizations, and motivation needed to succeed in life. It also added so much to my following years as a coach." Asked if he regrets missing the Olympics - cancelled in 1940 and 1944 - Jordan responded, " I never looked on it as a disappointment. Maybe I wouldn't have made it but, sure, I would like to have had the chance to try out for the team. However, I remember friends I made in the service, some of whom went off to war and never returned. So, my missing the Olympics isn't something I thought much about...nor likely did any other track and field athlete of my generation."

When Jordan retired from Stanford in 1979 he received letters from all over the Country. One such letter was from someone he had not seen in 36 years. Bruce Bellard, Professor, Department of Health and Physical Education, Bowling Green State University, wrote, "My interest in running started way back in 1943 when I was a cadet at St. Mary's Pre-flight School in the Navy. At that point a young Navy instructor was kind enough to spend considerable time with me giving me assistance. That instructor was YOU."

Jordan served as a U.S. Naval Officer during WWII, leaving active duty with the rank of Lieutenant Commander.

Jordan, an Associate Press Armed Services All-American in football.

6. In Redlands They Still Call Him Coach

"You gave it your all," Jordan said, "and that makes you a winner." - Mickey Bevis

Payton Jordan started his coaching career at Redlands High School in southern California just before his service in World War II then returned to Redlands after leaving the military in 1946. Interestingly, some of the same seventh graders that got to know him before the war were seniors in high school when he returned.

Jordan's first track team - Richard McCracken, Oddie Martinez, Bob Sewell, Jim Sloan, Manases Soto, Don Daniels, Roger Woodrow, Buzz Eldridge, Ed Taylor, Frank Jacinto, Harold Hartwick, Junior Amodt, Hartwell Davis, Harold Moore, Anthony Jacinto, Don Poe, Tom Farrington, Chuck Breyer, and former coaching and teaching partner Bob Scholton - all showed up some forty years later when they learned that Jordan was invited to speak about the Olympics to a local civic group in Redlands. Well, Bob Scholton's wife, Lois, had organized it, so Jordan shouldn't have been too surprised by the teammate turnout. The boys-turned-men Jordan had coached achieved success in their own right. Poe was a police chief. Martinez is a former mayor of Redlands and currently an elementary school principal. Taylor is a lawyer, Frank Jacinto is a manager of more than 1000 acres of citrus crops, and Tony Jacinto is an insurance salesman.

Following Jordan's move from Redlands to Occidental College in 1946, his good friend Bob Scholton became Redland's head track coach. Bob continued in that capacity until his retirement in 1970. The Jordans and Scholtons have remained close friends over the years. In fact, the couples celebrated their 50th wedding anniversaries together on a trip to Tahiti in 1990. Lois Scholton has passed away, but Bob and Payton still talk on the phone, regularly.

"It's just nice to have a group like this to honor Mr. Jordan," said Tony Jacinto. "He was our idol. They just don't make them like him." According to Ed Taylor, "He paid as much attention to the marginal athletes as he did the champions. To him everyone was a champion. He developed the will to win and the ability to lose with dignity. That was his concept of track and field and it has worked well in life." Jim Sloan noted in a letter to Jordan, "I've only had two very special idols in my life and turns out they were friends at USC: John Wayne (a.k.a.: the 'Duke') and Payton Jordan." Oddie Martinez reflected, "The name Payton Jordan is so well known. But to us he always will be Coach Jordan."

"These guys are not any different than the Olympic champs I coached. They have the same drive and willingness to pay the price," Jordan added.[12]

Mickey Bevis, a hurdler from Jordan's 1946 Redlands High School team, wrote an essay in 1999 titled *Coach* about his very special memories of Jordan. His essay follows.

"Many reports have been written about track superstar Payton Jordan. Jordan was captain of the University of Southern California track team of 1939 that won the title, 'America's greatest track team.' *LIFE* magazine featured the 21-year-old world-class sprinter on the cover. Later he became the Stanford University coach. In 1968 he

---

[12] Jim Long, "Jordan: In Redlands, they still call him Coach," *San Bernardino Sun*, 1986.

coached an all time record winning Olympic team. As a senior sprinter he holds an unprecedented series of world records and being inducted into the Stanford Athletic Hall of Fame in 1995 was well earned. But all the accounts of Jordan's career, to my knowledge, have overlooked one very important fact: he began his coaching career at Redlands High School.

"As a member of the 1946 Redlands High School track team I can truthfully say that I set no records. In fact I have no recollection of ever winning a single event, yet the prize I walked away with at the end of the season had more value than all the blue ribbons or gold medals I could have received had I won every event. It was just a few simple words from Coach Payton Jordan, but his dynamic delivery remained indelibly in my memory. So, when I had the opportunity to meet with him after 53 years, I could not resist. No, I was compelled.

"In 1946 I was just an average kid but one of the smallest trying out for the team. My performance in the 120-yard high hurdles, the one event I wanted to excel at, was mediocre at best. Even so, Coach Jordan encouraged me to enter the competition. After a poor showing at the first meet, he pointed out that the fastest runners took three steps between hurdles and I was working harder with my five-step method. I didn't think I could stretch my stride that much, but time after time I tried. When I stretched to four steps between hurdles, my running time improved, but this meant alternating the jumping leg and was awkward and not fulfilling. I tried harder and eventually succeeded in doing the three steps for about half the race.

"For the first time in track history, Redlands won the Chaffey Invitational and had a chance to compete seriously in the C.I.F. (California Interscholastic Federation, the division above our local Citrus Belt League). By some miracle I had qualified for the semifinals of the high hurdles. When I put my feet in the starting blocks, it was time to show my coach that his faith in me had not been misplaced. I was determined ... not just to run a good race, but to win. My muscles were toned and ready. If I had been giving one hundred percent in the other races, now I'd give a hundred ten percent.

"The starter raised his arm and issued the command, 'Get set.' The gun went off and the runners bolted forward. I cleared the first hurdle, the second and third. Out of the corner of my eye I could see that I was keeping stride with the leaders. This was my race. Over that last hurdle and no one would beat me to the finish line.

"Here, it would be wonderful to report the Hollywood ending, how I went on to fame and glory. But this story is not about me. As it turned out, my foot hit that last hurdle and I tumbled to the ground, skinning my arms and legs on the sandy surface while all the other runners went by. Coach hurried to my aid, grabbed my arm with his strong grip and helped me to my feet. I looked up and said, almost apologetically, 'I... I didn't make it. I didn't win.'

"Coach's blue eyes locked on mine and looked deep into my soul. 'You gave it your all,' he said, 'and that makes you a winner.' With that, he put his arm around my shoulder and walked me across the finish line.

"For fifty-three years, Coach's inspiration helped me over many hurdles in life, how to come back after a fall and cross the finish line. That's why I had to go to Santa Barbara, in August 1999 to see him. Former pro quarterback, Secretary of HUD, and vice presidential candidate, Jack Kemp played under Jordan in college and said it best when he said, 'I'd run through a brick wall for that man.'

"After our visit, I rose to say good-by. Coach put his arm around my shoulder, much like he did that day in 1946, and called me his 'early champion.' Fifty-three years melted away and I was a callow youth again under his spell. At 82 his charismatic magic still worked. Sometimes a personal experience is so private that you want to guard it like a forbidden treasure; this one was simply too good not to be shared. In my heart, Coach Payton Jordan is the greatest in the world." [13]

1986 Redlands team reunion.
Front row (left to right): Richard McCracken, Oddie Martinez, Bob Sewell, Jim Sloan, Manases Soto, and Don Daniels.
Middle row (l-r): Roger Woodrow, Buzz Eldridge, Payton Jordan, Ed Taylor, Frank Jacinto and Harold Hartwick.
Back row (l-r): Junior Amodt, Hartwell Davis, Harold Moore, Anthony Jacinto, Don Poe, Tom Farrington, Chuck Breyer and Bob Scholton.

---

[13] Mickey Bevis, *Coach*, 1999.

Mickey Bevis: author of "Coach."

Bob and Lois Scholton with Payton and Marge Jordan (50th Wedding Anniversaries). Bob was Jordan's first assistant coach at Redlands HS.

7. At "Oxy" They Call Him the "Coach of Champions"

*"You are a history maker both as an athlete and maker of champions.
Thanks for adding class to the coaching world." - Sammy Lee, M.D.,
Oxy grad and two-time Olympic Diving Champion (1948 and 1952).*

During Jordan's ten years at Occidental College from 1947 to 1956, he produced one of track and field's greatest dynasties. Occidental - fondly called "Oxy" by locals - is an elite academic institution in southern California with a coeducational enrollment of just over 1000 at the time of Jordan's tenure. His teams won ten consecutive league championships, an NAIA national title in 1956, were ranked second in the nation to USC in dual meet strength in 1955, and produced two top-five finishes in the NCAA Championships in 1951 and 1952. His athletes also set a world record in the distance medley relay, won four individual NCAA championships, and competed in the 1952 and 1956 Olympics.

Milestone Track & Field Performances
Following are some of the most memorable Jordan Era accomplishments on the track.

- That day in 1950 when Ted Ruprecht, Walt McKibben, John Barnes and Bill Parker raced to the mile relay victory over the mighty Morgan State in the Coliseum mile relay. Anchorman, "Bullet Bill" Parker, started even with Olympic champion and world record holder George Rhoden and beat him by a yard at the tape to give Oxy an unbelievable victory in the time of 3:10.1, second fastest collegiate race in history.

- Bob McMillen's mad rush to the tape in Helsinki in the 1952 Olympics. Bob didn't quite catch Luxembourg's Josy Barthel but he beat a guy named Roger Bannister, and his time of 3:45.2 made him a co-holder of the Olympic 1500-meter record with Barthel. According to Jordan, "Bob was truly one of America's all-time greats in the mile. No other modern-day American has placed higher in the Olympic metric mile, and no other American shared the Olympic record, as he did." Two years later (May 6, 1954) Roger Bannister would become the first person to break the four-minute mile with a time of 3:59.4. *Sports Illustrated* rated Bannister's breakthrough alongside the scaling of Everest as the most significant athletic feat of the 20th century.

- John Barnes' 1952 NCAA Championship victory in the 800 meters, setting a new meet record time of 1:49.6.

- The 1954 two-mile relay team of Ev Trader, Calude Fiddler, Eddie Shinn, and Jim Terrill breaking the then world record with a time of 7:36.1, yet coming in third to Fordham and California in a blistering-pace race.

- The 1956 Olympics when Oxy's pole vaulters Bob Gutowski won the silver medal and George Roubanis, also European Champion from Greece, won the bronze medal.

- Bob Gutowski's 1957 world record in the pole vault (15'8 ¼"), breaking Dutch Warmerdam's 15-year record. Tragically, Bob died in a car accident in 1960 at the age of 25.

Memories of the 1956 Drake Relays

Ty Hadley wrote an essay titled "Reflections of ... Drake Relays 1956, the Five-Man Two-Mile Relay." His account of the race is telling about their connection to Coach Jordan.

"You may never have heard of the 5-man 2-mile relay. This race, however, exists as one of my most precious memories while competing for Occidental College. Let me tell you what happened.

"I was a sophomore at Occidental College and I had never competed in a large invitational. In fact, I had never been out of the state of California. Coach Jordan informed me that I would be going to the Drake Relays in Iowa. With youthful innocence I asked, 'Why are we going to Iowa?' Coach Jordan gave me a simple reply, 'To win.' I remember getting off the plane in Iowa. The weather was absolutely beautiful. Of course I was dressed to the nines - sport coat, white buck shoes, red knit tie, blue flannel slacks and my sports bag packed precisely as directed by Coach Jordan. That was the way we traveled, then.

"That evening I went to bed with the usual excitement, anticipation and hint of fear that always haunted me the night before a competition. Sometime around midnight I was awakened by a loud rumbling noise. I looked out the window to observe an angry storm that had hit Iowa with severe intensity. In the morning the storm continued with winds at about 54 miles per hour with rain, ice, and sleet. Our relay team, composed of Eddie Shinn, Chauncy Pa, Larry Wray and myself, Ty Hadley, met in a huge field house with other athletes waiting and warming up for their own particular race. The field house was warm and almost cozy. I looked out at the track and it appeared to me there was about six inches of water in a strong current coming down. The track was elevated and the infield was at least ankle deep in freezing water. Coach Jordan was with us during warm-ups and it was then I learned I would anchor the race. I knew I could anchor the race. I was not sure if I could swim through the current to get to the starting line. I was excited, a bit scared, and certainly honored that my coach had the confidence in me to be anchor. Also, I knew I would be taking the baton from Larry Wray, my best friend and soul mate. Larry always gave me special inspiration and when taking the baton from him, I felt invincible. I looked at my teammates and my coach. We were ready. I knew in my mind that the storm would not stop us.

"At the designated race time we departed from the field house and in a leaning motion, we sidestepped across the track and then waded through the infield, which was ankle deep in freezing water. At times, we were pushed backward by driving rain and sleet. My hands were already numb and my face stung from being pelted by tiny spears of ice. On the track I looked around. There were superior teams lined up, each with the desire to claim victory. I felt the competitive juices beginning to flow. This was true competition. Not only were we matched against the other runners, but also the strength of the north wind.

"On the track I began to formulate my race plan. I was not sure if I should power the first turn or simply begin slapping out a fast Australian crawl. Since I was not a swimmer, I decided to put my head down and power the entire distance. It was then when the starter gun sounded and I remember the display of splashing water and black cinders. Before the first straight away you could not distinguish the different runners or uniforms - everyone was soaking wet and covered with black cinders.

"The race went pretty much as Coach Jordan had planned. After the first two legs, we were about 30 yards behind the leaders. Larry took the baton and began closing the distance. It was then that I noticed a very curious thing. The stands were empty! The storm had driven everyone into the comfort of the field house. Only one lone figure stood at the side of the track in the driving storm. It was Coach Jordan. For just a moment imagine how I felt as an athlete knowing my coach was with me no matter what the circumstances. All the other coaches were inside. He was with his team. Coach Jordan gave me a look that I had grown to admire and respect. It was that of pride, confidence, and determination. I glanced back at him and said to myself, 'coach there is no way we are going to lose this race.'

"Larry was now in the final 100 yards of his leg. I knew Larry as well as I know myself. We had run together in high school and had set a national record in the four-man two-mile relay. I had taken the baton from Larry many times and together we had never lost. I saw Larry straining to close the distance and I knew he had spent every ounce of his energy — he always did. I took the baton early determined to make up the distance as quickly as possible. The storm, however, seemed to have no respect for my maximum effort. It was brutal, furious and unrelenting. After the first lap it appeared I had not gained a single yard on the leader. On the backstretch I had closed some of the distance but, in my mind, certainly not enough. It then appeared that the front runner was slowing just a bit. I reached down deep searching for some extra strength. The storm and the pace had certainly taken their toll and, for the first time, I doubted if there was anything left in the tank. At the top of the curve a phenomenon occurred which I cannot logically explain even to this day. I suppose I was hallucinating. I was the anchorman but, strangely in my daze of fatigue, I was reaching forward in an effort to pass off the baton to a runner in front of me. The runner in front of me was reaching back, hand extended in an effort to receive the baton. In my state of hallucination I recognized the runner. It was Coach Jordan. I reached up to pass off the baton to him and then there was a blur of a runner on my left side. The next thing I knew I had crossed the finish line. We had won!

"Four men picked me up at the finish line. I was too spent to even stand up and, honestly, everything in my body hurt. But, as before, my body began to recover from the warm glow of victory. That was a day I will never forget. Four runners from Occidental College placed first at the Drake Relays in 1956. Each runner ran 880 yards. Coach Jordan went the entire two miles. We finished what I now call the five-man two-mile relay. It was a day when all five of us gave our very best and our reward was victory and beautiful reflections of the past." [14]

---

[14] Ty Hadley, "Reflections of ... Drake Relays 1956, the Five-Man Two-Mile Relay."

Freshman Football

Each fall, Jordan also coached Oxy's freshman football team, winning nine conference titles outright and tying for a tenth. Among the players he introduced to college football were former pro quarterback and vice presidential candidate Jack Kemp class of 1957 and tight end Jim Mora, who went on to a long coaching career in the National Football League. In 1992, Jack Kemp wrote an article in USA TODAY titled: "Values Learned on the Field." Referring to his dream one day to play in the NFL, Kemp wrote, "For me the inspiration came to me one memorable day as a freshman at Occidental College. Coach Payton Jordan called me into his office and told me - in great confidence - that if I worked hard and never gave up, someday I could reach the NFL. I walked out of his office on cloud nine and practiced harder than ever. Years later, I learned that Coach Jordan had the same "confidential" conversation with every player. All the same, he inspired me to live up to my God-given potential and never give up on my dream."

Jordan Remembered

In 2001, Occidental College granted Payton Jordan an honorary doctorate degree. During the presentation ceremony President Theodore R. Mitchell referred to a 1954 letter an anonymous Occidental senior wrote to a local sports columnist - a letter the veteran sportswriter called "not only the finest tribute to a living coach I have ever received from an athlete, but the only one of its kind." The student-athlete praised Oxy track coach and athletic director Payton Jordan not for his extraordinary winning record, but for what the student called Jordan's "man-making ability." He wrote, "Mr. Jordan can nurture that small spark of self-confidence that is hidden in so many of us, and through his patient way bring out the fire that makes for success in life as well as on the track." [15]

Jordan's support from his former faculty colleagues and student-athletes is demonstrated further by the following quotes.

- **Ben Culley** - Ben was Dean of Students at Occidental College commenting on Payton Jordan's retirement from active coaching, "Frankly, the sport of track & field has lost one of its Super-Stars and the comment relates to all phases of the sport. It has been largely through your efforts that the sport has attained the respect and recognition it now enjoys. The many coaches, athletes, administrators, faculty and students who have had the privilege of working with you will forever remain a testimonial to your influence."

- **Glenn Dumke** - Glenn was Dean of Faculty at Occidental College then later Chancellor of California State University and Colleges. "I know that over the years you have worked with human values as well as athletic achievement and this will be a lasting legacy."

---

[15] Theodore R. Mitchell, President of Occidental College, when he awarded Payton Jordan an honorary doctorate degree (5/20/01).

- **Bob Mathias** - Bob is a two-time Olympic decathlon champion, Stanford graduate, U.S. congressman, and long-time Jordan friend, "He modernized the sport. You know what he says is true. He is honest and caring." [16] Interestingly, during Bob's senior year at Stanford (1953) the Jordan-coached Occidental team upset Stanford in a dual meet. But, Jordan had a secret weapon on his Oxy team: Jim Mathias, Bob's younger brother.

- **Jim Mora** - Jim was a former Oxy tight end, assistant football coach at Stanford, and long-time NFL coach. "I just want you to know that of all the coaches I ever had or worked with, you stand at the top of the list. You have always been an inspiration to me and there have been many times when I asked myself, "How would Coach Jordan handle this?"

- **Jack Kemp** - Jack was a former Oxy and NFL quarterback and national political figure. "Your career and your many victories notwithstanding, are small when compared to the lives you've touched in positive ways."

Oxy Coach Jordan and his mentor USC Coach Cromwell reunite at their 1948 dual meet - Jordan the USC grad; Cromwell the Oxy grad.

1952 Olympic Games, 1500 meters, Helsinki, Finland. In the lead is Josey Barthel (#406), Oxy's Bob McMillen (#997), and Roger Bannister (#177) as they head for the finish line. Time: New Olympic Record of 3:45.2.

---

[16] Dave Newhouse, "Jordan: Ex-Stanford coach has been track's P.T. Barnum," Jul 12, 2001.

1956 Olympic silver medallist, Bob Gutowski.

European champion and 1956 Olympic bronze medallist, George Roubanis.

Tom Meyer, world-class shot putter, and Bob Gutowski with Coach Jordan.

First-year Stanford Coach Jordan congratulates Oxy's Bob Gutowski on his pole vault world record of 15'8 1/4" set at Stanford Stadium, April 27, 1957.

1950 Coliseum Relays: Oxy mile relay team (left to right: Walt McKibben, Ted Ruprecht, John Barnes, and Bill Parker) blazed to victory over heavily favored Morgan State in time of 3:10.1, then second fastest mile relay time in history.

8. Greece: A Timeless Friendship

"I knew I had to win or die." - *Stylianos Kyriakides, Boston, 1946*

In 1955, Jordan was asked by the U.S. Department of State to fulfill an urgent request it had received from their Embassy in Athens. The Greek track & field association was extremely eager to have a top flight U.S. track coach come to Greece to spend three months coaching their athletes, conducting clinics, and working with athletic officials and coaches to improve coaching and organizational standards. Jordan, of course, was excited with the prospect to play a small part in helping Greece - the birth place of the Olympics - move a little closer to the prominence in athletics that it once enjoyed. Within three months of Jordan's arrival, seven Greek national records had been broken. And, the young Greek athletes he coached went on to thrill their nation at the 1956 Olympics with a taste of ancient glory, as they made the best Olympic showing for Greece since the beginning of the Modern Olympic Games in 1896.

Behind the scenes in Greece making the request for Jordan, specifically, was Otto Simitsek, the Hungarian-born Greek-speaking coach of the Greek national team. Simitsek had met Jordan in California at the first international track coaches meeting, which Jordan had organized as President of the National Collegiate Track Coaches Association. After Jordan's arrival in Athens, Simitsek introduced him to Greece's legendary distance runner, Stylianos Kyriakides, then 45 and, like Jordan, retired from competitive running. Jordan was well aware of Kyriakides, the champion distance runner whose stirring win of the 1946 Boston Marathon had galvanized world attention to the plight of starving Greeks after World War II. The two were destined to become great friends.

Stylianos Kyriakides: a Greek Legend

There is an old saying: "show me your friends and I will know who you are." Payton Jordan's friendship with Stylianos Kyriakides reveals a great deal about Jordan. He was so moved by Kyriakides' life story that he wrote this article about Kyriakides, which was published in the *Los Angeles Times*.

"My life has placed me with many athletes but to sit as a dinner guest and share the traditional lamb roasted on a spit over the hot coals and listen to this little guy tell of his great efforts to travel to America for the Boston Marathon....

"It was 1946. Greece had been torn by strife, both external and internal, and there was little heart left in the masses. However, there was one, Stylianos Kyriakides, who by the very nature of his training was willing to try the impossible. For here is a game champion. When his feet would blister and could not stand the beatings of the marathons, he took it upon himself to toughen those feet.

"From his porch, tonight, he gestured to a far away mountain across a long valley and more hills. These were the places of his training runs at night following his long workday. Kyriakides would remove his shoes and vanish into the stillness of night and purposely race over stones and rocks to toughen his feet. There was one stretch of about six miles where he had it especially fine - he was able to run on the stone ballast of the railroad track! Then there was the evening when he fell to his knees from sheer exhaustion a mile or two from home. In his words, 'I was very afraid for a minute.' Then he thought that to go to America he must be ready, he could not fail.

"His trip arrangements to America were very complicated, financially and otherwise, but when things were darkest he came up with a monumental statement: 'Do I go as one or for all Greece!!' This gained him the necessary support and Stylianos Kyriakides finally boarded the first TWA plane to fly out of Athens with just $30 in his pocket.

"Upon his departure he was given two boxes of candy by a friend to deliver to a relative in America. He phoned the relative from Boston and was asked to get on a train - $3 fare - and take the candy to the relative. With an impish gleam in his eye Kyriakides told me, 'You know, I just sat down and ate all that candy myself. Where was I to get all that money when all I had to spend for the entire trip in America was $30?'

"To become the Boston Marathon champion is the greatest single honor that can come to a long distance runner. Kyriakides gained that honor. To say that he received a welcome fit for a king when he returned home is putting it mildly. Actually, thousands upon thousands of people jammed the streets of Athens to pay homage to the gallant little champion. And, it was right then that a new chapter in Greek history began. The hero of all Greece spoke nervously, but from his great heart, when he said, 'Thanks, my people. We must become one again. Forget the past. Turn and embrace each other for we are each of us Greeks! Let us fight no more, Communists or not. America wants to help us if we will help ourselves and this we must do!'

"Even as Kyriakides spoke to me his brown eyes became misty and then he smiled and shrugged. It has been done. I thought of another Greek who had run himself to death from Marathon to Athens to bring word of Grecian victory over the Persians. Now, again, another of Grecian blood had run another historic race for love of his people and country.

"I came here to be of assistance to the Greek track and field athletes but already I have gotten more than I shall ever be able to give." [17]

Return to Athens, 1996
Payton Jordan returned to Greece, 41 years after his coaching work in 1955 and 27 years since he had been a guest of honor at a banquet with Kyriakides. He had missed Kyriakides' funeral in 1987. But, now, it was good to be back in Greece to help celebrate the 100th anniversary of the modern Olympic Games. Accompanying Jordan on this trip was Rafer Johnson, 1960 Olympic champion in the decathlon and the person selected in 1984 to light the Olympic flame during opening ceremonies of the Games of the XXIII Olympiad held in Los Angeles, California.

Today, Jordan was in an Athens stadium to hand out medals for the European Special Olympics competition. A man approached Jordan to introduce himself. Jordan didn't

---

[17] Payton Jordan, "Greece and a Modern Touch to Ancient Glory," *Los Angeles Times.*

recognize him. "You don't remember me," the man smiled. He waited a moment then said, "My father was Otto Simitsek," the coach of the Greek Olympic team who had requested and hosted Jordan's 1955 visit. "If he were alive, he would be so delighted to see you again," the man said. The son had been only nine years old in 1955, when Jordan had come to help the Greek Olympic team.

Jordan wondered what had happened to those men he had helped train, so he asked Simitsek's son, "Are any of them here?" Simitsek told an official, "Take Mr. Jordan to the finish line to see if any of his athletes are here." Halfway across the track, Jordan heard shouts of delight and saw a group of men in their 60s, running towards him with tears in their eyes. They were the Greeks he had met and trained in 1955, athletes he had helped prepare for the 1956 Olympics. "Coach Jordan! You are back!" they screamed before surrounding him, hugging and kissing, and lifting him to their shoulders. Jordan began to cry, too, and the crowd in the stadium knew they were witnessing a very special moment in sport.

A couple days later, Jordan went to the ancient stadium at Nemea, where there hadn't been a competition for 2300 years. In ancient times, games were held at Nemea, Isthmia, and Olympia. Jordan was asked to run in games where he would win the 100 and 200 meters in his age group against a field of still accomplished older athletes. Afterwards, the competitors donned ancient togas to commemorate the spirit of the Olympics, which had begun in Greece in a prior millennium. But, Jordan's thoughts were with his old friend, Kyriakides, the warm evening in his Athens backyard where they had talked, the sunny day at Marathon where Kyriakides jokingly wore a laurel wreath, the kind he took to Boston in 1946 and wore when he won the marathon, and the vision of Kyriakides running down the dirt road from the ancient site where the Greeks had won the day for their country nearly 2500 years before.

Jordan still could see a happy, healthy 45-year-old man, his friend, in the full bloom of joy, a bright blue sky above and the plains of the old battlefield behind him. It was a serene sight so exquisite that it erased the horror and loss of the World War that had enveloped Greece little more than a decade before, a time that had given Kyriakides his destiny and real reason to run, the ghosts of those teammates who had not survived, and the men of Marathon, the fallen and the victors who, like Kyriakides, had saved their country.[18]

---

[18] Nick Tsiotos and Andy Dabilis, *"Running with Pheidippides: Stylianos Kyriakides, the Miracle Marathoner"* with a foreword by Johnny Kelley, Syracuse University Press, 2001.

Pasadenan Coaches Greek Track Athletes

Jordan and Otto Simitsek, the Hungarian-born Greek-speaking coach of the Greek national team.

Jordan and the Greek Team - Pasadena Star-News, Sept. 7, 1955.

Jordan with the Greek Team.

32

9. 1960 USA Olympic Trials

Over 125,000 people came to Stanford Stadium in July 1960 to watch the United States Track & Field Olympic Trials in what was, and still is, the best attended Olympic Trials in U.S. history. This was a record attendance for a two-day track & field event in the United States only to be exceeded two years later by the US vs. USSR track & field meet, also held at Stanford Stadium. "Al Masters, Stanford Athletic Director, who had a great love for track and field and the Olympic movement, told me to put in a bid to host the 1960 Olympic Trials," recalled Jordan. "We went for it and got it." It was a great time for track and field in the United States, and the Trials epitomized the popularity of the sport, particularly in the Bay Area.

World records were established by Ray Norton in the 200 meters (20.5), Don Bragg in the pole vault (15'9 ¼"), and John Thomas in the high jump (7'3 ¾"). But the highlights of the Trials for the local fans were Bay Area competitors who made the Olympic Team.

- Stanford's Ernie Cunliffe took the third and final spot in the 800-meters, as his 1:47.5 narrowly edged out the fourth place finisher, Jim Dupree, by inches. It took the judges two hours to rule on the photo finish. Ernie waited outside the review area and upon hearing the good news hurried back to the stadium to tell family and friends. The first person he recognized on the way to the Stadium was Cheryl Jordan, Payton Jordan's older daughter. Thus, Cheryl was the first person Ernie told the good news and hugged!!! On finding family and friends in the stadium, Ernie, went on a hugging, cheering, and crying jog, which probably was the most publicly emotional moment of the Trials. Tom Murphy and Cal's Jerry Siebert placed first and second, respectively. The three Americans did not medal at the Olympics.

- Lee Calhoun won the 110-meter hurdles at the Trials in 13.4, equaling the American record. Lee went on to win the gold medal in the Olympics. Stanford's Chuck Cobb placed fourth at the Trials to become an alternate on the team. "Coach Jordan had 60,000 fans in Stanford Stadium pulling for me as a hometown crowd, but earning the alternate slot was the best I could do that day," said Chuck.

- In addition to his record win in the 200 meters, Ray Norton from San Jose State won the 100-meters (10.4) in a finish that had Frank Budd about 18 inches behind in second and third through sixth all within 12 inches behind Budd. At the Olympics Norton made it to the finals in both the 100 and 200 meters but did not medal.

- Cal's Jack Yerman took first in the 400 meters (46.3). Earlier, Jack had won his qualifying heat in a personal best of 46.0. Yerman was ill just before the Olympics and did not reach the finals. Teammate Otis Davis won the gold in a world record time of 44.9. However, Jack recovered to run the lead-off leg on the USA 4x400 meter relay team, which won a gold medal in a world record time of 3:02.2.

- Rink Babka, a local favorite who lived about a mile from Stanford Stadium, won the discus with a toss of 192'3 ½". Al Oerter came in second in the Trials but went on to win the Olympic gold medal with an Olympic record toss of 194'2". Rink Babka won the silver.

The United States Olympic Committee, the press, the athletes, and the public at large extolled the careful organization and smooth execution of the 1960 Olympic Trials.

According to Pincus Sober, Chairman of the United States Olympic Men's Track & Field Committee, "The Olympic Trials held at Stanford were the finest meet ever held in the United States." [19] Ed Orman of the *Fresno Bee* reported, "The smooth manner in which Olympic officials, guided by the personable Stanford University track and field coach, Payton Jordan, conducted the meet, deserves nothing but praise. It was the finest run meet we have ever covered." [20] Several athletes noted their satisfaction with the proximity of living and dining facilities (Stern Hall), training facilities (Angell Field), and Stanford Stadium all within easy walking distance on the Stanford University campus.

---

[19] Pincus Sober, July 9, 1960 letter to Payton Jordan.

[20] Ed Orman, Sports Editor, *Fresno Bee*, July 1960.

10. 1968 Olympics: Trying Times - Greatest Team

"You are a great coach and a better friend." - John Carlos, 2002

The selection of Payton Jordan to be head coach of the 1968 USA men's Olympic team was quite logical to those close to track and field. In addition to his Occidental and Stanford coaching experience he had provided coaching assistance to the Greek Olympic team in 1955, the U.S. Maccabean team in 1965, the Yugoslavian Olympic team in 1967 and orchestrated the 1960 USA Olympic trials and the 1962 USA versus USSR dual meet. In 1964, Jordan served as first assistant coach on the USA men's Olympic track and field team, where he focused primarily on the sprints and field events.

But, in 1968 Jordan and those around him knew he would face both opportunities and challenges unlike any other USA Olympic coach before or after. The strength and depth of talent competing for positions on the 1968 men's team were some of the most impressive ever. Yet, there were social pressures at the time that threatened to distract athletes and coaches with the potential to adversely affect their performance in the Games. Coping with these pressures and bringing the individuals together as a team would be quite a challenge.

Also, there was a first-of-its-kind preparation challenge. The Games would be held in Mexico City, elevation 7340 feet; whereas, all previous Games had been held at or near sea level. Consequently, it would be necessary for the team to train at a similarly high elevation. So, a site was selected with an elevation of 7400 feet and a training camp built. The location was Echo Summit, California, on the south shore of Lake Tahoe. The camp included an eight-lane track and temporary living and dining facilities. The USA Olympic trials and two months of training between the Trials and the Games would be held here. The women's team would train separately at another high-altitude location near Los Alamos, New Mexico.

Turbulent Times

Turbulent social times surrounded the 1968 Olympic games. The Civil Rights Act had been passed four years earlier, the country was at the height of the increasingly unpopular Vietnam War, Martin Luther King had been assassinated April 3, 1968, and two months later Robert F. Kennedy, presidential candidate and civil rights advocate, was assassinated June 5, 1968. Clearly, all athletes and coaches were cognizant of the continuing struggle for civil rights that surrounded them, their families, and friends. Additionally, certain activists were reaching out to black athletes, proposing that they boycott the USA Team as a protest action against various forms of racial discrimination that still existed in society at large.

At a 1968 USA team reunion held in 2000, several of the athletes reflected back on the social pressures bearing upon them in 1968. "Most of us weren't interested in politics, but politics were put on our backs," said Lee Evans winner and world record setter in the 400 meters. "Our grandparents and our parents had their struggles, and we were born in the 1940s to carry that load into the 1960s." Larry James, who came in second to Evans in the 400 meters said, "There was so much going on in the 1960s that you had to take a stand. You had to run to, or run away." Madeline Manning-Jackson, then a 20-year-old runner, recalled the stressful days leading up to the Games. "The racial tension forced us to be close. We needed each other badly. We came to compete, and all of a sudden we were being asked about world problems and problems at home. People from the outside were telling us what to do. We got together and we said, 'We made the Olympic team. It's our blood, sweat and tears that brought us this far. Everybody's on their own now, but let's support each other, whatever we do.'"

Jordan's Leadership

Everyone on the team was well aware of the social issues being discussed and Jordan, too, acknowledged their existence. However, he insisted their mission ahead during the two months of final preparation at Echo Summit and through the "finish line" at Mexico City demanded their full and absolutely undivided attention. So, at the Echo Summit training camp and Mexico City Jordan would do all he could to protect his athletes from any distractions that could adversely affect their needed attention to every performance detail. Throughout, Jordan was all business, focusing on technique, final preparation, and the mental attitude needed to become an Olympic champion.

Teammates recall an incident at Echo Summit involving the now-deceased sports activist and proponent of the boycott action, Jack Scott. *[Note: Same common name and also Stanford track teammate but not the same Jack Scott who authored this book.]* Scott, an unauthorized visitor, was hassling Coach Jordan on the subject of the potential boycott. Mel Pender, one of the Olympic teammates, urged Mr. Scott in rather forceful terms to leave and not return. Teammates also recall an incident at the Mexico City Olympic Village when Jordan escorted TV sportscaster Howard Cosell away and instructed him to stay away from his athletes until after they competed.

Teammates recognized Jordan's personal credibility as a world-class sprinter and coach and his authentic interest in preparing each one of them to realize their Olympic dream. They noted his consistent support for his assistant coaches and their decisions. Jordan's view is that effective leadership must be based upon respect and loyalty as a two-way street. Thus, he was able to gain teammate confidence as a credible leader, channel their tremendous talent and commitment, and focus it all to performance on the track during their single greatest athletic opportunity.

Unselfishness Made the 1968 Team Special

Although racial tensions were common to the times, Jordan knew that his racially mixed team was forming a unique bond as they lived and trained together in the relatively isolated mountain location of Echo Summit. "That's the way it was. We all stood up for each other," said Jordan. "It's one of the teams that will go down in history as the best united and most friendly group of people in the highest level of competition." Jordan still marvels at their unselfishness. "I have never been able to explain very well about their team unity and their spirit to help one another. Whoever got first was secondary. If you can beat me, you'll be the winner and if I beat you, I'm the winner, but you still respect me and we'll love each other the same."

As an example, long-jumper Bob Beamon can thank Ralph Boston, then world record holder and former Olympic champion, for the help Boston gave him. The champion, Boston, turned to the soon-to-be champion, Beamon, and said, "You've got to get your steps straightened out." Beamon was having difficulty getting his timing right and Boston was more than happy to aid his teammate. Boston was a three-time Olympian who valued being a teammate, as opposed to being just another competitor. "He was having trouble on his run-up and in the qualifying you have three attempts to meet the qualifying standard," Boston said. "He had fouled twice. It was just a matter of settling him down and making some minor adjustments so he could qualify." With Boston's guidance, Beamon did qualify. Then Beamon went on to set a world record by such a margin that many thought it never would be beaten. Boston later joked with a smile, "That was pretty stupid of me, wasn't it? It was my world record that he broke."

When John Carlos authorized the release of his biography in 2002, he gave a copy to Jordan with a telling note inscribed on it, "To Coach Jordan, You have always been there for me in the good times and the bad times. You are a great coach and a better friend."

Unprecedented Team Performance
One of the mysterious attractions of Olympic track and field is that athletes train and dream for years to get to one brief moment of reckoning, where only results are measured. Sure this was a talented team. And, yes, they came well prepared. But, those are subjective judgments. What they did do was rise to the occasion - not as a few individuals but as a team - when and where only results are counted. These results proved to be unprecedented in modern Olympic history: twelve gold medals and six world records. Following is a recap of the twelve gold medal performances to put this team in historic perspective.

- Bob Beamon's long jump leap of 29 feet 2-½ inches smashed the existing world record by 1' 9-¾"! Beamon's record stood for 23 years. In 1991 Mike Powell improved it by less than two inches, and Powell's world record remains, today.

- Jim Hines won the 100 meters in a world record time of 9.9 seconds, equaling the then world record.

- Tommie Smith won the gold medal in the 200 meters in a world record time of 19.8 seconds. Teammate John Carlos, a former world record holder in this event, came in third.

- Lee Evans won the 400 meters in the world record time of 43.8. His record endured for twenty years. Teammates Larry James, a former world record holder, and Ron Freeman won silver and bronze medals, respectively.

- The USA 400-meter relay team (Charlie Green, Mel Pender, Ronnie Ray Smith, Jim Hines) won in a world record time of 38.2 seconds.

- The USA 1600-meter relay team (Vince Matthews, Ron Freeman, Larry James, Lee Evans) won in a world record time of 2:56.1

- The incomparable Al Oerter won his fourth consecutive Olympic gold medal in the same event (the discus) with an Olympic record toss of 212 feet 6-½ inches.

- Dick Fosbury won the high jump with an Olympic record leap of 7 feet 4-¼ inches.
- Bob Seagren won the pole vault with an Olympic record vault of 17 feet 8-½ inches.
- Bill Toomey won the decathlon with an Olympic record point total of 8193.
- Willie Davenport won the 110-meter hurdles with a time of 13.3 seconds, equaling the Olympic record.
- Randy Matson won the shot put with a toss of 67 feet 4-¾ inches.

Protest Action

While the athletes did not let social pressures affect their focus and performance, these pressures would not be ignored. When Tommie Smith and John Carlos went to the medal award ceremony for their 200 meters victory, each wore black socks and carried their shoes. The U.S National Anthem was played and Smith and Carlos bowed their heads and raised their fists. Tommie had a black glove on his right hand; John had a black glove on his left hand. Pictures of this ceremony became front-page news coverage. The President of the US Olympic Committee, Douglas F. Roby, was summoned to meet with members of the International Olympic Committee, headed by Avery Brundage. Following that meeting, Roby informed Smith and Carlos their competitor's credentials had been revoked and they were given 48 hours to leave the Olympic Village.

The protest action by Smith and Carlos received mixed reaction. "I'd defend them until hell froze over. They were part of the team. They did their job and competed like champions. That wasn't malicious or anything. We never had a harsh or a recriminating word," said Jordan of Smith and Carlos. Yet, some teammates reported they were saddened that Tommie and John would be forever known more for the controversy surrounding their award ceremony than their outstanding athletic accomplishments.

Protests continued, messages were communicated, but in a more subdued manner and without recrimination from the International Olympic Committee. In the 400 meters race, the USA team took first, second, and third. Lee Evans, Larry James, and Ron Freeman wore black berets to the victory stand, but removed them during playing of the national anthem. New long jump world record holder Bob Beamon came to the victory stand wearing no shoes and black socks. Legendary long jumper Ralph Boston came to the victory stand barefooted in silent protest.

Jordan later reported that Lee Evans came to him when all this was happening and said, "Coach, don't worry, we'll be there and do everything we have to do." Jordan later was quoted as saying, "I knew then that everything was going to work out. Our message was of greatness on the track and the other message was of greatness in a social statement that had nothing to do with the athlete. It had everything to do with society."

Reflections Over Thirty Years Later

Tommie Smith reflected back on his protest and ejection from the Games. "We didn't do it for the dinero," Smith said. "We love our country, but we wanted people to take a look at what's wrong. I don't think these kids who wave the flag to please their sponsors love their country any more than I do."

John Carlos' authorized biography released in 2002 is a story of triumph and perseverance, of courage in the face of opposition. Carlos has spent a lifetime - not just a moment - helping young people and fighting racism. John has never regretted that shining moment despite the prejudices and personal struggles that moment aroused. "I have made a statement that went down in history, and if I had to do it all over again, I would do it without hesitation. God bless!"

Madeline Manning-Jackson wondered if today's athletes, with their agents and sponsors and bank accounts, aren't in danger of missing something. "We hope they don't lose the camaraderie and relationships with their fellow athletes," she said. "Everything is so self-contained now, the priceless gift of friendships is being lost. Look at us after 32 years - we all have love and respect. This is a family." [21]

Al Oerter, legendary discus thrower, is the only person ever to win four consecutive Olympic gold medals in the same event. Since Al knew Jordan over an extended period and at the level of world-class athletics, I wanted to ask his perspective on Coach Jordan. His recent reply follows. " Payton Jordan was perhaps the most important part of my run up to the 1968 Mexico Olympic Games. I can still recall his presence at the side of the ring while we were training up at Lake Tahoe prior to the Games. I was well down the world's list that year and really not anticipating doing well in Mexico City. But Payton just seemed to lean on me to work at advanced levels that I had not experienced prior to Lake Tahoe. The result was that my distances improved quickly and I certainly started to feel that a fourth gold medal was possible. The man's influence was not only positive and direct but also lasted through the competition itself. I can think of no other coach that I have been with that had that influence on my competitive life."

Ralph Boston is a three-time Olympic medal winner, former Olympic and world record holder in the long jump, and Administrator at the University of Tennessee who commented in a letter to Jordan, "You are more than just a great coach, you are a great human and I am proud to be linked with you in perpetuity. I can never repay what you and all the gang have done for me, but rest assured I am eternally grateful."

Randy Matson, an Olympic silver and gold medal winner in 1964 and 1968, world record holder, and first to exceed 70 feet in the shot put, said in a letter to Jordan, "I really believe that those few minutes visiting with you helped me get back over 70' that last three meets. You helped me to remember some things that I had just forgotten. Looking back, I feel that if I had gone to see you in 1972 before the Olympic Trials, I would have another gold medal and still have the world record. I tried some different things in my technique back in '71 and never did get straightened out. Anyway, you can bet that if I have any more trouble, I'll know where to go for help."

---

[21] John Zant, "Reunion of 1968 Olympians recalls remarkable times," *Santa Barbara News-Press*, July 2000

Larry Young is the 1968 Olympic bronze medal winner in the 50k walk and USA Track & Field Hall of Famer. He wrote to Jordan recently, "The 1968 Track and Field Olympic Team was a special group of athletes and coaches. You certainly had a lot more to deal with than most Olympic coaches and history has shown that you dealt with it very well. Your integrity shines through it all! I'm proud to know you and to have had you as my coach."

Looking back on the team, now, Jordan says, "Each person has a very special place in my heart. And, the team has a very special place in my heart. There's no greater team in history. The record shows it. I speak for what the experts say, now: more gold medals, more world records, more silver medals, more bronze medals, more American records, the greatest team in Olympic history."

Challenges Met
The talented athletes proved their greatness by supporting their teammates and delivering outstanding results. Social pressures, too, were great and athletes and coaches expressed their convictions. Coach Jordan had taken on the role of head coach with his reputation as a great motivator and team builder. The outstanding results and teammate support, both on and off the playing field, verify that he was the right person for the right job.

1964 First Assistant USA Men's Track and Field Coach Jordan with well known Bay Area sports writer Walt Gamage (left) and the legendary Olympian Jesse Owens (center).

1968 Head USA Men's Track and Field Coach Jordan.

Mike Portonova, Head Manager, with Head Coach Payton Jordan.

1968 USA Men's Track and Field Coaches and Managers (l-r): Lodge, Roesch, Lewis, Durbin, Jordan, Portanova, Potts, Oelkers, Haydon and insert of Jordan with First Assistant Coach Stan Wright.

Payton Jordan and Stan Wright 1968 Olympic Coaches - Mexico City

Larry Questad (#297, USA and Stanford) during 200-meter dash. Cover of *Olympia Handbuch, Heribert Lechner, 1972.*

WALT LITTLE, PAYTON, RAY NEWMAN, BILL BOWERMAN, SAM BELL, GIL BISHOP

Fellow track and field coaches, not on the Olympic team staff, who provided their volunteer help at the Echo Summit training camp.

Al Oerter wins his fourth consecutive Olympic gold medal in the discus.

11. Stanford Jordan-Era: Facts and Stats

(1957 through 1979)

During Payton Jordan's 23 seasons as head track and field coach at Stanford he produced 31 All-Americans, 7 individual NCAA champions, 10 Olympians, 6 world records, and 9 inductees to the Stanford Athletic Hall of Fame. Here is just a summary of these accomplishments. Further details can be found in the Stanford Jordan-Era Track and Field Supplement," [22] also part of this book.

- All-Americans
  - 1958 - Chuck Cobb, 120-yd high hurdles
  - 1959 - Ernie Cunliffe, 880-yds; John "Jake" Kelly, triple jump.
  - 1960 - Ernie Cunliffe, 880-yds; John "Jake" Kelly, triple jump; Jerry Winter, shot put
  - 1961 - Dave Weill, discus
  - 1962 - Dave Weill, discus; Art Batchelder, javelin; Harry McCalla, cross country
  - 1963 - Dave Weill, discus; Steve Cortright, 120-yd HH; Larry Questad, 100 & 220-yd dash
  - 1964 - Harry McCalla, cross country
  - 1965 - Bob Stoecker, discus; 440-yd relay team of Eric Frische, Dale Rubin, Bob McIntyre, Larry Questad
  - 1966 - Bob Stoecker, discus
  - 1968 - Peter Boyce, high jump; Tom Colby, javelin; Brook Thomas, cross country; Greg Brock, cross country
  - 1970 - Casey Carrigan, pole vault; Don Kardong, 3-mile and cross country
  - 1976 - James Lofton, long jump
  - 1977 - James Lofton, long jump; Terry Albritton, shot put
  - 1978 - James Lofton, long jump; Roy Kissin, 10k

- Team NCAA Champions
  - 1957 - Fifth place
  - 1962 - Fifth place
  - 1963 - Second place
  - 1968 - Second place (cross country)

- NCAA Individual Champions
  - 1962 - Dave Weill, discus
  - 1963 - Dave Weill, discus
  - 1963 - Larry Questad, 100-yd dash
  - 1965 - Bob Stoecker, discus
  - 1976 - James Lofton, long jump
  - 1977 - James Lofton, long jump; Terry Albritton, shot put

---

[22] In the course or researching this book the authors sought and received input from over 150 former Stanford teammates, representing each year Jordan was at Stanford. In appreciation for this teammate support the authors have created a "Jordan-Era Track and Field Supplement." The supplement includes: Payton Jordan - Awards and Positions Held; Assistant and Volunteer Coaches; Team Captains; Current Top-10 Stanford Marks with Jordan-Era marks highlighted; Varsity Team Rosters; and Teammate Write-ups.

- Stanford Athletic Hall of Fame
  - 1960 - Ernie Cunliffe
  - 1963 - Dave Weill
  - 1965 - Harry McCalla
  - 1966 - Larry Questad
  - 1967 - Bob Stoecker
  - 1971 - Don Kardong
  - 1972 - Duncan Macdonald
  - 1976 - Terry Albritton
  - 1978 - James Lofton

- Olympians
  - 1960 - Chuck Cobb, 110m hurdles, alternate
  - 1960 - Ernie Cunliffe, 800m, 6th
  - 1964 - Dave Weill, discus, bronze
  - 1968 - Casey Carrigan, pole vault
  - 1968 - Peter Boyce, high jump, Australian team
  - 1968 - Larry Questad, 200-meters, 5th
  - 1972 - Chuck Francis, 100-meters and 4x100 relay, Canadian team
  - 1976 - Don Kardong, marathon, 4th place
  - 1976 - Duncan Macdonald, 5k
  - 1980 - Tony Sandoval, marathon (US boycott)

- World Records
  - 1961 - Ernie Cunliffe, 1000-yds (indoors), 2:07.3
  - 1965 - Frische, Rubin, McIntyre, Questad, 440-yd relay, 39.7
  - 1967 - Jim Eshelman[23], pole vault (indoor), 16'11 ¼"
  - 1973 - Curl, Kessel, Hogsett, Anderson, 880-yd relay (indoors), 1:27.4
  - 1974 - Hogsett, Bagshaw, Mason, Kring, mile intermediate hurdle relay, 3:37.8
  - 1976 - Terry Albritton, shot put, 71-8 ½

---

[23] In the 1967 Santa Barbara Relays, Eshelman also was first collegiate vaulter to clear 17 feet outdoors. The height was measured according to NCAA procedures. After the meet concluded another meet official adjusted the height down 3/4 inch, because the runway had been resurfaced and the "box" allegedly was 3/4 inch below the runway "plane." Jim remained his usual "stoic" self; his teammates were less restrained.

12. Stanford Years - 1957 through 1961

"My dad gave me love and direction; Coach gave me confidence, motivation, determination, and friendship."- Hank Roldan (Class of 1957).

When Payton Jordan arrived at Stanford in the summer of 1956, he replaced Jack Weiershauser, a former Stanford track star and a man well respected by his teammates. However, with his coaching success at academically oriented Occidental and his developing international prominence, Jordan was recognized as America's most promising young track and field coach. Stanford, of course, has never been shy about pursuing the very best. Thus, support grew quickly to recruit Jordan. Common wisdom suggested that if Stanford didn't act soon, the University of Southern California clearly would go after Jordan when their then successful coach, Jess Mortensen, retired.

At first, a number of teammates were skeptical of Coach Jordan's inspirational talks wherein he tried to convince them they could become some of the very best. They also were a little skeptical of his signs in the locker room and his other inspirational messages. However, within a few months, most totally accepted his philosophy of excellence with all the required commitments of discipline, training, and other preparations needed for peak performance. "Like a great evangelist, Coach Jordan converted me," said future All-American and Olympic hurdler Chuck Cobb.

"In the beginning, I resisted Payton Jordan's coaching philosophy and methods, but I soon realized that I had inherited a new coach with special talents in motivating athletes to perform at their maximum levels," said still top-10 ranked javelin thrower Hank Roldan. "His pre-meet pep talks injected such a strong adrenaline rush in my system that I felt I could move mountains! No coach (football, basketball, baseball, and track) had ever been able to elevate me emotionally and physically to such a height of readiness and determination in all my years of competition. I soon found myself mesmerized by his every word when he spoke to us during his pep talks. I also learned from Coach Jordan that if I could imagine something, I could accomplish it. He was not afraid to be an innovator in putting on our track meets. It was actually exciting to compete in our home meets. I especially enjoyed the Stanford band and cheerleaders performing at our Occidental-Stanford home meet."

Social Environment Affecting the Student-Athlete during this Time Period

As the first timeframe, 1957-61 was most conservative by nature. These students were born into the later years of the Great Depression and before the US was to enter WWII. To this generation, a college education was considered a privilege; and the opportunity to attend Stanford a unique one at that. This student-athlete also was most likely to be the first-generation in his family to attend college.

There was a strong sense of optimism despite the Cold War. The so called "space race" with the Soviet Union had begun. Prospects were bright for opportunities evolving in the developing electronics industry finding its home right around Stanford.

The student-athlete was respectful to authority, teachers, and peers and was eager to learn. Students sought to do well academically and athletically in a university environment that was generally conservative.

Jordan's Coaching Philosophy

Jordan arrived with a reputation both as a technical expert, particularly in the sprints and relays, and a great motivator. But, he also brought with him a philosophical sense of meaning to running, competing, winning, and being a champion. Samples of his "teachings" follow; others will be introduced in subsequent chapters.

1. The need for concentration in running

Performing well is not something that happens by mistake. If you watch opera singers or actors, for example, they become an island unto themselves before performing. You have to push everything aside and totally enter silent concentration so you can plan what you are going to do. You must plan ahead and use your concentration to make things happen. You can't always make them happen the way you want, but you definitely can come closer. You sense what's going to happen. You visualize the race and almost know how it will turn out.

2. Real winners help others to succeed, too

Great athletes are willing to share even if it costs them a victory. They don't like to see someone else fail, so they help. Maybe they lose in one sense, but they don't lose in the true sense; they gain. Some would never help anyone because they think it would hurt them. But I think that when you feel that way, you are losing something very vital that you really need in your life - the fact that you shared with someone, that you helped someone, they helped you, and you both evolved a greater respect and a greater feeling because of that.

I [Jordan] remember Jesse Owens in a national championship meet. All the sprinters, including Owens, and the starter were on the line getting ready to go, when a teammate of mine broke his shoelace. Jesse Owens said to the starter, "Wait a minute," then walked across to his bag, pulled out a shoe, pulled the shoelace out and went over and laced the guy's shoe for him. Again, this was for the National Championship! Jesse then proceeded to beat him. That's the kind of man Jesse Owens was: a very rare breed. But that's what he was like. He had no doubts in his mind about his ability, and he didn't feel it was going to hurt him to take time for somebody else. Then, he went ahead and did what he had planned to do all the time: win.[24]

3. Innovation

Jordan created an innovative and exciting setting at Stanford track meets. He put names on uniforms. He introduced the athletes before their events. He used rotating signboards so spectators could follow the field events. He hired colorful announcers and ringed the track with pennants. He even gained the support of the Stanford Band to play at key track and cross-country meets. And, behind the scene he built team morale by obtaining a special dressing room for the track team. He then covered the walls with pictures of former Stanford stars. To be eligible to use the team room athletes had to better a list of

---

[24] Sri Chinmoy, "Sri Chinmoy With His Himalayan Champion-Coach," 1984.

required marks in the various events, as set down by Coach Jordan. Also prominently displayed were the current "best marks" for each event. This had an added incentive to the trackmen, as they battled to improve their position on the so called "challenge board." Not surprisingly, attendance in excess of 10,000 for dual meets at Stanford stadium was common. One thing is certain - no one fell asleep at a Jordan-produced track meet at Stanford.[25]

Teammate Remembrances

"Ole coach"... still a sprinter
One day Coach Jordan decided he would teach us sprinters a thing or two about fast starts from the blocks. So he lined us all up (Dean Smith, Ben Anixter, Kurt Hauser and maybe Chuck Cobb was there too). Payton handed the starting gun to the freshman coach, Floyd Strain, then Payton lined up to race with us. This was just for 50 yards he told us. Well, all of us were determined to beat the coach, so we were like high-strung coiled springs. So, right before the gun fired, Jordan would flick his arm and at least one of us would false start. After about four false starts, away went the coach with about a 3-yard lead and we could not catch him. Result: a very effective non-verbal lesson on the need for focus and concentration. [Norm Pease]

An amazing journey from Norway to Stanford
We [Bertil Lundh and his wife pregnant with twins] landed at Oakland airport in early December 1958 after a 15-hour trip from New York. Nobody was there to meet us so we "had to scramble to find Palo Alto." A Greyhound bus was all we could afford. Having arrived in Palo Alto, we set out to Stanford and to find the Athletic Department. We walked up Palm Drive on a very warm Saturday morning, still dressed in our New York winter clothing -hot! We found the Athletic Department, but it was closed. Someone suggested we go to Angell Field where a track meet was going on. We went out on the field and I introduced myself to Coach Jordan. His response was: "Hi, how are you. Nice to meet you," and then turned around and walked away. Strange greeting to someone who had traveled 6,000 miles by sea, air, and land! But shortly thereafter, he turned around and said: "What's your name again?" Coach Jordan then said: "My gosh, you were supposed to be here next Monday." We got tremendous help from the coaching staff to settle down and adjust to America and California and campus life. Coach Jordan got a family doctor for us, and a night watchman job for me, as well as a cute cottage in Palo Alto. The coaching staff, as well as my teammates, gave us tremendous support for which we are eternally grateful. Thanks you all! [Bertil Lundh]
The trip by sea to New York is a story unto itself - see his write-up in Jordan-Era Track and Field Supplement.

Football player turned discus thrower
Freshman football: I suffered three brain concussions in one week - first in a home game against USC, second in practice, and third in Los Angeles against UCLA. Doctors advised an early retirement from football if a Stanford education was to be valued. Stanford's track and field coach, Payton Jordan, a former football coach, encouraged me to try the discus. Having no clue who this Coach Jordan guy was other than knowing that he had posed for a cover of LIFE magazine around the time of my birth, I followed

[25] Walt Gamage, "Jordan's system makes big hit with Stanford track, field team."

his advice. And, it was not too long before his background at USC and Occidental College was learned. It is hard to believe that we now have a son a little older than Coach was when he came to Stanford in 1956, my freshman year.

With no real experience in track and field, I found the discus to be the best event suited for me. Besides that, the competition in the javelin, shot put, and high jump, my favorites, was beyond my capabilities, talents, skills, and desires. And, the discus ring was hidden down and away from Coach Jordan's eagle eye. Not that laziness had anything to do with it, but having to run was a strange endeavor. Why run? After all, the discus ring is only 8 feet in diameter! But, Coach put running on the workout sheet daily anyway. The weight event guys rolled their eyes when the original weight-men's relay was suggested against USC. But it turned out to be a popular event in our meets with the top collegiate track powers. Chalk up another successful innovation by Coach Jordan! [Harlan Limmer]

An All-American digs deep
It was 1959 and we had not beaten UCLA for years. I was barely leading in the long jump, was slightly hurt, and had one jump left. Jordan came over and told me to go to the trainer to get ready for the low hurdles. This was at UCLA. A cheer went up from the crowd near the long jump pit. Jordan ambled over and said we had a problem. He got me off the table and we headed for the pit. Another cheer went up and I was in third place. Coach put a damp towel on my head and squeezed my shoulders. Someone in the crowd yelled, "Give it up Jordan, he'll never do it." My friend Paul Gillespie, without my knowing, put a paper marker in the pit, 8 inches farther out than I requested. My next jump was the best jump in my life up to that time, putting me back in first place. I also beat Jimmy Johnson in the low hurdles for a third place. We won the meet on the relay. [John "Jake" Kelly]

The "red coats" are coming
In 1960 a group of teammates, Art Batchelder, Dan Moore, and Don Bell, came up with the idea that teammates and coaches should wear cardinal red blazers and ties when traveling as a team. Coach Jordan quickly endorsed the idea. Fortunately, Art Batchelder's father, who worked for the Emporium, arranged the purchase. Of course, it took the resources of a major retailer to accommodate the sudden spike in demand for cardinal red blazers. On the one hand, this traveling uniform created a sense of team identity. On the other hand, there are many stories of teammates asked to handle luggage in airports and hotel lobbies. Nobody, however, seems willing to own up to any tip income. This track team innovation eventually spread to other Stanford sports. [Dan Moore]

A world-class hurdler in development: Chuck Cobb
During my senior year in 1958, which was Coach Jordan's second year at Stanford, I had not only totally "bought in" to Coach Jordan's program and regime, but had become one of its top advocates. I was honored that my teammates elected me captain, but I am not sure if I would have been elected without Coach Jordan as my campaign manager.

Teammates Look Back on the Influence of Coach Jordan

On learning to compete successfully

My memorable experiences on the Stanford track team revolve mostly around learning to compete and what it takes to be successful. Coach Jordan was a constant reminder of the need for dedication to the task at hand to be successful. I always remember Coach saying that you have to want to win to win. It was true then and is still true today. [Craig Barrett - *now CEO of Intel*]

Following in the teacher/coach footsteps

After the military, I returned to Stanford to finish my Masters Degree and teaching credential, then start my career in education in San Jose, California. With Coach Jordan's influence a huge factor in my career choice, I coached track and field for 16 years at the high school level at Pioneer and Leland High School. I spent the last nine years as Principal of Leland High School and served as President of the Central Coast Section and represented the Section on the California Interscholastic Federation Board for four years. I also chaired the CIF track and field and cross-country committee for two years. Besides my dad, Coach Jordan was the greatest role model I ever had. His influence made me want to follow the same path: work with young people in education in general and coaching in particular. [Don Bell]

Inspirational leader

Jordan is simply the best. He has positively influenced my life since I met him in college in 1957. He is upbeat, encouraging, and inspirational - a national treasure. His precepts reach out to myriads of young men and women. They don't make people like Payton Jordan very often. We who know him are very lucky. [Ben Anixter]

What makes a champion

Even though I set no records nor received All-American honors, Coach Jordan called me Champ anyway! I often asked him why he did that. Through the years, Coach often told me that I was a Champ in his eyes because of my attitude and effort to improve and using the most God gave me. This discus thrower was called self-made by the *San Francisco Chronicle*. I must have earned over a dozen Personal Best certificates! Having no track legacy from high school, this discus thrower was just an injured football player throwing a dish. But the truth is that Coach Jordan should get much of the credit for what was learned each year ... about throwing a discus and about life. Jordan never discouraged or manifested any doubt. Even when I was greatly disappointed that I was not considered to be team captain, Coach vigorously encouraged me to be all that I could be and to be myself. More from Coach Jordan was given to me than was deserved. [Harlan Limmer]

From a private person and incredible talent

Coach Jordan had many inspirational sayings posted in the locker room. As a very private person the one I most remember and tried to follow in my personal life was: "Champions are Gracious and Humble." One day a teammate added the words "AND FAST" after Humble and unfortunately that didn't apply to me! [Ernie Cunliffe]

The personal connection and friendship
Payton Jordan set, and is, the gold standard for following through on what one says he
will do. I've never known anyone who does this as consistently as Jordan. I have tried to
follow his example in conducting my life in this area - sincere caring and remembering
the efforts of all those around him. He still makes you feel important, now and back
then, when you talk with him. He lets you know, regardless of your ability, that the place
and time spent together was special and worthy of remembrance. [Bill Flint]

Not only is there such warmth and charisma in his person, but also a very special
penetrating effect in his manner that tells the person he or she is capable of doing better.
He is a master at creating self-esteem in all those whose lives he has touched. In this age
of extreme liberal attitudes, Jordan stands on the side of morally correct issues. A man's
real prominence in his life is measured by the many friendships he acquires. On this
issue, his legacy is secure. Here is a man recognized throughout the world, and yet he
possesses complete humility. I believe that while Jordan has contributed so much to the
character development and motivational growth of thousands of individuals, he would
not have had his own self-esteem working as continuously for him without the powerful
influence of one Marge
Jordan, his wife. Few people
have the opportunity in their
lifetime to possess such a
meaningful relationship as the
many of us that have been
part of Jordan's extended
family of friends!
[Al Cheney]

Coach Jordan and Chuck Cobb, Stanford team captain,
All-American, and 1960 USA Olympic team alternate.

50

Coach Jordan with Ernie Cunliffe, All-American, 1960 USA Olympic team member, and Stanford Athletic Hall of Fame.

13. Stanford Years — 1962 through 1967

"The man continues to amaze me with his memory, zest for life, and his sincere interest in other people." - Larry Questad, Olympian and Stanford Hall of Fame

The early 1960s arguably were the golden years of track and field in the United States. 125,000 spectators attended the 1960 Olympic Trials and 155,000 attended the 1962 dual meet between the United States and the Soviet Union, both held at Stanford Stadium. It was not uncommon to have crowds of 60,000 at the Coliseum Relays in Los Angeles to witness the likes of Peter Snell breaking a four-minute mile along with other great performances. And, dual meets were a mainstay at Stanford Stadium with attendance frequently in excess of 10,000.

Social Environment Affecting the Student-Athlete during this Time Period

While there are not clear cutoff dates, this period (1962-1967) was one of transition with the early years a continuation of trends that existed in the 1957-1961 timeframe. That is, this period began as one of relative harmony with a focus on academic and athletic excellence and love and respect for country. The outlook on life generally was positive, despite the Cold War overhang. The student-athlete was an independent thinker, yet generally receptive to authority and learning. There was an openness and respect for their teachers and peers. The focus was on learning without any pre-set agenda or anti-authority chip-on-the-shoulder attitude. Track teammates sought to do well academically and athletically in a university environment that generally was conservative. Extremist liberal faculty and administrators existed but were a relatively quiet minority.

The latter years of this period represented the beginning of what may be called the "Age of Rebellion." External social issues were beginning to be pushed and authority was being questioned. Liberal administrators and faculty were becoming greater in number and more vocal. The safe and conservative atmosphere of "the farm" was being inundated with outside influences - attitudes and protest actions towards the Vietnam War and a strident swing against authority figures. By 1967, the student body president, David Harris, would be sent to prison for refusing to answer his draft call. Arsonists had torched the ROTC building on campus, and anti-war demonstrations had become a common lunchtime occurrence. Even the track team was not immune from this. A freshman sprinter from England, Pat Morrison, refused to conform to the written Athletic Department appearance standards regarding the length of his hair. His refusal and resultant removal from the team became "news." This became a distraction that divided teammates and detracted from teambuilding and on-track performance.

Jordan's Coaching Philosophy

Having been a champion athlete and coach, Jordan often was asked, "What makes a champion?" Those fortunate enough to be coached by Jordan knew that being a "champion" had far deeper meaning than mere elapsed time, height, or distance on a given day. In 1967, the beginning of some very turbulent social times, Jordan was interviewed by the *Stanford Observer* and asked his view of what makes a "champion." An excerpt from the article follows.

Being a champion

It is a combination of commitment, coachability and goals. These may appear to be three somewhat prosaic words in the dictionary but their combined meaning adds up to one declaration: champion.

Commitment comes from accepting responsibility. A champion must take responsibility along with the privileges, and he must accept rules and yet not feel that his individuality is encroached upon. He has the responsibility to himself, his family, his teachers, his coach, and his team. The champion must be totally committed to a cause. Commitment is not a one-way street. In devoting himself to the committed areas, the athlete's life is enriched. An athlete can experience in one explosive moment virtually every emotion known to man: sacrifice, pride, disappointment, hurt, pain, exhilaration, sharing, and giving of himself. And with commitment, pride emerges. Pride is the ingredient that makes possible the great performance.

Coachability transcends the mere ability to take direction. A coachable athlete has respect for a leader, whether that leader is identified as his family, coach, fellow athletes, or his teachers. A champion does not follow blindly, but when he is asked to train and perform with reason and logic he will respond with his highest performance.

The athlete must have dreams and goals - without them there is no mission. Psychological endurance - mental and moral toughness - is necessary to achieve the goals an athlete sets for himself. He must face issues as they are and work them through. He must sacrifice and give of himself to reach those goals.[26]

Visionary principles

During my freshman year at Stanford [1962/63] Payton had me write a research paper on the effects of using steroids to enhance performance. He wanted me to learn how steroids could hurt my body. But most importantly, how it gave what he considered an unfair advantage. In those days many weight throwers used steroids, and of course this year's 2004 Olympics has been clouded by drug controversy. Payton was, as always, way ahead of the game with his clear image of the student athlete and the life style that dedication to sports should embody. [Bob Stoecker]

Alumni Association support

Another perspective on his coaching philosophy can be seen through the support he received from the Alumni Association Board. Following is an Alumni Association Board resolution issued in support of Jordan's focus, performance, and results.

WHEREAS for the six years of Payton Jordan's tenure as Director of Track and Field at Stanford his constant emphasis on mental and moral as well as physical development has created an image of which all Stanford alumni can justly be proud;

AND WHEREAS his consistency of performance in word and deed constitutes an outstanding example for youth, which commands the admiration and support of all who have observed his efforts;

---

[26] *Stanford Observer*, 1967.

AND WHEREAS the success of the student athletes under his charge, who have established new University records in nearly a score of track and field events during the past six years, amply demonstrates that strong emphasis on moral and mental growth is in no way incompatible with outstanding athletic performance;

NOW THEREFORE BE IT RESOLVED that this Assembly, representing the 23,500 members of the Stanford Alumni Association, considers that Payton Jordan above all others provides the qualities essential in any man entrusted with the proper development of young track and field athletes;

AND BE IT FURTHER RESOLVED that this Assembly extend to Payton Jordan, for his contributions to Stanford, the appreciation of the members of the Stanford Alumni Association, and expresses the hope that he will remain as Director of Track and Field for many years to come - thereby assuring that Stanford will recapture its great track and field heritage of the past.

Gordon F. Hamptons
President

Robert L. Pierce
Director

Teammate Remembrances
On being a Stanford student-athlete
It is difficult (and perhaps impolitic) to explain to others what a tremendous place Stanford is and how terrific the athletic program can be. I know my Stanford colleagues who read this generally will agree, but then we all shared similar experiences. What Payton taught were those qualities of success that work well anywhere - in sports, business, or public service. He started with a high level of careful organization, taught hard work and preparation, offered very skilled technical guidance, and, most of all, gave constant positive, but honest, reinforcement. Surrounded by motivated and successful student-athletes, coaches, and teachers, participating at a high level in Stanford athletics did seem routine - especially with the high level of competition we experienced. [Bud Walsh]

The Stanford experience
Coach Jordan was so terrifically organized and he too had a very special charisma about him. I had met him at the all-comers meets, but I did not realize how great a coach he really was. Although his expertise was in the sprints and field events, he quickly realized my potential and gave me the attention I needed. Sometimes I wonder what it would have been like to train with Bill Bowerman at Oregon or Jumbo Elliott at Villanova where there were TONS of better distance runners than I. But in retrospect, I flourished at Stanford, and I treasure the great academic experience. [Harry McCalla]

Jordan elects to stay at Stanford
In 1962, Jess Mortensen, the long-time track coach at USC, died suddenly and unexpectedly. Immediately, there was great speculation as to his successor; and quite naturally, Coach Jordan was at the top of the list. At that time, USC was still undefeated in over 100 consecutive dual meets, and was the perennial national champion. A tremendous amount of pressure was put on Jordan to return to USC to assure track and field dominance for many years to come. He had letters, phone calls, and petitions from virtually all of the past and present Trojan greats, Olympic Champions, World Record holders, from Parry O'Brien to Rex Cawley, and others. As speculation grew, other universities approached Jordan for the head coaching position and athletic director. I know he agonized over that, and I'm sure USC would have paid him far more than he was earning at Stanford. At our awards ceremony that year he announced that it was his intent to stay at Stanford, and to continue to build a successful program where he was. He had committed to the challenge of doing that, and, though flattered by the solicitations of his alma mater, he was going to stay! There was not a dry eye in the house. He had already attained a lofty estimation in the hearts and minds of all of us who knew him, but that act elevated him to an even higher level. [Dan Moore]

Stanford track is a team sport
Coach was the premier promoter of track and field as a team sport. One of his innovations was the addition of the weight-men's 440 relay to our meets. What a sight seeing those big guys sprint around the track! He encouraged the team to ring the track in support of Ernie Cunliffe's assault on the school 880-yard record and the 4-minute mile. He was an inspiration to all of us. I remember the great dual meets with "speed city," San Jose State; and the dual meets with Cal, UCLA and USC with crowds of 10,000 people. Led by Dan Moore, Larry Questad and Dave Weill, the 1963 team was one of Coach's most successful, taking second place in the NCAA's. [Len Breschini]

Lesson learned re commitment
By the beginning of my junior year, I was faced with a choice of doing better academically or leaving school. In an effort to put my failing college career back together, I planned to try track again and I was surprised that Coach wasn't overjoyed to see me. I recall a brief but to-the-point discussion about commitment. After a short verbal thrashing, he did give me the chance for which I will always be grateful. That was in the 1962-1963 season. We trained with more intensity than I was used to as a sprinter with a lot of weight and distance work. Someone got pushed off the track without pushing back, so we runners all had to take boxing instruction during the off-season. As a slightly heavy sprinter with short arms, I was not suited for the boxing ring. I wasn't the only one to suffer, as Larry Questad got a bruised spleen. I recall the sessions we had with the sports psychologist and the megavitamin packs that I must now confess I didn't take because they made me feel sick. Most of all I recall Coach Jordan's admonition to "let out the animal in you" or to "let out the artist in you." We all learned we were capable of accomplishments on the track we had not thought possible.
[Eric Frische - *member of the world record 440-yard relay team; now an orthopedic surgeon*]

Fall training for weight men

During the first couple years I split my time between football and track, but eventually decided to spend my time in the track program. Little did I know what awaited me that first non-football fall season. Apparently Jordan had become confused about the different needs of weight men and distance runners. Sure, he encouraged us to lift weights but - and this is where he got confused - he also had us out on the damn golf course running inconceivable distances. And he told us it was fun! When I looked around at Don Bell, Art Batchelder, and Dave Weill, I just did not see much gleeful frolicking. Though we persisted, Jordan could not be convinced that we were in danger of hurting ourselves out there. It was straining our loyalties until Don began finding perfect spots where we could walk unseen by the coaches and, even better, he found a shortcut that got us back with impressive, but not suspiciously impressive, times. [Steve Arch]

On missed opportunity

My biggest disappointment while running cross-country for Stanford was that our team never got to compete in the NCAA championships held every year at East Lansing, Michigan. I am personally convinced we would have dueled with our archrival San Jose State for the top spot in any of the four years I was at Stanford. But back then, the Stanford cross-country team didn't even merit a photo in the year book, which put us below soccer, water polo, golf and boxing in the pecking order. In 1963, I was scheduled to go to the NCAA meet along with Harry McCalla, but President Kennedy was assassinated the day before our trip and our plans were cancelled. When I catch myself feeling rueful about my missed opportunities, I always think of Jordan who was the best sprinter of his era and yet was never able to compete in the Olympics due to WWII ... but knowing the sacrifice others made, he never ever mentioned it! [Weym Kirkland]

The "flip-flop" downward baton pass

Jordan, always known for innovation, had his relay team work on a new approach to the baton pass that he was convinced would be more efficient. The passer would extend the baton forward but pointed down. The receiving runner would take off, not look back, but extend his receiving hand back with thumb and index finger spread. When the baton touched his hand he would close his grip and drive his arm forward. Well-disciplined timing, of course, is essential. Burt Nelson of Track & Field News reported, "It is only fitting that Stanford, which achieved the most perfect series of exchanges I have seen in 30 years of relay watching, was rewarded with the world record. Each exchange achieved maximum advantage and it was a beautiful sight, indeed. With such perfection it was inevitable that the record would fall." After the world record, the "flip-flop" became commonplace. [Jack Scott]

Stanford versus San Jose State, April 2, 1966: psychology and a little magic

"Psychology never scored heavier than it did in the Stanford-San Jose State track meet, Saturday," noted Dan Hruby of the *San Jose Mercury News*. "San Jose's Tommie Smith, one of the world's greatest athletes, was hoping he could wrap up a victory in the long jump with one or two jumps, then get on to his running assignments. However, Stanford "Iron-man" Bud Walsh suddenly leaped 23'11-¾', which meant Smith would have to return to the long jump after his 440-yard run. Smith put in a blistering 440, winning in a U.S. best time of 45.7. But, that pace, plus the need to return to the long jump to crank out another jump to win, was draining even for the great Tommie Smith. Stanford's Larry Questad had won the 100 yards over San Jose's premier sprinter, Wayne Herman. Then, in the 440-yard relay, Jordan presented his team with the "magic" baton. This was the same baton that a Stanford team had used the year before to set a world record in this event. The baton also had never lost in nine previous outings. Wayne Herman led his San Jose team in the opening leg but a series of weak passes, compared to three excellent passes by Stanford, gave Questad, Stanford's anchorman, a five yard lead on Tommie Smith, San Jose's anchorman. Larry sped on to victory.

Earlier in the week, Jordan had met with his team and doped out every event. *[In those days "doping" meant developing a plan as to who was needed to take what place in each event, so that the team could win.]* Jordan stressed to his runners that they needed to keep the flashy San Jose runners from winning the 100, 220, 440, and the two relays. Questad's winning the 100 and the team victory in the 440-relay were critical to the Stanford win. In the field events Bob Stoecker excelled with wins in the shot put, javelin, and discus. Jordan admits that Stoecker was great but Jordan's nomination for "hero" was little Bruce Johnson at 5'10', 134-pounds, a senior who had never won a varsity letter but who took second in the two-mile run with a 9:17.8 clocking. This was almost 8 seconds better than his personal best. Stanford's Bill Fyall also got off his all-time best in the shot put and pulled a back muscle in the process. Jordan cited this as typical of the courage and determination displayed by athletes on both squads in one of the best college dual meets ever held at Stanford.

In the stands San Jose professor, Bruce Ogilvie, who makes studies of what motivates athletes, shook his head. "And some people say psychology means nothing in sports," he chuckled sardonically." [27]

An Olympic sprinter in development: Larry Questad
Arriving at Stanford in the fall of 1961, I really wanted to play football, but Coach Jordan persuaded me that, if I was going to make it in track, there would be no football. Weight lifting and long distance training in the fall proved to be a new experience. I took a lot of starts with the Coach - damn, he was quick for an old guy! School was very hard and there were lots of distractions. I survived, luckily, and track season finally got there. I was able to win most of the time and established new freshman records in the 100 and the 220.

The fall of 1962 was different. First, I knew what to expect, and I began to build a "father-son type" relationship with Coach. By the time we began the outdoor season, Coach had my confidence up; I was in good shape and ready to run. The specifics of the 1963 season, other than I won both sprints in the conference meet, are vague until the NCAA's. But I do remember Albuquerque! 100-yard dash - national champion - fastest man in college. And then to almost win the 220, losing only to Henry Carr, who either was or would become the world record holder.

---

[27] Dan Hruby, "Psychologists - Take a Bow", *San Jose Mercury News*, Apr 3, 1966.

But, the season wasn't over. Coach got Dave Weill, Steve Cortright, and myself invited to Moscow to compete in the Communist World Championships. This was really something - parade of flags, opening ceremonies, 80,000 people, and drinking vodka. Absolutely the most exciting thing I had ever done. Then to top it all off, I won the 100 and 200 meter races, set stadium records; and then was selected the outstanding performer.

The fall of 1963, it was back to Stanford and off-season training, which was interrupted by an invitation to compete in Tokyo. It was a pre-Olympic competition and turned out to be a great trip. I had very high expectations and my goal was the 1964 Games. Then, the injuries began. In the 100-meter finals at the Mt. SAC Relays, I pulled a hamstring. But, by the time Nationals came around, I was running very well. Only one competition prior to the meet, but all I needed to do was place in the top 6 to qualify for the Olympic Trials. During the 100m heats, I had a starting block break, fell onto my face, somehow managed to push myself back to my feet and placed third. With blood running all over the place, I was informed that only 2 people moved on. No one had seen the equipment failure and despite all the protesting from Coach Jordan, I was out. End of dream! ... *perhaps not.*

The obvious highlight of the 1965 season was the Fresno Relays. There were very strong fields in both the 100 and the 440-yard relay. It was definitely my night! I ran a 9.3, several watches were 9.2, the existing world record, and then came the relay, my favorite event. Our team blistered the field and set a new world record of 39.7. This was the first time a university team had ever held this record. Previously, it always had been held by "national" teams.

Teammates Reflect on the Influence of Coach Jordan
On blending motivation, teamwork, innovation, and dedication
What can I say about Coach Jordan that hasn't been said? He had an ability to get the most out of everyone on his teams. A perfect example was our 440-yard relay team. He had us use a new hand-off technique, which is now used by everyone; and we practiced it over and over! The team consisted of two good sprinters, a world-class sprinter and me, an average quarter miler. One night in Fresno in 1965, everything, including the new hand-offs, came together. Several years later, during a telecast in Eugene, Oregon, I heard O.J. Simpson comment on our relay team and the importance of the hand-offs. He stated, "They are the most important part of the short relay. A Stanford team set the world record in 1965 with perfect passes and only one true sprinter." [Bob McIntyre]

As I think back on team meetings before big meets, a feeling of enormous pride comes over me for the opportunity to attend Stanford and the association with Coach Jordan. He prepared us physically and mentally. His media guides inspired me to be a better runner. There was an article in the *San Francisco Chronicle* that talked about my being the first "Negro" middle distance runner at Stanford. It's funny, I never thought about it at the time, Coach Jordan certainly never went there, and there was no reason to do so. So in summary, I got a great education and in the process became an All-American and collected a total of five track and field and cross-country NCAA championship medals. [Harry McCalla]

One of a kind

As the years go by, two things have grown in magnitude. First, how lucky a person is simply to make an "Olympic Team," let alone the 1968 Team, which is being touted as the "Best Ever." Secondly, how fortunate to have met a man so remarkable as Jordan. Looking back at my college days, I was as much of a problem as I was an asset to the school. There were many rules of life I needed to learn. If it had not been for Coach, I probably would have made many more bad decisions. I'll never be able to thank him enough for just being the "Ole Coach." Whether it was the Fall of 1961, when I first met him, or the days of body surfing at Catalina, or just last year when we were eating ice cream, the man continues to amaze me with his memory, zest for life, and his sincere interest in other people. He is an amazing individual. I love the man and, when he is gone, the world will have lost someone very special! [Larry Questad]

Coach Jordan emphasized not only physical preparation and training, but he also emphasized the need for mental preparation. His ability to inspire confidence in one's ability was a message that transferred onto my years in the business world - when you are prepared, you can be confident that you can get a job done. [Dave Weill]

Coach helped me learn to believe in myself, and to know that I could compete and win against anyone - and that quitting is not an option. I have applied that philosophy throughout my life and it always works. And maybe I can't pole vault anymore, but I never doubt that there is anything I can't do or overcome if I set my mind to it. Thanks, Coach. [Chuck Smith]

Jordan always was an inspiration to us - as a person and as a coach. I remember he used to work out along with the sprinters. He was in great shape. He gave inspiring pep talks and worked with us individually to create and achieve our goals. He always encouraged us to work hard in our studies as well as on the field. When we traveled, he reminded us that we were representing Stanford and that we should dress well and walk tall. [Harlan Andrews]

Some other great memories of Coach Jordan were times we spent as a team at his house. He would show us some of his awards, medals and watches and later his fighting cocks. I think he thought his chickens fought harder than we ever did! [Bob McIntyre]

A few years later when I was in grad school I got to know Jim Tuppeny, former assistant coach at Villanova and then head coach at the University of Pennsylvania. Jim offered an interesting observation about Coach Jordan. He told me that, in his opinion, Coach Jordan didn't want just to manage a pool of outstanding one-dimensional athletes, even if it meant consistent NCAA championships. Rather, Jordan was motivated to influence the character development of broadly talented young men through track and field. As I reflect on those comments, now, I wonder if anything could be more consistent with Jane and Leland Stanford's mission in founding their great University. [Jack Scott]

Coach let me keep my track scholarship (post-surgery) after I'd become about as useful to the track program as a traffic cone. Coach said, "Don't ask that you win. Ask that you do your best. If you've done the preparation and believe in yourself, you'll prevail." He was the first person in my life to define charisma by personal example. His emphasis on preparation and self-belief have been touch-stones ever since - I haven't always prevailed, but I've always known that I honestly gave it my best shot, and, thanks to Coach, I always felt good no matter what the result. [Chris Hungerland]

Difficult time ahead
The 1960s were also difficult years of social unrest and protest on campus, primarily because of the Vietnam War, but also because of rapid social change and civil rights issues. I never got the sense that Jordan had any major difficulty in dealing with all the change going on around us all, although I am sure he had some. He tried to interact with all athletes as athletes first. No one gave him more challenge that a young sprinter from England named Pat Morrison, with his brilliant sprinting style, long curly hair, and openly socialist philosophy. I remember that UCLA coach Jim Bush used a picture of Pat as the reason one shouldn't go to Stanford. In the end, Pat did himself in with his behavior, and left the team and school. Jordan suffered through the publicity and criticism as well as could be expected although it was undeserved. He always urged us to keep our eyes on our goals, which is very good advice, indeed, for all of life. [Bud Walsh]

Dave Weill, Olympian and Stanford Hall of Fame, with Coach Jordan. Credit: cover of COACH & ATHLETE magazine, April, 1963.

Summer 1963, Stanford All-Americans (l-r) Dave Weill, Steve Cortright, and Larry Questad with Coach Jordan were invited to participate in the Znamensky Memorial Meet in Moscow.

1963 Stanford team, which placed second at the NCAA Championships.

Front row 1 (left to right): Russ Peterson, Sheridan Downey, John Groeling, Dave Weill, Harry McCalla, Dan Moore, Bob McIntyre, John Beck, Dan Prono.

Row 2 (l-r): Eric Frische, Phil Arnaudo, Robin Ruble, Harlan Andrews, Gary Walker, Phil Lamoreaux, Len Breschini, Paul Schlicke, Rick Scherer, Jim Johnson.

Row 3 (l-r): Weym Kirkland, Allan Chapman, Bill Pratt, Bob Miltz, Rich Chesarek, Doug Bruce, Jack Chapple, Steve Arch, Lorne Peterson.

Row 4 (l-r): Bill Gilstrap, Phil White, Steve Cortright, Larry Questad, Ken Fraser, Graham Gilmer, Ken Emanuels, John Fontius, Jay Marik, Clayton Raaka.

Stanford world record 440-relay team: (left to right): Larry Questad, Eric Frische, Coach Jordan, Bob McIntyre, and Dale Rubin.

Jordan with Harry McCalla (All-American and Stanford Hall of Fame distance runner) on the left and Steve Cortright (All-American hurdler) on right.

Bob Stoecker, team captain, NCAA Champion, and Stanford Hall of Fame.

Pole vault world record holder, Jim Eshelman (right), and Stanford teammate, Jack Scott (left), compete at the 1969 Armed Forces Track and Field Championships.

14. Stanford Years — 1968 through 1973

"Coach's positive approach made me believe I could reach into the self I did not know and become something that I did not know existed" - Russ Taplin (Class of 1968)

This timeframe often is characterized as "The Age of Rebellion" in terms of values; and pursuing athletic greatness wasn't part of the "zeitgeist." According to teammates, it was hard to rev up for track competition when Vietnam politics were front-and-center. But, despite these formidable external distractions, very noteworthy accomplishments were achieved by trackmen of this era - testimony to their strength of character and greatness.

Social Environment Affecting the Student-Athlete during this Time Period

Major social trends, which started in the late 1962-1967 timeframe, continued to take on even greater dimension during 1968-1973. Considerable civil strife was prevalent and track and field was not immune. The non-violent civil rights movement of the early 1960s took on a different tone with the "black power" movement. There was an unsuccessful call for black athletes to boycott the 1968 Olympics. Several athletes utilized various forms of protest during awards ceremonies to demonstrate support against racial prejudice. Demands for equality on several fronts often pitted people against each other. Suspicion and distrust led to polarization between blacks and whites, men and women, supporters of the military and those against, rich and poor, educated and less educated, religious and atheists, and young and old (i.e., over 30). The university environment became a major site of protest speeches, sit-ins, demonstrations, boycotts, and demands for change. Many Stanford faculty and administrators became pro-active and supportive of such protest actions.

Relations between coaches and student-athletes in general became more "arms-length" and frequently antagonistic. In hindsight this was a natural consequence of the anti-authority rhetoric common to the times. Many parents and faculty encouraged youth to think independently and to question authority. During these times of turmoil, many in positions of authority demonstrated that their core competencies were more rooted in consensus administration rather than leadership. As passions heightened and views became polarized, one's values often became defined more in terms of what one was "against" rather than what one was "for."

The role of a college coach, particularly at Stanford, became quite difficult. There was an atmosphere of open debate as to whether an elite academic institution of Stanford's caliber should compete among the top Division 1 athletic programs. After all, comparable elite academic institutions in the Ivy League did not. Yet, Stanford coaches still were tasked to attract and develop individual and team talent, instill a spirit of dedication, focus, teambuilding, and deliver tangible and measurable results consistently against some of the strongest athletic programs in the country.

Could Stanford really have it both ways? If we fast-forward to the present, we now see Stanford remains a top academic institution and also is the leading recipient of the Sears Cup, awarded to the university with the most outstanding overall athletic program. In fact, Stanford has won the Sears Cup for the last ten years in a row beginning in 1995! Much of this success can be traced to the dedication and perseverance of some Stanford coaches, notably Payton Jordan, during some very trying times.

Jordan's Coaching Philosophy

After the 1968 Olympics, Jordan arguably was the highest profile college coach in the country. There was even an effort to get him to run for California Secretary of State within Governor Reagan's administration. Those who experienced his leadership knew very well the depth of his convictions, particularly with respect to leadership, discipline, dedication, and teamwork. During the year or so following the 1968 Olympics, Jordan accepted dozens of speaking engagements around the Country. A few excerpts from these speeches provide insight into his views towards leadership and discipline, particularly in the coach-athlete relationship.

1. On Leadership

Jordan frequently referred to an article titled "The Penalty of Leadership" in his presentations. "In every field of human endeavor, he that is first must perpetually live in the white light of publicity. The reward is widespread recognition; the punishment, fierce denial and detraction. When a man's work becomes a standard for the whole world it also becomes a target for the shafts of the envious few. If his work be merely mediocre, he will be left severely alone - if he achieves a masterpiece, it will set a million tongues a-wagging. Long, long after a great work or a good work has been done, those who are disappointed or envious continue to cry out that it cannot be done. The little world continued to protest that Fulton could never build a steamboat, while the big world flocked to the riverbanks to see his boat steam by. The leader is assailed because he is a leader, and the effort to equal him is merely added proof of that leadership. Failing to equal or to excel, the follower seeks to depreciate and to destroy - but only confirms once more the superiority of that which he strives to supplant. If the leader truly leads, he remains - the leader. That which is good or great makes itself known, no matter how loud the clamor of denial. That which deserves to live - lives." [28]

Those familiar with Coach Jordan's office remember a sign prominently displayed. It speaks to his views on principled leadership.

Cowardice asks the Question, "Is it Safe?"
Expediency asks the Question, "Is it Politic?"
Vanity asks the Question, "Is it Popular?"
But the conscience asks the Question, "Is it Right?"
And there comes a time when one must take a position that is neither safe, nor politic, nor popular, but he must take it because conscience tells him it is right.

2. On Discipline

I am convinced in my 30 years of coaching, that our role as educators, as coaches, provides us a unique opportunity to help the young to become fit, to become committed, and to become disciplined good citizens. We're overrun today with the idea that everybody should "do his thing." However, in athletics you can't very well do your own thing. You have to work together. At any other role in society where you are working towards group goals you must work in unity, not individually doing your thing at the expense of the freedom and opportunity of others. In coaching we have a great opportunity to help develop these important character traits - to help build the whole person.

---

[28] "The Penalty of Leadership," the Cadillac Motor Car Company, *The Saturday Evening Post*, Jan 1915.

The serious athlete knows that he's got to have discipline. As trite and corny as it may sound, he's got to pay the price and he knows it. He won't get there and beat the other person, the one that is paying the price, if he doesn't. And, as coaches and educators of the young, we're often the role models these kids look to. If the parents haven't instilled discipline in the youth, then our job is that much harder. But, we still need to do it. These kids come to us looking for guidance and leadership. They are going to test us. I don't mind testing. I don't mind dissent. But, I want to have a chance to be firm, when I believe something is correct in the role that I play as a coach within a team.

Coaching responsibility is something about which I'd like to hear something said a little more often. An essential, albeit unpleasant, aspect is that the coach should have the fundamental right - in fact the fundamental responsibility - to bounce whomever he wants off of the team in cases where the individual's behavior impairs team discipline. This is because such behavior diminishes the prospects of team success, thus encroaching upon the rights and opportunities of all teammates. It is the coach's duty not only to teach his sport but also to create a learning environment that fosters discipline, team unity, morale, and the highest of ethical standards.

Jordan often concluded his presentations with the following personal comment. "In my heart I feel deeply about what I say. I am fundamentally an educator. I don't want to be of faint heart. I have had 30 years in education and it means too much to me. I love these kids and they know it."

Teammate Remembrances
Smart running; winning finish
I had run 4:07 for 2 straight weeks in the mile and was up against a 4:04 miler from UCLA with a great kick. Before my warm-up for the race, Coach Jordan suggested that I start my kick early to take away the finish of the UCLA runner. I felt good with 500 yards to go, so I jumped into the lead and gained 20-25 yards on my opponent with one lap to go. I could hear Jordan yelling, "Keep your form and pump with your arms." I held on to first place by five yards, finishing in my personal best of 4:06. [Jim Letterer]

On bringing out the best in you
Coach said I could beat Olympic team and NFL star Earl McCullough over the first hurdle. He was wrong; but I did get my best start ever and almost caught him at the tenth hurdle, running my best time at the Coliseum. [Grady Means]

Canadian Olympic sprinter comes to "the farm": Charles Francis
I really enjoyed my time at Stanford, even if they did call me Chuck at the track. I first heard of Stanford from two members of my home track club, Ian and Dave Arnold, who went there ahead of me. It sounded good from their accounts and I figured the weather would not be too bad in Connecticut. It sounded better when I found out it was in California; but, fortunately, I did not hear much more about the place or I might have been too intimidated to apply. My mother bought me a copy of Payton Jordan's book *From Childhood to Champion Athlete*, which impressed me greatly and made me want to get down there to find out how to do the eggshell drills!

Teammates Look back on the Influence of Coach Jordan

Character development on "the farm"
To say the least, my first year at Stanford was an uncomfortable period of adjustment. While I set a freshman record in the vault, I also established another record for switching majors in one year - math, physics, and engineering. The track team offered an identity to a somewhat lost kid and Payton Jordan was a pier of stability. Throughout my four years on the team, I always saw Coach Jordan as the most dedicated individual I had ever met and I think I gained some strength from his example. It wasn't that he was focused solely on winning, although he was most certainly a winner. It rather was his emphasis on putting out your best effort in everything you did. He made it very clear in both his actions and words that win, lose, or draw, you could walk away proud if you knew you had prepared well, fought hard, and accepted the outcome on your own terms. To him, it was as much about character as it was about being a winner and to be a true champion in life you had to have both. [Clint Ostrander]

Clarity in a time of uncertainty
Coach Jordan presided over this collection of egotists and characters with grace and determination. He hated excuses and he hated to lose. He did not care to compromise with the long hair and social changes that washed over us all in the 1960s, but he was a genuine friend to every trackman who ever made an honest effort. To borrow a phrase, he was a man of clarity in a time of uncertainty. [Roger Cox]

Support and leadership
At Stanford, the lasting impressions of Coach Jordan are support and leadership. He took a very strong interest in each athlete, from the first day of freshman year. And through good times and bad, he was a great leader - the locker room sign, "lead, follow, or get out of the way." He researched every event and was extremely helpful on the fine details of technique and training. And, he coached attitude. Who could forget visiting his home and having him compare his athletes to the fighting cocks that he raised. He said he could tell from the attitude of the boys (and the birds) how they would do from how they walked, how they held their heads, how they approached competition. He loved brave, tough attitude. [Grady Means]

Role model
I remember Coach Jordan's pep talks before every track meet. His encouragement to do our best, compete fairly, and represent Stanford to the best of our abilities was terrific. But most important of all to me was Coach Jordan's personal talks with me when I was injured my sophomore year in track season. He encouraged me to get therapy every day. As I healed, he emphasized not coming back too quickly or risk re-injuring my hamstring. I did come back stronger my junior year and finished as Stanford's number one runner in cross-country and ran personal bests in track. Coach Jordan was one of my positive role models in my entire life. He was a great pillar of integrity and honesty with high moral and religious values. He will forever hold my admiration and respect.
[Jim Letterer]

Positive attitude
It is safe to say that Coach Jordan and I are of quite different personality types. I am not always able to muster the everyday enthusiasm that Coach Jordan always conveyed to us. As it is for all of us, he has certainly had his disappointments, some of them major I know, but he has managed to embrace all that has been good in his life and to allow that to determine his attitude and his demeanor with those around him. It is a quality that I have tried to call upon in difficult moments and times, particularly since I have received more than my share of blessings. A major inspiration at such times is Payton Jordan. [Peter Boyce]

On reaching and becoming
On receiving the request for input to Jordan's biography, I simply took the first three words that came to mind in describing him: positive, enthusiastic, and kind. Not all of us were or could be record holders or super stars but all of us could have repeat personal bests. Coach was infectiously positive, a true believer, and his persona at its core was simply and completely upbeat. Negativity had no place at Angell Field. Coach's positive approach made me believe that I could reach into the self I did not know and become something that I did not know existed. [Russ Taplin]

1968 Cross Country team placed second at the NCAA Championships.
Left to right from the front row:
Row 1 (left to right): Allen Sanford, Bob Anchondo, Brook Thomas,
and Chuck Menz.
Row 2 (l-r): Greg Brock, Don Kardong, and Coach Marshall Clark.

Stanford distance running powerhouse (l-r): Don Kardong (1976 Olympian, 4th in the Olympic marathon, and Stanford Hall of Fame), Arvid Kretz (Stanford All-Time #4 in 2-mile and #3 in 3-mile), and Duncan Macdonald (1976 Olympian in the 5K, Stanford Hall of Fame, and first Stanford runner to break the 4:00 mile).

Jordan with Assistant Track Coach and Head Cross Country Coach Marshall Clark.

Jim Ward, third-fastest Stanford 440-yard dash and team captain, with Jordan.

Peter Boyce, Stanford and Australian Olympic high jumper, with Coach Jordan.

For Jordan nurturing is a way of life: athletes, birds, flowers, fruit trees, etc.

15. Stanford Years — 1974 through 1979

"90 percent of the people never go head-to-head, you win or you lose, no excuses, making those who do a somewhat rare breed." - Matt Hogsett (Class of 1976)

This was a period that produced some truly outstanding athletes. James Lofton was a three-time All-American and two-time NCAA champion in the long jump, a strong relay runner, and later a member of the NFL Hall of Fame. Terry Albritton was an All-American, NCAA Champion, and world record holder in the shot put. Three teammates made the USA Olympic team: Don Kardong and Duncan Macdonald in 1976 and Tony Sandoval in 1980. The depth of talent and commitment went far beyond these standout athletes. Now, teammates reflect back with the benefit of decades of hindsight not just on athletic accomplishments but the important life's lessons learned.

Social Environment Affecting the Student-Athlete during this Time Period

Although anti-authority social trends of the 1968-1973 timeframe continued at the beginning of this period, there was a slow swing back towards the trusting and respectful relationships that existed between coach and student-athlete characterized by the first and some of the second timeframes of Jordan's tenure. These student-athletes seemed less influenced by the rhetoric of dissidents. They were able to compartmentalize their thinking, so that they could focus attention to excellence as a teammate on the track and excellence as a student in the classroom. And, they learned to enjoy life while being aware of, but not controlled by, dissident influences that were waning somewhat on and off campus. They were self-motivated to succeed and knew certain authority figures, such as coaches, could help "enable" them to succeed. They didn't spend much time dwelling on what might be generational, philosophical, or political differences.

Jordan's Coaching Philosophy

1. On mutual respect

Jordan's coaching relationship is not one of domination, intimidation, or cheerleading. Rather, his relationship with his athletes is grounded in mutual respect. He demonstrates this same respect for each of his athletes, whether they were one of his high school athletes at Redlands or great Olympic champions. He has the unusual ability to recognize in an individual athlete when the athlete can use a little help or when the athlete needs some space to work things through on his own. Perhaps a sign of a truly great coach is one that also can recognize when not to coach. "In 1964 Payton was at the side of the ring during a training session when I tore the cartilage off my ribcage. I think he felt as bad as I in that I believe he thought the Olympic Games were not in the cards for me. What I did appreciate was his not referring to the injury on a continuing basis and his willingness to let me get on with the competition, if I felt I could. None of the nonsense: you can do it, disregard the pain, or this is your one chance to win a third gold medal that few have done before. He allowed me to figure it out for myself without his influence - it was much appreciated," said Al Oerter - four-time Olympic Champion.

2. On winning

In an interview with Sri Chinmoy, Jordan shared his view on what constitutes winning. "My feeling is that the winner can come from any level - first, second, third, fourth, fifth or very last - providing he sets goals, works hard, achieves a new pinnacle in his life, and just takes part to the best of his ability. This is a winner, and to just worship at the shrine of number one is a mistake because everyone is a part of the process. If there were not a lot of people there, there couldn't be a winner. If you were all by yourself, you couldn't place first. You've got to have other people. So everyone plays a part in making the winner a winner. We all take part. We all have a piece of the action. We all do something and we all contribute and share." [29]

The teacher and philosopher at heart, Jordan wrote a poem on the subject of what constitutes winning.

To Be the Best One Can Be - by Payton Jordan

To warm up on the billowy sod
Behold the closeness to God
I will fly under the beauty of the skies
In the freedom that no one denies

Then to the rebound of the tartan
I will run like the bold Spartan
Oh, to the greatness of God, is the greatness within
To run the best one can is to win

3. Championship reflections – Jordan's personal notes for a team meeting

"We have told the story. Father-son relationships. Belief in each other, being the best one could be athletically, academically, and as good human beings. Did we learn life skills, did we learn respect and love for others, to carry oneself with pride and confidence while presenting one's best self to the world. Did we come to learn we were gentle persons first and then athletes with pride...groomed well, committed, disciplined and coachable, reaching for the stars, dreaming dreams, setting goals, and holding an inner faith while striving to be the best we could be." [30]

4. Innovation and collaboration among coaches

With credible experience in both football and track Jordan sat down with Stanford head football coach, Bill Walsh, to made his case that some highly talented wide receivers and running backs could become even better football players if they ran track. Walsh agreed with Jordan's reasoning, so a number of football players were selected to run track in lieu of spring football practice. These future NFL greats (e.g., James Lofton, Darrin Nelson, Gordon Banks, and Ken Margerum) proved the collaborative development plan initiated and orchestrated jointly by Jordan and Walsh would produce tangible results for the Stanford teams and enhanced professional opportunities for the individual student athletes.

---

[29] Sri Chinmoy, "Sri Chinmoy With His Himalayan Champion-Coach," 1984.

[30] Quotation from Payton Jordan.

71

Teammate Remembrances

Image lesson from the "ole coach"
Following a particularly hard fought, second-place finish in the 400 intermediate hurdles in the USC dual meet at the LA Coliseum, ole coach put his arm around me in apparent support and whispered, "Tuck in your shirt, Tiger, you're on national TV."

Now, nearly 30 years later, having thrived in the suit and tie world, not a day passes without a thought about or a lesson learned from ole coach. Long forgotten are the rebel encounters with Coach Jordan, the authority figure - "Get your hair cut, Champ"; "Tuck in that shirt, Tiger." Those memories have been replaced by a timeless, enduring sense of integrity, self-respect, and personal accountability. As I parent my three children, coach their teams, listen to their dreams, and attempt to imprint solid values, I am never far from Payton Jordan and his teachings. [Kenny Kring]

The personal connection
The most memorable thing I remember about Coach Jordan is the day I first met him. I definitely was not a recruited athlete, nor had I filled out any sort of questionnaire regarding my high school track career. I merely hoped to be accepted as a walk-on. I had heard the cross-country team would be working out the week before freshman orientation, so I made arrangements to stay with some relatives in Mountain View, California until the dorms opened. When I first arrived on campus I made my way through the maze of hallways that eventually took you to the track office, and poked my head through the doorway and introduced myself to Marshall Clark, whose desk you could see from the door. Marshall greeted me and steered me toward the inner sanctum, Coach Jordan's office, and introduced me to him. Much to my shock and amazement, Coach Jordan proceeded to tell Marshall about all my high school accomplishments, as if he had known me for some time. Talk about making a sheepish freshman feel right at home! Here was the legendary coach of the 1968 U. S. Olympic Team rattling off the best times and jumps of a two-bit high school kid from Vallejo! From that day on Coach Jordan has always had a special place in my heart, and he is a large part of my motivation for coaching middle school kids, as I do today. [Jim Bordoni]

Special trip
Because of his 1968 Olympics connections, Coach Jordan arranged for the Stanford team to be invited to compete against the Mexican national team in Mexico City in 1977. The local track officials greeted him with full regalia and honors. We had a blast. Coach Jordan could have visited his friends without us and not have taken the trouble to haul us along. But he did. [Clay Bullwinkel]

Success continued
Coach Jordan retired at the end of my freshman year. I don't think there was any connection between my arrival and his departure. Anyhow, using the lessons that I learned from him, as well as his successor Brooks Johnson, I went on to have a reasonably successful track career, highlighted by stints as one of our team captains in 1981 and 1982, a ranking at graduation as Stanford's no. 4 all-time 400 hurdler, and a semifinal berth in the 400IH at the TAC National Championships in 1984 (50.72 PR) while attending Stanford Law School. [Garry Schumway]

In the game
I now tell my kids that 90 percent of the people never go head-to-head - you win or you lose, no excuses, making those who do a somewhat rare breed. For those I have encountered during my life who consider athletics to be brutish, I have told them there is one time in your life when you are the strongest, the fleetest, the most alive - those young years in a person's life, when you choose what you are, whether you are in the game or not. For the great or, like myself, the not-so-great, the lesson is the same. [Matt Hogsett]

Profile of an Olympic marathoner: Don Kardong
In the spring of 1976 I decided my future might be in the marathon. I entered the Olympic Trials Marathon that spring and surprised a few people by taking the third spot behind Frank Shorter and Bill Rodgers. My experience in the Montreal Olympics was even better, although bittersweet, as I finished fourth in 2:11:16. I ran faster than the Olympic record. Unfortunately, so did the three guys ahead of me. I missed the bronze medal by three seconds.

Teammates Look Back on the Influence of Coach Jordan

Definition of a champion
In the spring of my senior year, I received a medical school acceptance, culminating my years of study at Stanford. I ran to the Coach's office to inform him. He was already down at the track with the sprinters and field event guys. When I informed him of my news he suddenly picked me up by the waist, hoisted me in the air and announced my good fortune to the team. He then told me to run to the golf course to inform my distance coach, Marshall Clark. "You're a champion, Hadley," he said, "on and off the field." I ran through campus to the golf course with tears in my eyes, pleased by my good fortune, but most pleased that Coach Jordan was so proud of me, one of "his guys." Finally, it was an honor to receive the Al Masters Stanford Track and Field Scholastic Achievement Award at the conclusion of my senior season and a Stanford blanket signifying four consecutive years as a varsity athlete. [Mark Hadley]

Lessons learned
No one ever knew better what young men and women can do or how better to motivate them to do it. Coach Jordan has my greatest admiration and gratitude. But, of course, with his sense of humility he would be the last to acknowledge it. Such is the man. I hope he knows what a legacy he has left. [Matt Hogsett]

You taught me a lot about track, but more about how to behave as a gentleman with humility, humor, passion, etc. and for that I am eternally grateful. [Terry Albritton]

My most memorable experiences with Coach Jordan revolve around the one-on-one attention he was always willing to give me. He treated me like he was not only proud of who I was, but also proud of what I could become. Little pointers like not wearing socks (less slippage in the shoe), finishing a longer run with a sprint (putting in the extra effort when you think you have nothing left to give), and showing me proper running form and insisting that I maintain it. Finally, I will never forget two of the most important moments I shared with Coach Jordan: the day I met him in his office, before I was even accepted to Stanford, and the day I sat down with him in his office and resigned from the team. He understood my decision, and felt my loss and pain; however, he understood. He knew that I learned a lot more than about sprinting from him over the previous two years. He knew that I would not forget him, the team or the lessons he taught me about sprinting and life, the parallels. He was right. [David Schreiber]

Coach Jordan reinforced in me the merits of dedication, training, preparation, sacrifice, and a positive work ethic. He asked us to believe in ourselves, in our team, and our coaches. He taught me that the whole, the team, is bigger than the parts, the individuals. He reinforced the concepts of team achievement and the value of every member's contribution, no matter how small. He celebrated our wins and taught us how to lose with dignity, although never to be comfortable with losing. He taught us never to rest on our laurels but to consistently prepare to do our best - because on any given day the mighty might be defeated by the lesser known. He helped us set our sights and goals and showed us how to achieve them. He helped me translate my athleticism and the lessons learned in the athletic arena into my scholastic and personal life - and ultimately into my professional life. Coach Jordan was (and is) much, much more than a world-class athlete and track coach. [Mark Hadley]

Vineyard consultant to the ole coach
One of my favorite memories of Coach Jordan is as his vineyard consultant about ten years ago. When he heard that I had gotten into grape growing and winemaking, he asked if I could come by the Rancho in Los Altos and guide him in his pruning. His interest in grapes, fruit trees, flowers, gardening, and birds continued after his retirement from coaching. So for a few years, until he got the hang of it himself, I would go over to his place every spring and spend an afternoon with him in his incredible back yard pruning back the myriad varietals he had growing back there amongst the chicken coops and the fruit orchards. About this time I also started coaching track at my sons' grammar school. My boys were in the third and fifth grades at the time; but, not being real confident in my coaching abilities, I thought I might bring in a true expert as a guest coach one day. Of course, Jordan never hesitated to say yes to my request, and he spent a memorable afternoon mesmerizing a dozen or so kids who did not really grasp the magnitude of their good fortune. One of my favorite pictures is the group shot I took of the kids with Jordan. To me it just sums up how magnanimous the Coach is: a true gentleman and ambassador of the sport. [Jim Bordoni]

Fundraising for Stanford track & field.
We ordered and waited for our food. Whether sitting or standing, Coach Jordan comes across as energized and spry. I could not help but start thinking of my loss of my father four months earlier. I mentioned dad. Coach Jordan said a few things that showed he remembered him well. Ole' Coach could read my face all the way. He showed complete acknowledgement when he nodded a few times. Nothing more on that topic needed to be said. A feeling came over me as if I was with a close relative. But with whom? Not a grandfather. An uncle? A much (much!) older brother? I thought about all those athletes naming their son Payton. Then it dawned on me. I sat up in the booth smiling ear to ear

at Coach Jordan. We returned to the topic of fund raising. It took me 19 years, and a dear loss, but I finally understood him, and he understood me. This fellow was not only an athlete, a coach, a teacher, a mentor. His greatest mission, his foremost gift, is to be there when a person needs something a bit more heavy duty. Fatherliness can incur risks. Kindness is not always returned. Yet he does it readily, repeatedly, and graciously. [Clay Bullwinkel]

Two NFL greats remember their ole coach
Coach Jordan taught me how to run. I was very quick and had the potential to be very fast. After my freshmen year of football, I was instructed by Coach Bill Walsh to run track. I was not allowed to participate in spring football. It turned out that Bill and Payton spoke and about halfway through my freshman football season - the coaches got together and decided I would run track. Coach Walsh assumed running track would help me in football in the long run. He was right. Running track at Stanford made me a number-one pick in the NFL draft. [Darrin Nelson]

The most meaningful time I had with Coach Jordan was in March of 1978. Coach Jordan and I traveled to Detroit for the NCAA Indoor Championships. I had just finished my senior season of football, played in the Senior Bowl, and our Stanford team had won the Sun Bowl. I was getting ready for an NFL career. It was just the two of us traveling. Coach Jordan talked about my upcoming NFL career and what life would be like as a pro athlete. Coach Jordan instructed me on continuing to train like a "champion." He talked about how to conduct yourself like a "champion." I recalled the sign above the track locker room door, "Champions Should be Gracious and Humble." To me that is the essence of Coach Jordan.

It is quite an understatement to say he had a great effect on my athletic career. All the pro football Hall of Fame coaches I played for - Bart Starr, Forrest Gregg, and Bill Walsh - were only the tip of the iceberg compared to Payton Jordan. He made me believe in myself as a champion! Thank you for everything and more. [James Lofton]

Bonds are strong
My strongest memory of Coach Jordan took place just a short time ago [in 2002]. Coach Jordan was asked to speak at the eulogy for Coach Marshall Clark at the Saratoga High School Gym. I was introducing myself to members of the 1968 Stanford cross-country team, which Clark coached to a second place finish in the NCAA championships. Coach Jordan strode in with his wife and upon seeing the faces of the 1968 squad burst into tears. The normally ebullient and talkative Jordan was speechless. [Stacy Geiken]

James Lofton, the finest sprinter/long jumper ever to attend Stanford, crosses the finish line in a winning 400-meter relay. Lofton still holds the Stanford long jump record and has been inducted into the NFL Hall of Fame.

Jordan with Bill Walsh, Stanford football coach.

Former NFL greats with their ole Oxy football coach, Jordan. (l-r) Ron Botchan, Jack Kemp, Marge and Payton Jordan, and Jim Mora (2004).

Jordan with shot put world record holder Terry Albritton (1976).

Jordan with Kenny Kring, outstanding
decathlete and assistant coach.

16. Post-Jordan Era: Coach of the Coaches

"You and the athletes you coached always gave your best in representing the University; and when others gave in to passing fads, you stood firm in championing those ideals which the founders of the University decreed." - Albert S. Bradford,
Stanford Class of 1955

Jordan retired from his head coaching position at Stanford in 1979. Of course, as Track Coach Emeritus, he would never stay too far from track and field and the young people so important to him. He subsequently played a lead role in fundraising and overseeing the renovation of the Angell Field track on the Stanford campus. The new Cobb Track and Angell Field complex, now, is one of the premier track and field facilities in the country. And, his influence on younger Stanford coaches in many different sports, as they began their coaching careers, has contributed to the athletic program success Stanford enjoys to this day - ten straight Sears Cup titles beginning in 1995.

Mentor to Younger Coaches

Beyond the scope of track and field, Jordan proved to be a role-model mentor to the younger Stanford coaches starting out their coaching careers. "I take pride in what role I may have played in helping them succeed in their coaching careers, both in terms of the results on the playing field and even more importantly the influence they have had on the character development of so many fine student-athletes in the process," said Jordan.

1. **Football: Dick Vermeil** - Dick was a young assistant football coach at Stanford in the late 1960s, and then went on to become a very successful coach in the National Football League. According to Dick, Payton Jordan was instrumental in Dick getting his first opportunity in the NFL. "George Allen, then head coach at the Los Angeles Rams, was an old friend of Jordan's from Jordan's Occidental days. When George was looking to hire someone for a new position he conceived (Special Teams Coach), he called his old buddy, to see if Jordan might know of a young assistant college coach that would fit Allen's needs." Jordan recommended Vermeil. According to Dick, "George hired me and I found out years later that he didn't even interview anyone else." When asked why folks rely so much on Jordan's judgment, Dick replied, "I think it is his combination of credibility and authenticity."

2. **Football: Pete Kettela** - quarterback coach. " I shall always remember your competitiveness, hard work and honesty in dealing with people."

3. **Football: Dave Tipton** - defensive line coach. "You are one of my all-time favorite people. I hope I look and feel half as good as you when I grow up! You will always be my hero. Payton, you are the epitome of what Stanford is all about."

4. **Baseball: Mark Marquess** - Mark, a member of the Stanford Athletic Hall of Fame, started with Stanford baseball as a player in 1967-1969, then as an assistant coach from 1972-1976, and head coach since 1977. Through 2003, his teams have reached the College World Series in each of the last five years. "I have played for

and coached with some of the finest college coaches in the nation. But, Payton, you are head and shoulders above any coach I have ever seen - you are the very best and will always be the coach I respect the most! I just hope that in my coaching career I can have half the positive influence on my athletes that you had on the athletes you coached. Thank you for all your help in my career! You showed me that you could be a winner and still be a man of integrity and class. You took no shortcut - you always did things the right way!"

5. **Women's Swimming: Richard Quick** - Richard has been Stanford women's swimming and diving coach since1987. His Stanford teams have won seven NCAA titles and finished lower than third only once during his sixteen-year tenure. Quick has won a total of 12 NCAA titles during his collegiate coaching career, the most in the history of Division 1 coaching. "Every time I see you, it reminds me of the reason I became a coach and teacher. Your record in athletics, both as a coach and competitor, is beyond belief, but your positive influence on all those that have had the honor of your association is more valuable than can be put into words. I will forever be extremely grateful that I have had the opportunity to understand why Bob Timmons, all your peers, and all your athletes think so highly of the Great, Gentlemanly, Legendary Coach. Thank you for being so kind to a newcomer to 'the farm'."

6. **Men's Swimming: Skip Kenney** - Skip has been Stanford men's swimming and diving coach since1979. He has guided Stanford to 22 straight PAC-10 titles and seven NCAA titles. In addition to Stanford, Skip was the 1996 USA Head Olympic Swimming Coach, assistant Olympic coach in 1984 and 1988, six-time NCAA Coach of the Year, and recently inducted into the International Swimming Hall of Fame. "As I have grown as a coach, I have come to appreciate more than ever the truly good people who are devoted to the principles of teaching and have a genuine concern for the coaching profession as a whole. In my view, no one has been more influential and instrumental as an advocate of those principles of professionalism and instruction than Payton Jordan."

7. **Women's Tennis: Frank Brennan** - During Frank's tenure as Stanford women's tennis coach from1980 to 2000, they captured ten NCAA titles. "I'll never forget how the legendary coach was so friendly and generous with this rookie coach back in 1979-80. You made me feel so welcome! I try but rarely succeed, to make rookies feel at home following your example. You are my idol!"

8. **Men's Tennis: Dick Gould** - Dick has been head coach of the Stanford men's tennis team for the past 38 years. His teams have won 17 NCAA titles and finished in the top five 29 of the last 34 years. "You have had a very definite positive and profound effect on my coaching methods and my attitude towards things in general. From the time I was a student in the late 1950s in your track and field 'methods' course on up to the present, I have continued to learn a great deal from you and the way in which you handled yourself and other things. In short, Payton Jordan symbolizes 'class' in every respect and I shall always be grateful to you for the impact you have had upon me and my personal and professional growth."

9. **Volleyball: Don Shaw** - Don has coached both men's and women's volleyball for the past 20 years. "You'll always be one of my role models and I'm proud to be able to say I've been associated with you."

10. **Men's Track & Field: Marshall Clark** - former assistant track coach and head cross county coach commenting on Jordan's induction into the Stanford Athletic Hall of Fame. "Possibly the young Turks in the current power structure were impressed enough with "Chariots of Fire" to look back into the record books and see what track and field was like when the public was interested enough to come out and watch the meets. You are most deserving and certainly one of the track legends of my life."

11. **Men's and Women's Track & Field: Vin Lananna** - Vin was Director of Track & Field/Cross Country at Stanford from1992-2003. He guided Stanford to five NCAA titles in track and cross-country for both men and women. In 2003, Vin accepted the position of Director of Athletics at Oberlin College. "Your support, optimism, advice and friendship will always be appreciated. You're a great coach and an inspiration to our staff and track teams. Cobb Track and Angell Field is a dream come true - thanks."

Peer Coaches
In addition to his favorable influence on younger Stanford coaches, Jordan also is well respected by peer coaches both at Stanford and elsewhere.

1. **UCLA Track: Jim Bush** - long-time UCLA Track Coach. "This is a great honor to be able to write a letter about the man and coach that I've admired for so many years. If I had to pick a person that would best represent what we are looking for in a coach...Payton Jordan would be the man. I'm just starting my 53rd year in coaching, and I have not found anyone who has all the qualities that he possesses. Payt is one of the most knowledgeable track coaches I've ever met. He is one of the greatest organizers, motivators, dedicated to helping teach all his athletes not just about track, but also about life in general. When I coached at UCLA, my teams were some of the top teams in the nation. But the team that gave us the best competitive competition was the Stanford team. We always had more talent than Stanford but we had to compete all out, because we knew the Stanford team would. His athletes really loved him as a man and coach. I got to know most of his athletes, and we had a very friendly relationship. I would like to relate a story to prove what I just said. I had a team of seven great athletes in Dublin, Ireland in 1963 that were going to compete against the Irish.

Three of the athletes were members of Stanford's 1963 NCAA squad; two were NCAA champs. These three young men kept talking about what a great coach and person Payton was. One of the other athletes said, 'I'm tired of hearing, Payton this, Payton that, etc.. You act like he is God!' The three athletes looked at each other and with a little smile, all said in unison, 'Maybe he is!' The complaining athlete got mad and walked away. What went through my mind was how lucky to have athletes admire you that much. To know Payton Jordan is to love him. I regard Payt as one of my very best friends and really miss not seeing him at all our track meets. Thanks "Payt" for being my friend."

2. **USC Track: Ernie Bullard** - former great USC track coach. "If there is a notion of the quintessential mentor, it would be Payton Jordan. His talents for preparing the individual to developing major events are a matter of record.

Nineteen-sixty-eight was a time when elements of the fabric of society began to unravel. Payton's performance as the Olympic coach was vital! His sense of firmness, flexibility, and fairness allowed the complex situation to conclude successfully. Without his leadership, track & field could have been a disaster. The members of that team respect him, today.

The late Bud Winter [former San Jose State coach] and I often spoke of Payton in the highest terms. Frankly, I never heard Bud say a negative thing about his friend. That is unusual among coaching foes.

My professional goal was to coach at USC. Payton's support was instrumental in making that a reality.

My competing and coaching memories are an intricate part of my life. In particular, I have enjoyed and cherished the company of Payton Jordan."

3. **UCLA Basketball: John Wooden** - legendary UCLA basketball coach. "We taught through a special era. I was very fortunate to be able to share it with you and others with similar philosophies. However, since I am about ten years your senior, please do not refer to yourself as old. This will be more clear to you ten years from now."

4. **Stanford Baseball: Dutch Fehring** - retired Stanford head baseball coach. "I've always considered you to be the best friend I ever had at Stanford and will always appreciate having been there with you to share in your many, many wonderful qualities."

5. **Stanford Gymnastics: Wes Ruff** - retired Stanford gymnastics coach. "The department will in time recognize the quality of your program and the class you brought to it. Those of us who know the situation have long admired the kind of program you have conducted and appreciated the frustration circumstances have caused you. I am honored that you call me your friend."

Academic Faculty and University Administration

At the core Jordan is a teacher, a builder of character. Consequently, his support from Stanford academic faculty members and University administration is particularly meaningful to him.

1. **Joe Franzini** - Joe was an engineering professor, now Emeritus Professor, at Stanford. "I have always admired your basic philosophy and have tried to apply some of your concepts in the classroom - try hard, do your best, play fair, be honest. I want you to know that the impact of your philosophy extended beyond the bounds of the men of the track team. I sincerely mean that."

2. **Dick Johns** - Dick was Dean of the School of Earth Sciences at Stanford. "Since those long-ago days when I watched you as a USC football player, I have admired you as a winner. That admiration remained even when I was at Cal Tech, helping judge track and field events while your Occidental teams were beating our ears back. I reckon it was mainly because you always have been a clean, hard competitor, with enormous and fine influences on younger people."

3. **John Bunnell** - John was Admissions Officer. "When I think of all the joy and class you've brought to Stanford University and the Bay Area over the years, Payt, I put you in the 'national treasure' category. It's not 'cool' to have heroes these days, but I proudly include you among the top as one of my all-time favorites."

4. **Douglas Walker** - Doug also was an Admissions Officer. "Ever since I first came to know you at Stanford, I always admired you for your high standards. It made no difference whether it related to the athlete's performance on the field or in the classroom. You have high standards and you expected the same from your men. Perhaps that is why you were able to turn out some mighty great champions."

5. **Don Carlson** - Don was Directory of University Relations. "You will not remember, but after your first year at Stanford and while I still was in the Southern California office, I tagged along on one of your recruiting visits to a high school track star and his family. I have never forgotten the impression you made on that family, that youngster, and not the least, me. A man as positive about life as you are is bound to have critics among the less positive people who seem to populate most of the earth. I've dealt with a few of them, each time beginning with my memory of you off the field, in that family's living room, where the starting blocks for a special friendship were set for me."

6. **Jo Blue** - Jo was head of food and dormitory service. "Some of the most pleasant memories of my Stanford days revolved around the US-USSR track meet and I realize what made them so memorable was Payton Jordan! Your understanding and helpfulness to the Stern Hall Food Service Director in trying to provide meals that would please a variety of nationalities was tremendous. You always had time for those not in the limelight."

Athletic Department

Within the Department of Athletics administration Jordan's unique contribution is recognized not only as a world-renowned coach but also as a teacher and mentor to student-athletes and other coaches. Jordan also was close to all the folks in the Athletic Department support operations, who made major events come off so successfully.

1. **Joe Ruetz** - Joe was Stanford Athletic Director from 1972-1978. During his tenure, he merged the men's and women's athletic programs. "I am fully aware of the difficulties under which you worked in trying to build a competitive track program at Stanford. What you were able to do with the limited help you were given by others and me was simply remarkable. Even more than that is the positive influence you had on the young men who were privileged to be coached by you. That is a far better measure of success than the wins or losses that might have accrued had it been different in other ways."

2. **Gary Cavalli** - former Stanford Sports Information Director. "Your personal warmth, integrity, energy, enthusiasm, high standards, fairness, and sense of responsibility are things that I've admired and tried to emulate in my own life. You are one of only a few great men I've known."

3. **John Kates** - John was Director Major Gifts. "Words can't begin to express the admiration, respect and love Gene and I have for you. You are truly a Champion of Champions."

4. **Alf Brandin** - retired Director of Development. "I've always thought of you, Payton, as one of the greatest of all track coaches! And not only because of your professional ability and competence in your field, but because as a great leader and inspirational coach you have helped direct young men towards the right values of life."

5. **Jon Denney** - Assistant Athletic Director (Development). "You've been a source of inspiration for so many people associated with Stanford Athletics over the years. Thank you for making such a big impact on this great University."

6. **Ray Purpur** - Associate Athletic Director (Operations). "You're such an inspiration to work with. I think of all the things we worked on to make the track [new world-class facility] a reality and I know it could not have been done without your watchful eye. I wish everyone who runs on the track could know what you put into it and to the entire athletic program."

7. **Gary Migdol** - Media Relations Director. "Your legendary status will live forever in "Home of Champions." You are truly one of the great Stanford coaches of all time."

Jordan with Dick Gould, Stanford men's tennis coach.

Jordan with Jim Bush, former UCLA track coach.

17. Post-Jordan Era: Stanford Women's Athletics

Cross Country and Track and Field

Stanford women's track and cross country teams really started to develop after the passage of Title IX in 1972. Ann Thrupp was one of the first women to compete in cross-country and track for Stanford. Thrupp was also Stanford's first All-American in women's cross-country, winning the honor three times from 1976-1978.

When Thrupp first went out for the Stanford track team, there was not a women's team, so Thrupp asked Coach Jordan if she could train with the men. Coach Jordan welcomed her with open arms and encouragement. Jordan also welcomed and helped any woman who wanted to come out and run for Stanford, even though track was not yet a varsity sport for women.

Laurel Treon was the first "official" women's track and cross country coach at Stanford. Treon helped elevate women's track to a varsity sport in 1979 and was instrumental in building a solid foundation for the success of the women's teams in the 1980s.

Treon recruited some of the best athletes in the nation. For example, Treon signed Kim Schnurpfeil in 1979, and then signed Ellen Lyons in 1980, one of the top distance runners and a national high school cross-country champion in 1979. Treon also helped Stanford sign another national high school cross-country champion, Ceci Hopp, in 1981, as well as the multitalented Regina Jacobs. Because of Treon's recruiting and coaching skills, Stanford was well on its way to becoming one of the top running programs in the nation.

With Treon's guidance, the women's success came almost immediately. The women's team placed third at the inaugural NCAA Cross Country Championships in 1981. Treon decided to leave after the season, but she had already laid a great foundation for Stanford's women's cross-country and track teams.

As the women's program kept getting better, Stanford became a national force and placed second in 1983, 1984 and 1985 at the NCAA Cross Country Championships. The Stanford women's teams have won the NCAA Cross Country Championships twice - 1996 and 2003 - and placed second in 1997.

The women's teams have dominated the Pac-10 Cross Country Championships by winning the past eight titles 1996 - 2003.

The first NCAA Outdoor Track and Field Women's Championships were held in 1982 and Stanford had two individual champions: Kim Schnurpfeil in the 10,000 meters and Ceci Hopp in the 3,000 meters. In 1984, the Stanford women's team placed third at the NCAA Outdoor Track and Field Championships; and in 1992, the Stanford women took second at the NCAA Indoor Track and Field Championships.

The women's progression in running has been amazing considering that at the 1956 Melbourne Olympics, the longest distance women were allowed to run was 200 meters. And, at the 1972 Olympics, in Munich, the longest distance woman were allowed to run was 1,500 meters. Women were finally able to run longer than 1,500 meters when the women's 3,000 meters and marathon were added in the 1984 Olympics.

Women's Athletics Overview

Stanford has always been on the leading edge of promoting equality and giving people the opportunities to succeed. For example, Stanford was coeducational from its inception in 1891, at a time when single-sex colleges were the norm. In 1904, Jane Stanford said, "Let us not be afraid to outgrow old thoughts and old ways, and dare to think on new lines as to the future of work under our care." Stanford has not only lived up to Jane Stanford's dream, it has exceeded it both academically and athletically.

Currently, there are 16 women's varsity sports and 15 men's varsity sports. Stanford is one of the top academic schools in the world and Stanford has won an unprecedented tenth straight Sears Directors Cup titles (1995-04), which honors the top overall athletic program in the country. This is a feat unmatched by any other school. Additionally, Stanford women have won 29 NCAA Women's titles - more than any university in the nation.

The history of the tremendous advancements and successes of women has proven that we need to keep our minds open in accepting new ideas, ideals and people. We need to continue to help everyone succeed, if we want to continue to improve and evolve as a human race. Let us always strive for excellence in all walks of life. Let us follow the wonderful example of Jane Stanford and coach Jordan.[31]

---

[31] Source: Ellen Lyons Santiago, Stanford track and cross country teams and Class of 1984.

18. A Masters Runner Enjoying the Quality of Life ...
Not Just the Quantity

"Nothing ever just happens ... we have to make it happen. So life is what we make it ... and we should always experience the moment, and joy of living a vital and rewarding life all the way through our years." - Payton Jordan

When Masters competitions really got started in the 1970s, Payton Jordan decided to enter a few of what he referred to as "old-timers" races. He was 55 at the time. He then went on to set 26 age-group world records in the sprints and lose only once in a quarter century of Masters competition.[32] This certainly dispels the old myth that "those who cannot compete, coach." Also, his prowess came as absolutely no surprise to his former track athletes. Well into his 40s, his Stanford sprinters feared his demonstrating next to them the technique of a proper start. Well into his 50s, his field event men dreaded the possibility of a "fun sprint" joined by the Ole Coach. Murray Olderman of the Redlands, CA Daily Facts once even wrote of Jordan, "If the pro football scouts didn't check birth certificates, they'd sign him up as a defensive backfield prospect, or maybe a wide receiver. Members of those species in the National Football League are considered super-fast if they can run 40 yards in 4.5 seconds. Payton Jordan at age 65 is in that class without drawing a deep breath." [33]

Jordan says his training philosophy today is about the same as in younger years. The basic difference, now, is the increased amount of rest required before races. As he has aged, he has shifted the balance of his training mix considerably from running, which now places too much strain on joints, to more flexibility exercises and stretching. This routine seems to work well because he has been virtually injury free. "I probably work harder than people think I do ... It's not just natural, natural is a result of hard work and knowing what you have to do to get the job done. One can have talent, but nothing is strictly natural ... you still have to work at it and discipline yourself to do so," Jordan said.

Jordan isn't opposed to jogging, but he feels there are more efficient ways to get into condition. He prefers quality, not quantity. By that he recommends shorter runs with a faster tempo. For example, he recommends a series of 70-yard runs, gradually building up speed. As you get into better condition, increase the distance of these "intervals" towards 220 yards, then 330 yards. He wrote a pamphlet on this titled, *Running for Fun and Fitness for Everyone.* The Tea Council of the USA printed eleven million copies and distributed them for free, in the early 1970s.

Jordan also is quick to point out his view that one should live a balanced life, not just excessive training. He believes today, just as he always has, that it's about choices and knowing that we have some control and influence over what we do with our lives. And, he's firmly committed to enjoying the quality of life ... not just the quantity.

Finding joy in whatever you do ... Jordan believes, is one of the most essential aspects of growing older in a healthy, vital way. He says it doesn't matter what the activity is, so

---

[32] *Don Bloom, The Sacramento Union, May 9, 1982.*

[33] Murray Olderman, Newspaper Enterprise Association, *Daily Facts, Redlands, CA, May 5, 1982.*

long as it brings that zest and happiness to one's life. He believes it's totally a personal thing - no one's responsibility but one's own - to find outlets that keep your spirit engaged in life. Without this, he believes life loses some of its meaning.

"I love gardening ... it's very therapeutic," Jordan said. "Being in the yard with nature and the flowers, the earth's soil is very healthy and invigorating for me. I guess it's part of the nurturing that is such a strong part of my being, just like with coaching ... it's a wonderful feeling watching things grow and tending to their efforts," Jordan commented.

"I am so thankful to have activities that I thoroughly enjoy and ones I can be involved with in a variety of capacities," Jordan said. "I may not be running for the rest of my life, but you can be assured I'll be involved with running and track in some other capacity that will fulfill me in a positive way. Aging is about growing; we don't just get old. We grow older ... and therefore we should be growing all of our life. You don't just stop growing because you are older, and if you do ... then you're giving up and that's a problem," he contends.

Jordan is concerned about the many people who seem to want to blame age for all their problems. He says that for those who think age is a disease, they're in big trouble because there's no cure for it. However, he believes there are ways to slow the aging process down. He encourages everyone to get out and get the body moving.

"First and foremost, you've got to breathe," Jordan said. "But not just your normal breathing, I mean deep breathing, because one of the first things to go is the capacity to use oxygen. So any time, no matter where you are, people should try to expand those lungs as much as possible. Second, we do lose flexibility with age, but we can retain a great deal of it if we just work on stretching our body every single day. The creaks and cracks and sore joints people often complain about and blame on age, are actually the body not getting enough movement ... so stretch, it's easy and very beneficial. Third, it's strength because muscle mass does seem to disappear as we get older, so you've got to replace it in order to keep on functioning. Without muscle, you'll have a hard time getting up out of a chair, or bed for that matter, and that can make a significant difference in one's quality of life," Jordan advised. "And, always be sure to do these activities safely and correctly, otherwise the results could be detrimental."

Jordan firmly believes it's an exciting time to be growing older. The extraordinary breakthroughs in scientific and medical research have enabled people to not only live longer lives than ever before, but perhaps more importantly, healthier, active lives for a longer period of time.

"Our generation is really on the cutting edge and we can be role models to those younger than ourselves," Jordan said. "Retirement does not mean sitting down, doing and saying nothing. Why waste the wisdom, creativity, energy and God-given gifts. We must continually create lives of value by meeting daily challenges. Our later years can be a heck of a ride, if we get in touch with ourselves and others."

Jordan continues to practice what he preaches and believes age has nothing to do with being a champ. He says the ingredients of a champion are simple steps that anyone can take. First, you have to have the desire to make the commitment. Second, you have to be unafraid to dream and set goals. Finally, you have to have the discipline to make it all happen. Payton Jordan: always the true champion, role model, and teacher.[34]

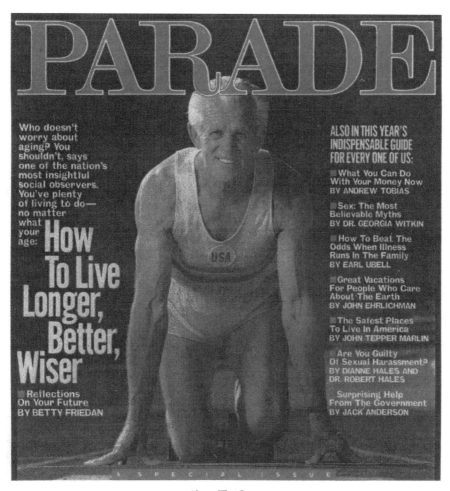

About The Cover

Payton Jordan of Los Altos, Calif., won his first track meet in 1931. This lifelong athlete later became coach of track at Stanford University and was head coach of the 1968 Olympic track-and-field team. He retired in 1979 and competed in masters meets(for athletes 40 and over), setting a series of world records sprints. What keeps Jordan, who turned 77 yesterday, "on track"? Besides Marge, his wife of 53 years, and his family, he says: "My philosophy is to find joy in whatever you do--whether it's music, art or running. Sport is only one of the many things that bring zest and happiness to life. That's why I do it. When are we are too old to do anything that makes us happy?"

Jordan on cover of PARADE, March 20,1994.

---

[34] Kelly Ferrin, "What's Age Got to Do With It?" Feb 99. Several references in this chapter were based on an interview gerontologist Kelly Ferrin did with Payton Jordan in preparation for her book.

Jordan on cover of Stanford Today, *March/April 1998.*

Jordan on cover of WARMUPS, *May 1999.*

Oregon track coaching legend Bill Bowerman, Barbara Bowerman, and Jordan at 1998 Nike World Games, plus insert of Bill Bowerman.

Jordan with USC track teammate and life-long friend, Lou Zamperini, whose life's story is chronicled in his book, "Devil at My Heels."

Payton and Marge Jordan with Sri Chinmoy, as Jordan receives the Sri Chinmoy Lifting up the World Award (2004)

19. Namesakes

At a Stanford track reunion a few years back I asked Payton Jordan, "As you reflect back on your entire career as a competitor and coach, what stands out as your most proud memory?" Without hesitation he responded, "The humbling fact that a number of my athletes, fellow coaches, and friends have honored me by naming their sons and daughters after me." Recalling that conversation, it seems only fitting to recognize these eighteen important namesakes in this book about him.

1. **Michael Payton Delevante** - Born 7/30/41. Son of Jamaican Athletic Official, Ivan Delevante. Ivan was deeply involved with planning and officiating the 1941 Jamaican Olympiad. Here Ivan and his wife got to know well the two American athletes who were invited to participate: Payton Jordan and Hubert Kerns. Michael Payton Delevante currently lives in Mississauga, Ontario, Canada.

2. **Jordan Sloan** - Granddaughter of Jim Sloan. Jim was Payton's first sprinter at Redlands High School in 1942.

3. **Jon Jordan Cunliffe** - Born 9/25/62. Son of Ernie and Lois Cunliffe. Ernie was a Stanford All-American, Stanford Athletic Hall of Fame, world record holder in the 1000 meters (indoors), and 1960 USA Olympic team member in the 800 meters.

4. **Payton Peck** - Son of Russ and Marjorie Peck. Russ was a Navy track and football teammate of Payton Jordan's in 1943 and also a Stanford pole vaulter and football player. Payton Peck lives in Hawaii.

5. **Jordy Terrill** - Son of Jim and Peggy Terrill, Occidental trackman, 1954, and assistant coach at Stanford from 1958-1962.

6. **Payton Carling** - Son of Bill Carling, Occidental sprinter, 1954.

7. **Jordan Pease** - Son of Norman Pease, Stanford sprinter, 1959.

8. **Payton Carr** - Son of Henry Carr, 1964 Olympic champion in the 200 meters, and Olympic record holder.

9. **Jordan Long** - Son of Bret Long, the son of Leo Long, 1954 NCAA champion and Stanford javelin thrower.

10. **Payton Wray Lewis** - Born 12/10/94. Son of Kasey and Belyn Lewis. Kasey was a pole vaulter on a USA touring team to Europe in 1963.

11. **Jordan Shaw** - Daughter of Don and Carolyn Shaw. Don was the head coach of the Stanford women's volleyball team for over 15 years.

12. **Kayley Jordan Nellessen** - Daughter of Sandi and Jack Nellessen. Family friends. Jack was a Masters sprinter.

13. **Payton Seals** - Son of Mr. and Mrs. Seals, family friends who live on Catalina Island.

14. **Jordan Edward Blakely** - Grandson of Tom Farrell, 1968 USA Olympic bronze medal winner in the 800 meters.

15. **Anthony Jordan Reid** - Son of Ron Reid, former sports writer for the *Palo Alto Times*.

16. **Greg Payton Jordan** - Son of brother, Dale, and Bette Jordan.

17. **Payton Fuller** - Son of Hugh Alexander Fuller, Jamaican sprinter who competed with Jordan in the 1941 Jamaican Olympiad.

18. **Jordan Ann Reid** - Granddaughter of Ron Reid, former sports writer for the *Palo Alto Times*.

20. Concluding Comment

Having obtained input from literally hundreds of people who have known the "Jordan magic" from his days as a competitor through his coaching/teaching career, the authors would like to close with the words of Pitch Johnson. Son of an Olympic hurdler and Stanford track coach, Pitch Johnson (Class of 1950) quite literally "grew up" in and around track & field. Pitch and his brother both competed for Stanford and he has supported Stanford track & field for decades, thereafter.

"Payton Jordan has been a winner in every sense of the word, athletically and ethically, from the early 1930s at Pasadena High School until today. Building on a core of desire deep within himself, he was inspired by Charlie Paddock (1920 Olympic sprint champion) in high school and shaped by his great mentor at USC, Dean Cromwell, into a champion athlete and person for his whole lifetime. Payton not only knows how to be a champion himself on and off the track, but he has the gift of inspiring others to be champions as well, as his years at Oxy and Stanford will attest. Underlying all this success is his deep love of the sport. This love gave him the drive to promote the sport on campus, in the press, and to put on the finest and best-attended dual track meet of all time, the USA-USSR meet at Stanford in 1962. Everybody who runs, jumps or throws things, or enjoys watching those who do, owes Payton Jordan his or her deepest gratitude."

21. Epilogue

Marge and Payton Jordan have been married since 1940. They have two daughters, Cheryl and Marnie. Cheryl and her husband, Bill, have a son and daughter, Kevin and Megan. Marnie and her ex-husband, Mike, also have a son and daughter, Brett and Mandi. There also are three great grandchildren: Delaney, Riley, and Gracie Marie. Marge and Payton Jordan now reside in Santa Barbara, California.

Marge and Payton Jordan at Jordan Olympic Obelisk, Cromwell track, USC (left) and Jordan Plaza, Stanford (right) (1999)

Brother, Dale Jordan, and his wife, Bette (1998).

*Marge with daughters Cheryl (l)
and Marnie (r) at 50th
wedding anniversary.*

*Daughter, Cheryl,
and husband, Bill.*

*Great grandchildren: Kevin (and Jeanne's) children Delaney holding Riley
and Brett (and Val's) child Gracie Marie.*

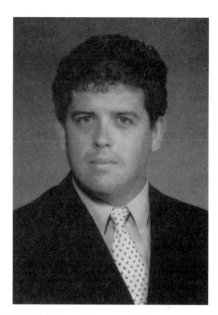

Grandchildren (left to right): Cheryl (and Bill's) children Megan and Kevin.

Grandchildren (left to right): Marnie (and ex-husband Mike's) children Mandi and Brett.

INDEX

While not included in this index, a wealth of additional information about Stanford Jordan-Era Track and Field can be found in the Supplement at the end of the book.

A

ABC network 2
'Age of Innocence' 13
Albert, Frankie 17
Albritton, Terry 43, 44, 70, 73, 77
Allen, Bob vii
'America's Greatest Track Team' 19
see also Jordan, Payton, schools attended by
Amodt, Junior 19, 21
Anchondo, Bob 67
Anderson, John 44
Anderson, Mickey 12, 13
Andrews, Harlan 59
Angell Field (Stanford) renovation 78
Anixter, Ben 49
annual scrapbook
see Monteverde, Abraham Lincoln
Apolliad, The 12
see also Jordan, Payton, writings of
Arch, Steve 56
Archibald, Dave 3
assassinations
see social and political impact on athletes
Atterberry, Willie 3

B

Babka, Rink 3, 33
Bagshaw, David 44
Banks, Gordon 71
Bannister, Roger 23, 27
Barnes, John 23, 28
Barrett, Craig vii, 49
Barthel, Josy 23, 27
Batchelder, Art 43
Beamon, Bob 37, 38
Beatty, Jim 3
Bell, Don 49
Bell, Sam 42
Bellard, Bruce 17

Berlin Wall 1
see also social and political impact on athletes
Berlinger, Harold 3
Bevis, Mickey 19–21
Birukov, Badin 1, 4
Bishop, Gil 42
Blakely, Jordan Edward 93
Blue, Jo 82
Bordoni, Jim 72, 74
Boston Ralph 37–39
Boston Marathon 1946 31
Botchan, Ron 76
Bowerman, Barbara 90
Bowerman, Bill 42, 90
Boyce, Peter 43, 44, 67, 69
Bradford, Alfred 78
Bragg, Don 33
Brandin, Alf 83
Brennan, Frank 79
Breschini, Len 55
Breyer, Chuck 19–21
Brock, Greg 43, 67
Brown, Coco 16
Brumel, Valeri 3
Brundage, Avery 38
Budd, Frank 33
Bullard, Ernie 81
Bullwinkel, Clay 72, 75
Bunnell, John 82
Bush, Jim 80, 84

C

Calhoun, Lee 33
Captain of Champions 10
see also LIFE magazine
Carling, Payton 92
Carlos, John 35, 37, 38–39
see also social and political impact on athletes
Carlson, Don 82
Carr, Henry 57, 92
Carr, Payton 92
Carrigan, Casey 43, 44
Cavalli, Gary 83

Cawley, Rex 3
Chaffey Invitational 20
'champion'
as spoken to young Payton Jordan 7, 10
Champions, Maker of 10
see also Coach Dean Cromwell
championship reflections 70
Chem, Samrath viii
Cheney, Al 50
Chinmoy, Sri 71, 91
Clark, Marshall 67, 68, 80
Coach by Mickey Bevis 19–21
Coach Carl Metten (Pasadena High School) 11
Coach Dean Cromwell (USC track and field) 7, 10, 26, 27, 94
influence on Payton Jordan 10
Coach Howard Jones (USC football)
1939 Rose Bowl 10
influence on Jordan's decision to coach 10
Cobb, Chuck iv–vii 33, 43–44, 48, 50
meeting Coach Jordan 45
Colby, Tom 43
Cold War Era 1–6
see also social and political impact on athletes
Coliseum Relays (1950) 26
camaraderie
see Jordan, Payton, philosophy on teamwork
Conley, Phil viii
Connolly, Hal 3
Cortright, Steve 43, 58, 60, 62
Cosell, Howard 36
Cox, Roger 66

Cromwell, Dean
   see Coach Dean Cromwell
   (USC track and field)
Cromwell Track at USC   95
Cuban Missile Crisis   1
   see also social and
   political impact on athletes
Culley, Ben   26
Cunliffe, Ernie 33, 43–44, 49,
   51, 92
Cunliffe, Jon Jordan   92
Curl, Ken   44

D

Daniels, Don   19–21
Davenport, Willie   38
Davis, Hal "Hurrying"   17
Davis, Hartwell   19–21
Davis, Otis   33
Day, Bud   12
Delevante, Michael
   Payton   92
Denney, Jon   83
Drake Relays, Iowa   23-24
Drayton, Paul   3, 5
Dumke, Glenn   26
DuPrau, Eunice   2
DuPree, Jim   33
Durbin   41

E

Echo Summit, California,
   training camp   35–36, 42
Eldridge, Buzz   19–21
elevation challenge for
   1968 Olympics   35
   see also Jordan, Payton,
   coaching positions of
Eshelman, Jim   44, 62
Evans, Lee   35, 37, 38

F

Farrington, Tom   19–21
Fehring, Dutch   81
Fiddler, Calude   23
Figueroa, Aurelia   vii
Five-Man Two-Mile Relay
   by Ty Hadley   24–25
Flint, Bill   50
Forbes, Gordon   vii
Fosbury, Dick   38
Fowle, Kristin   viii
Francis, Chuck   44, 65

Franzini, Joe   82
Frische, Eric   44, 55, 61
Freeman, Ron   37, 38
Fuller, Payton   93
Fulton, John   13
Fyall, Bill   57

G

Gamage, Walt   3, 40
Garrett, Michael   10
Geiken, Stacy   vii, 75
golden boy   vi
Gould, Dick   79, 84
Greek Olympic Team
   see Jordan, Payton,
   character of, as
   'sports ambassador'
Green, Charlie   37
Gutowski, Bob   23, 28

H

Hadley, Mark   73, 74
Hadley, Ty   24–25
Hartwick, Harold   19–21
Hayes, Bob   3
Hendershott, Jon   1
Herman, Wayne   57
Hillenbrand, Laura   vii
Hines, Jim   37
Hogsett, Matt   44, 70, 73
Hopp, Ceci   85
Horn, Larry   11
Howard, John   2
Howard Cosell   36
Humphrey, Jim   12
Hungerland, Chris   60

I

idol to young Payton Jordan
   Charlie Paddock   7
International Olympic
   Committee in response
   to protest actions   38

J

Jacinto, Anthony   19–21
Jacinto, Frank   19–21
Jacobs, Regina   85
Jamaican Olympiad   15–16
Jamaican Amateur
   Athletic Association   15
James, Larry   35, 37, 38
Jeffrey, Clyde   13

Johns, Dick   82
Johnson, Brooks   72
Johnson, Bruce   57
Johnson, Pitch   vii, 94
Johnson, Rafer   30
Jones, Howard
   see Coach Howard Jones
Jordan, Greg Payton   93
Jordan, Payton
   character of
      defending athletes 35, 38
      as having a positive
         outlook   4
      as history maker/
         legend   vi, 15, 23
      as instilling
         confidence   24, 26, 39
      as person of
         integrity   26
      as 'sports
         ambassador'   15–16,
         26, 32 (*see also*
         Supplement)
         1955 Greek
            Olympic team   35
         1965 Maccabean
            Olympic team   35
         1967 Yugoslavian
            Olympic team   35
         1996 return trip to
            Athens, Greece   30
   coaching, philosophy of
      being a champion   53
      discipline   64
      innovation and
         collaboration
         among coaches 46, 70
      leadership   64
      motivation   10
      mutual respect   70
      need for concentration
         in running   46
      teamwork/
         unselfishness   36–37,
         46
      visionary principles   53
      winning and
         losing/competing   13,
         19–20, 70
   coaching positions of
      (*see also* Supplement)
      1944–46 Redlands High
         School   15, 19–22
         reunion picture   21

1946–1956 Occidental College 23–28
  football team record 26
  track dynasty 23
1956–1979 Stanford University 43–86
  track and field statistics 43
1968 Olympics vi, 8, 19–20, 35–42, 59, 63, 72, 93 (*see also* Jordan, Payton, character of)
  medal count 8, 10–14, 19, 37, 38
  family of
  children, Cheryl and Marnie, grandchildren, and great grand-children vii, 7–8, 16, 33, 95–97
  parents and sibling 7–8, 14, 95–97
  wife, Marge (*nee* Marjorie Bettannier) 8, 14, 76, 91, 95
  (1941) trip to Jamaica 15,16
  (1990) trip to Tahiti 19, 22
  full name of 7
  major organizational feats of 1960 US Olympic Trials 4, 33–35, 50–51
  1962 US v. USSR dual meet at Stanford vi, 1–6, 94
  first international track coaches meeting 29
  mentor of 10-11
  military service of (1942–1946) U.S. Naval officer 17–18
  namesakes for 92, 93
  personal achievements of *see also* Supplement
  1935 junior-college national record 220-yard 11
  1938 world record 440-yard relay vi, 13
  1939 NCAA championships, USC team captain vi, 12

1941 US National AAU Championships 100-yard 12
1941 world records on grass 15
1942 wins last official race, beating fastest man 12
1944 Officer in Charge of enlisted personnel 17
1996 masters 100- and 200-meter 31
2001 honorary doctorate from Occidental
National Collegiate Track Coaches Assoc. President 29
  president of men's student body Pasadena High School 8
  U.S. Navy rank of Lieutenant Commander 18
  USC track scholarship vi, 10
  proudest memory of vi, 92
  schools attended by (1937–1939)
    USC 10–14
    football 14
    track dominance of 11–12
  (1935) Pasadena High School 8, 94
  see also personal achievements
  sources of inspiration (*see* Coach Dean Cromwell; Paddock, Charlie)
  thoughts on missing the 1940/44 Olympics 17
  writings of 12–13, 71, 87

K
Kappa Alpha fraternity 12
Kardong, Don 43, 44, 67, 68, 70, 73
Karlgaard, Rich vii
Kates, John viii, 83
Kelly, John "Jake" 43, 48

Kemp, Jack vii, 21, 26 27, 76
USA TODAY article, *Values I Learned on the Field* 26
Kennedy, John F. 1
Kennedy, Robert F. 35
Kenney, Skip 79
Kerns, Hubert 15, 16
Kessel, John 44
Kettela, Pete 78
King, Martin Luther 35
Kirkland, Weym 56
Korobkov, Gavriel, Soviet Coach 2–6
Krueger, Al "Antelope" 11
Kretz, Arvid 68
Kring, Kenny 44, 72, 77
Kuznetsov, Vasily 3
Kyriakides, Stylianos 29–31

L
LaFond, Lee 12, 13
Lake Tahoe training camp 39
Lannana, Vin 80
Landsdell, Granny 11
Lee, David vii
Lee, Sammy 23
Letterer, Jim 65–66
Lewis 41
Lewis, Payton, Wray 92
Liebendorfer, Don 2
LIFE magazine *Captain of Champions* feature vi, 11–12, 14, 19
Limmer, Harlan 48, 49
Little, Walt 42
Locker, Ed vii
Lodge 41
Lofton, James 43–44, 70–71, 75–76
Long, Jordan 92
Los Angeles Coliseum 14
Lundh, Bertil 47
Lusis, Janis 3

M
Macdonald, Duncan 44, 68, 70
MacDonald, Herbert 15
Maker of Champions 10
  see also Coach Dean Cromwell

Manning–Jackson,
Madeline   36, 39
Margerum, Ken   71
Marquess, Mark   78
Martinez, Oddie   19–21
Mason, Reginald   44
Masters, Al   2, 33
Mathias, Bob   vii, 27
Mathias, Jim   27
Matson, Randy   38, 39
Matthews, Vince   37
Mauro, Jim   vii
McCalla, Harry   43, 44, 54, 58, 62
McCracken, Richard   19–21
McIntyre, Bob   44, 58, 59, 61
McKenley, Herb   16
McKibben, Walt   23, 28
McMillen, Bob   23, 27
Means, Grady   65, 66
Mentz, Chuck   67
Metten, Carl
    see Coach Carl Metten
    (Pasadena High School)
Meyer, Tom   28
Migdol, Gary   83
Milliman, Dave   vii
Mitchell, Theodore   26
Monteverde, Abraham
    Lincoln   11
Moore, Dan   48, 55
Moore, Harold, 19–21
Mora, Jim, 26, 27, 76
Murphy, Bob, vii
Murphy, Tom, 33
mythical 1940/44 Olympic
    track teams
    see Olympic Games

N

Naval Air Station,
    Ottumwa, Iowa   17
Nave, Doyle   11
Nellessen, Kayley Jordan   92
Nelson, Darrin   71, 75
Nelson, Mel   2
Newman, Ray   42
Norton, Ray   33

O

Occidental College
    alma mater of Coach Dean
    Cromwell   10
    (see also Jordan, Payton,
    coaching positions of)
Ockerman, Eunice   vii
Oerter, Al   3, 33, 37
    four consecutive Olympic
    gold medals in the same
    event   39, 42, 70
Ogilvie, Bruce   57
Olderman, Murray   87
Olympic Games
    1896 Athens   29
    1912 Stockholm   10
    1920 Antwerp   7, 10, 94
    1924 Paris   10
    1928 Amsterdam   10
    1932 Los Angeles   4, 7, 10
    1936 Berlin   10, 12
    1940/44   12, 15, 17
    1948 London   10, 23
    1952 Helsinki   23, 27
    1956 Melbourne   23, 28, 29, 31, 86
    1960 Rome   v, 30, 35, 50, 51, 92 (see also Jordan, Payton, major organizational feats)
    1960 Olympic Trials at
    Stanford (see Jordan, Payton, major organizational feats of)
    1964 Tokyo   vi, 35, 39, 40, 58, 92
    1968 Mexico City
        high altitude of   35
        (see also Jordan, Payton, coaching positions of)
    1972 Munich   39, 42, 86
    1976 Montreal   68, 70
    1980 Moscow   70
    1984 Los Angeles   30, 86
    1988 Seoul
    1992 Barcelona
    1996 Atlanta   30
    2000 Sydney   vi
    2004 Athens   vi, 53
Orman, Ed, 34
Ostrander, Clint, 66
Owens, Jesse, 40, 46

P

Pa, Chauncy   24
Paddock, Charlie
    idol to young
    Payton Jordan   7, 94
Parker, Bill   23, 28
Pease, Jordan   92
Pease, Norm   47, 92
Peck, Payton   92
Pender, Mel   36, 37
Peoples, Bob   12
Peters, Keith   viii, 3
Phi Epsilon Kappa physical
    education fraternity   12
Poe, Don   19–21
Portonova, Mike   41
Powell, Mike   37
President John F. Kennedy   1
Press, Harry   3
Press, Tamara   3
Purpur, Ray   83

R

Reid, Anthony Jordan   93
Reid, Jordan Ann   93
Rhoden, George   23
Roby, Douglas F.
    President of the US
    Olympic Committee   38
Roesch   41
Roldan, Hank   45
Ron Freeman   37
Rose Bowl   10–11
Roubanis, George   23, 28
Rubin, Dale   44, 61
Rudolph, Wilma   3
Ruetz, Joe   83
Ruff, Wes   81
Ruprecht, Ted   23, 28
Russians   2

S

Sabina Park, Kingston,
    Jamaica   15
Saddler, Ray   3
Sandoval, Tony   44, 70
Sanford, Allen   67
Santiago (Lyons), Ellen   vii, 85, 86
Sayers, Roger   5
Schindler, Amby   11
Schnurpfeil, Kim   85

Scholton,
  Bob and Lois   19–22
Schreiber, David   74
Schumway, Garry   72
Scott, David Barrett   iii
Scott, John B. "Jack"   v, 56,
  59, 62
Scott, Jack   36
Scott, Maggie and son
  Michael   vii
Seagren, Bob   38
Seals, Payton   93
Sears Cup   63, 78, 86
Seibert, Jerry   3, 33
Sewell, Bob   19–21
Shaw, Don   80, 92
Shaw, Jordan   92
Shinn, Eddie   23, 24
Shindler, Amby   11
Sholton, Bob   19, 22
Sholton, Lois   19
Simitsek, Otto   29–32
Simmons, Steve   vii
Skull and Dagger, honorary
  service organization   12
Sloan, Jim   19–21, 92
Sloan, Jordan   92
Smith, Chuck   59
Smith, Ronnie Ray   37
Smith, Tommie   37, 38,
Snell, Peter   52
Sober, Pincus   34
social and political impact
  on athletes   36
  Great Depression   10, 45
  WWII   12, 15, 17
  Greece torn by strife   29
  Cold War   1, 45
  1968 protest
    actions   35-36, 38
Sokolov, Nikolai   3
Soto, Manases   19–21
Soviet News Agency
  TASS   1
St. Mary's Pre-Flight
  School   17
    competitive sports
    teams   17
    Moraga, California   17
Stanford, California   2
Stanford Hall of Fame   13
Stanford, Jane   86

Stanford University
  see Jordan, Payton,
  coaching positions of
statistics   43
  see also Supplement
Stoecker, Bob   43, 44, 52,
  57, 62

T

Taplin, Russ   63, 67
Talley, Adrian   12, 13
Taylor, Chuck   2
Taylor, Ed   19–21
television, first
  coast–to–coast track
  broadcast   1–2
Terrill, Jim   23, 92
Terrill, Jordy   92
Thomas, Brook   vii, 43, 67
Thomas, John   4, 33
Thrupp, Ann   85
Tipton, Dave   78
Tipton, Eric "The Red"   11
Toomey, Bill   38
Trader, Ev   23
Traynor, Pat   3
Treon, Laurel   85
Trojans (University of
  Southern California)
  see Jordan, Payton,
  schools attended by
Tsibulenko, Viktor   4

U

University of Southern
  California
  see Jordan, Payton,
  schools attended by
U.S. Ambassador
  Sue Cobb   v
U.S. Amateur Athletic
  Union   2
U.S. Navy, service of
  Payton Jordan   17

V

Vermeil, Dick   78
Vickery, Earl   12
Vietnam War   35

W

Walker, Douglas   82
Walsh, Bill   71, 76
Walsh, Bud   54, 56, 60
Ward, James S.   v, 68
Ward, Julie and sons
  Travis, Nick, Zack,
  and Grayson   vii
Warmerdam, Dutch   23
Weill, Dave   43, 44, 58,
  59, 60
Williams   Ulis, 3
Winter, Bud   81
Winter, Jerry   43
Wojcik, Joe   vii
Wooden, John   vii, 81
Woodrow, Roger   19–21
Wray, Larry   24
Wright, Stan   41
WWII, *see* social and
  political impact on athletes

Y

Yerman, Jack   33
Young, Bob   2
Young, George   3
Young, Larry   40, 57

Z

Zamperini, Lou   12, 91
Zimmerman, Paul   4

STANFORD JORDAN-ERA TRACK AND FIELD SUPPLEMENT

In the course of researching this book the authors sought and received input from over 150 former Stanford teammates, representing all years Jordan was at Stanford. In appreciation for this teammate support the authors have created this Supplement.

I.   Payton Jordan: Awards and Positions Held as Sports Ambassador

II.   Assistant and Volunteer Coaches

III. Team Captains

IV. Top-10 Stanford Marks with Jordan-Era Marks Highlighted

V.   Varsity Team Rosters

VI. Teammate Write-ups

I. Payton Jordan: Awards and Positions Held as Sports Ambassador

Awards -

- Track & Field Coach, Emeritus - Stanford University
- President of National Collegiate Track & Field Association - now Emeritus
- Member of National Collegiate Rules Committee - 8 years
- Member of National A.A.U. (Now USATF) Track & Field Committee - 8 years
- Track Coach of the Year - 1963
- N.A.I.A. Track & Field Hall of Fame - 1967
- Occidental College Athletic Hall of Fame - 1970
- Helms Athletic Foundation Track & Field Hall of Fame - 1973
- National Collegiate Track & Field Coaches Hall of Fame - 1975
- "Cap" Haralson Memorial Award for outstanding service to USATF - 1980
- National Track & Field Hall of Fame - 1982
- Mt. San Antonio Athlete & Coach Track & Field Hall of Fame - 1983
- University of Southern California Heritage Award - 1990
- Senior Athletes Hall of Fame - 1992
- Stanford University Athletic Hall of Fame - 1995
- United States of America Track & Field Masters Hall of Fame - 1997
- San Jose Sports Hall of Fame - 1997
- Arete Award for Pursuit of Excellence and Courage in Sports - 1997
- United States Track Coaches Hall of Fame - 1997
- United States Sports Academy - Dwight D. Eisenhower Fitness Award - 1999
- Santa Barbara Athletic Round Table Hall of Fame - 2000
- Occidental College Doctor of Humane Letters - 2001
- Payton Jordan U.S. Open Track & Field Meet - 2004 ... part of the USA Track & Field's Golden Spike Tour. (The only U.S. meeting that is part of the International Association of Athletics Federation's worldwide Grand Prix Circuit.)
- Sri Chinmoy Lifting up the World Award - 2004
- University of Southern California Athletic Hall of Fame - 2004

Positions Held -

- 1968 Head Coach of USA Olympic Track & Field team at Mexico City, Mexico
- 1967 Advisory Coach to Yugoslavia National Track & Field team for European Championships in Budapest, Hungary
- 1966 Head Track & Field Coach for World University Games at Tokyo, Japan
- 1965 Head Track & Field Coach of USA Track & Field team for Maccabiah Games in Israel.
- 1965 Head Track & Field coach of USA team in World Deaf Olympics in Maryland
- 1964 First Assistant Coach of USA Men's Olympic Track & Field team in Tokyo, Japan

- 1963 Head Coach of USA Track & Field team versus Russia, Poland, Hungary and Great Britain
- 1962 Meet Director of USA versus Soviet Union dual meet at Stanford, California
- 1960 Meet Director of USA Track & Field Olympic trials at Stanford, California
- 1958 Assistant Coach of USA Track & Field team versus Russia, Poland, Hungary and Greece
- 1955 Advisory Coach to Greek National Track and Field team for the 1956 Olympics in Melbourne, Australia

II. Assistant and Volunteer Coaches

To All of my Stanford Assistant Track Coaches:

I have been blessed by having all of you as Assistant Coaches during my years as Head Coach of Stanford track and field. All of you were so positive, knowledgeable, enthusiastic, and loyal. Each of you gave of yourself, caring much about the program, and the athletes. You did your jobs with integrity always.

It has been a great satisfaction to me that each and every one of you grew professionally and in stature while coaching with us to the point you were sought out for professional advancement to be Head Track and Field Coaches and leaders in other professional fields.

To each of you, I am, and will always be grateful for those many contributions you made in building the amazing tradition of track and field on the "farm".

The memories of the good times we shared will be with me always, and above all I treasure your friendship.

Always, with appreciation, respect and love,

Coach Payton Jordan

Floyd Strain - 1956-58
Floyd served in the Marine Corps in World War II then enrolled at Occidental College. He was a highly ranked 440-yard intermediate hurdler and one of the top decathletes in the country. He joined our staff at Stanford in 1956 and served through 1958. He then moved on to become National Track and Field Coach for American Samoa. His contagious enthusiasm has served him well in his coaching endeavors.

Jim Terrill - 1959-62
Jim is another of Jordan's Occidental College track and field champions, who also served a stint as an Air Force Officer after college. Jim had times of 1:48.8 in the half mile and 4:09.0 in the mile, plus he ran anchor on a world record setting two-mile relay team. Jim became Assistant Coach at Stanford in 1959 and served admirably through 1962 when he accepting the position as track coach at Yale. Jim was an extremely capable all around coach, very creative, and well organized. Jordan felt fortunate to have him on his staff. A great deal of credit must be given Jim for his valuable contribution to two of the finest track and field meets in history. The 1960 Olympic Trials, held at Stanford, had the largest attendance ever for a meet in the US. This was followed by the 1962 USA versus USSR meet, also held at Stanford, that many consider the finest international dual meet, ever.

Carmon "Jess" Bova - 1963-65

Jess was an outstanding USC track athlete. After graduating from USC Jess was a teacher in the U.S. Armed Forces Overseas Teaching Program. He served in locations such as Germany, France, and England. Jess was an assistant coach at Stanford then accepted an administrative position in Recreation for the Los Angeles City School System.

Jerome "Jerry" Barland - 1964-67

While a student athlete at the University of Kansas, Jerry competed in track and field under Bill Easton. Prior to coming to Stanford as an assistant coach, Jerry was the track coach at Bishop Amat High School. He created the very popular Bishop Amat Metric Distance Invitational Relays. At Stanford Jerry quickly established himself as a motivating leader and in his first season as head cross country coach he developed the best harrier team in Stanford history. His squad was unbeaten and won the West Coast Intercollegiate Championships. Jerry was a tireless worker and his abilities were recognized. He moved on to be the head track coach at Iowa State.

Phil Conley - 1964-79

Phil is Jordan's "dollar a year" javelin specialist and loyal long-time friend, who unselfishly donated his services to the Stanford track program. Phil was a great thrower in his own right and competed in the 1956 Olympics. He is a graduate of Caltech in Pasadena.

Marshall Clark: the Man Jordan Called Co-Coach - 1968-78

After serving in the U. S. Navy, Marshall Clark attended the University of Southern California, where he was a three-year varsity letterman in cross-country and track. Marshall began his coaching career at Los Altos High in Hacienda Heights in 1958, then Seaside, and on to Stanford in 1968.

Marshall's impact on the Stanford program was immediate. The cross-country team he inherited was coming off a decent season in 1967. Nevertheless, it still had been beaten handily by both USC and San Jose State. Marshall transformed that team into a national power. In his first meet as a Stanford coach, he guided the team to a one-point upset of nationally ranked USC at the Sacramento State Invitational. The team went on to trounce USC two more times while compiling an undefeated season and finishing second at the NCAA Championships in New York City. Two runners, Brook Thomas and Greg Brock, were All-Americans. Brock repeated as a cross country All-American the next year. By the end of his second full year at Stanford, Marshall had inspired runners to break school records in the mile, the two mile, the three mile, the six mile, and to tie the record in the steeplechase. He coached the first Stanford runner to break four minutes in the mile, Duncan Macdonald, and his success continued throughout the decade he was affiliated with the Stanford program. Three of his athletes, Macdonald, Don Kardong, and Tony Sandoval, went on the make USA Olympic teams, although Sandoval was deprived of the opportunity to run because of the 1980 US boycott. Marshall accomplished all of this with minimal scholarship support. After the 1968 NCAA Cross Country Championships, Track and Field News went out of its way to report that one of the runners on the winning Villanova team was a walk-on. It did not mention that only one of the athletes on the Stanford team that went to New York and came in second was on a track scholarship.

After Stanford, Marshall was then head track & field coach at Montana in 1978-1980 and San Jose State in 1984-1988. After that program was disbanded, he moved to coach at Saratoga High School. Marshall's sudden passing in 2002 at the age of 69, due to an apparent heart attack, was devastating to all who knew him.

All-American Brook Thomas summed up Marshall's influence and legacy. "Marshall was such a successful coach in large measure because he understood human beings as well as he understood track. He knew that different runners responded differently to different workout programs and different means of motivation. He adjusted his approach to individuals while still being able to mold those individuals into a team. He knew that it was fun to excel and that runners were more likely to put in the effort they needed to excel if they were having fun. He inspired devotion from his athletes because they knew that he placed their interests first and because he treated them all - the fastest and the slowest - with respect. He gave his runners some of the most important education they would receive in their time at the farm."

Commenting on his assistant coach - whom Jordan insisted on referring to as his Co-Coach - Jordan said, "Only a very few people were as caring, loyal, and of such integrity that he possessed. I will miss him, and his friendship will be something I will treasure always. He was a person who made a very special difference in the lives of those privileged to know him." [1]

Bill Moultrie - 1971-73
Bill served a dual capacity, as a staff member for football in the area of recruiting and as an Assistant Coach for Stanford track and field during his short two-year term on the farm. Obviously his talent search for football helped us in track because he was able to recruit athletes able to do both sports at the University. Bill was a very engaging person and related well with the two-sport athletes. He was a very enthusiastic and hard worker who brought much to our program. He was hired as head track Coach at Howard University.

Emerson "Bud" Spencer - 1970-79
A treasured friend, the late Emerson "Bud" Spencer was a rarity in Stanford track and field and in the history of the sport. Bud was an NCAA and IC4A champion, 440-yard dash world record holder, and an Olympic gold medal winner in the 1600-meter relay at the 1928 Games held in Amsterdam.

For a short two years after his graduation from Stanford Bud also coached track and field at Stanford. But, he soon decided to take a turn at writing and covered sports for thirty years at the San Francisco Call-Bulletin, eventually as Sports Editor. He always demonstrated a critical eye and a vast knowledge of athletic techniques and a "human interest touch" to make his stories live for the reader.

---

[1] Source: Brook Thomas, Stanford track and cross-country teams, All-American, and Class of 1969.

Our friendship covered decades so when he retired from the newspaper, I was not about to let his talents go to waste. I convinced him to become our "dollar a year" assistant consultant-coach with the only stipulation that his little mutt, Poobah, be a part of the package as our team mascot. During our close association coaching together we constantly exchanged observations and opinions about the "nuts and bolts" of athletic technique and questioned our athletes and fellow coaches, as we examined the practical significance of performance at a high level. In time we were moved to collaborate on a book, "Champions in the Making." This was an assemblage of all of the opinions, anecdotes, and mechanics and conditioning fundamentals essential to the skills of track and field performers that Bud and Payton had gleaned from their track and field athletes and colleagues. Of course Poobah - Bud's dog - kept a critical eye on their doings and supervised carefully.

These were fun years of sharing and deepening of a very special respect and friendship Bud and Payton enjoyed. And by the way, it should be known that Bud could make a mighty tasty clam chowder that he and Payton shared over many a long lunch while telling a few tall stories. And, it was obvious to one and all, that the little mutt, Poobah, brought lots of class into their world and helped keep their Stanford tracksters on their toes! As Bud would say, "That's 30."

Vern Gambetta - 1970-71
Vern served very effectively as a graduate assistant. He was a keen student of track and field and an expert technician. His contributions to the team and Stanford athletics were appreciated greatly. He has continued in his track career with distinction, making many excellent contributions to the profession. He is a highly sought after clinician.

Dick Reese - 1969-71
Dick served outstandingly as a graduate assistant with special attention to the jump area of track and field. He was an extremely thorough teacher and a very sound technician. His relationship with his fellow coaches and athletes was superb. His personality was infectious and his abilities as a motivator were outstanding. Dick was a former USC trackman, where he competed on the same team with Marshall Clark. Interestingly, Jordan found in him many of the same qualities possessed by Coach Clark: caring, loyalty, and integrity.

Kenny Kring - 1975
Kenny was one of Stanford's greatest all-around track and field performers and one of the nations most outstanding decathletes. A leader and team man, Kenny was highly regarded by his teammates who chose him to be team captain. He had all of the qualities of a solid coach. He was a natural teacher, solid in fundamentals, excellent motivator, great empathy, and nurturing personality. He was respected and admired by all those he coached. His caring, loyalty, and integrity would make him highly valued in any profession. He left track and field to pursue a business career, where he has been very successful in the executive search business. He is CEO of Diversified Search Company in Philadelphia.

Jim Royer - 1975
As a 1974 graduate, Jim agreed to serve as a graduate assistant coach while pursuing his post-grad degree. Jim was an outstanding leader and was chosen to be co-captain of his team with Kenny Kring. During his varsity career he was the top Stanford discus thrower. His duties as a graduate assistant were to administer the team strength program and tutor the discus and shot putters where he could contribute much to their development. He left Stanford to accept a position with the city of San Luis Obispo.

George Berry - 1975
A fine middle distance runner for Stanford as an undergraduate, George assumed responsibilities as a graduate assistant to handle all the details of administration for the track team operation, such as meet management, travel, equipment, team statistics, etc. And, in addition he assisted with our middle distance runners. He was a law student so not surprisingly his organizational abilities were superb. His intense love for track and field, plus his terrific enthusiasm brought much to the team and individual athletes. He was a "team player", extremely loyal, and ethical in his relations with others. He has gone on to become a highly successful and respected attorney in Los Angeles.

Bernie Oliver - 1977-79
Bernie was a very valued member of the Stanford coaching staff for three years. His major responsibilities were to handle the long jump, triple jump, and high jump, but if needed he was very capable of coaching in all areas of the program. While pursuing his Ph.D. at Stanford, it was evident he had much ability and all of the qualifications to become an extremely capable administrator and track & field coach. These qualities were recognized and he was afforded the opportunity to serve as an Administrator of Education in the State of Texas.

Terry Albritton - 1978
Terry is one of Stanford's greatest track and field athletes. He was a world record holder in the shot put (71-8 ½ in 1976) and indoor and outdoor NCAA champion. While serving as a graduate assistant, Terry worked with the entire team's weight-strength program and gave special and expert attention to the shot putters, discus throwers, and hammer throwers. His enthusiasm, caring, and loyalty added much to our track and field program. The qualities that made him a champion, he brought into his coaching efforts. He is a big imposing man, but he has great empathy and patience and brings the best out of those fortunate enough to have his mentoring. He continues his influence on young people as a very successful coach at St. Anthony High School in Maui, Hawaii.

Marvin Holmes - 1978
A highly valued Stanford track athlete, Marvin chose to serve as a graduate assistant. He was a mainstay sprinter during his four years on the farm. He contributed greatly to the successes of our sprint and relay events. Having experience as leadoff runner for both the 440 and 880 relays, it followed that his experience and expertise brought much success to the teams he coached. Marvin also made a smooth transition from athlete to coach. His sense of professionalism brought respect for his guidance. His high standards and loyalty contributed much to the program during his year on the Stanford coaching staff.

Dave Wells - 1979

A three-time letterman as an undergraduate middle distance runner, Dave served as a graduate assistant while pursuing an advance degree in education. In the fall he assisted Marshall Clark in cross country and thereafter worked in all phases of the track program, particularly with the middle distance events. Dave was the recipient of the Payton Jordan Coach's Award in recognition of outstanding physical ability and mental attitude. Dave Wells has continued in the coaching field and his been highly successful in northern California since leaving Stanford.

Archie Owens - 1979

Archie brought a wealth of experience to the program when he accepted the position of assistant coach. He was a well-known figure in northern California, as the organizer and director of the Bay Area Striders. He is a graduate of Morgan State, where he competed on the track team. Archie also served in the Marine Corps and was the Corps sprint champion. He was head track coach at Douglas High School in Baltimore, where his team won three league titles and two district championships during a five-year span. He returned to Morgan State to serve as assistant track coach for 1965-66. Archie is very knowledgeable in the development of strength programs for track & field athletes, which he was asked to do for our Stanford program. He was assigned to the jumps as well and the athletes he tutored realized outstanding results. We were most fortunate to have a man of Archie's abilities to join us. He brought so much energy and enthusiasm to the program and athletes. Too, he is a man of integrity and loyalty.

Dean Clark - 1979

Dean was an All-American distance runner at Washington State University. During his competitive career he won the Pac-8 northern division mile title and finished third in the three mile the same year. He graduated as an eight-time letterman in track and cross-country. Prior to coming to Stanford, Dean served three seasons as head cross-country coach and as an assistant track and field coach at Oregon State University. Although our time together was short, Dean was everything a head coach could ask for in an assistant coach. He is cooperative, competent, loyal, an enthusiastic teacher, and contributed to the program and our track and field athletes 110%!

III. Team Captains

Year	Name	Hometown
1957	Phil Fehlen	San Francisco, CA
	Frank Herrmann	San Jose, CA
1958	Chuck Cobb	Fresno, CA
1959	Don Chesarek	San Francisco, CA
1960	Ernie Cunliffe	Claremont, CA
	John "Jake" Kelly	Palo Alto, CA
1961	Don Bell	Alameda, CA
	Rich Klier	Oakland, CA
1962	Dave Weill	Walnut Creek, CA
1963	Harry McCalla	Berkeley, CA
	Dan Moore	Salem, OR
	Dave Weill	Walnut Creek, CA
1964	Steve Cortright	Long Beach, CA
1965	Bob McIntyre	Medford, OE
	Paul Schlicke	Spokane, WA
1966	Bob Stoecker	Los Altos, CA
1967	Bud Walsh	Coos Bay, OR
1968	Jim Ward	Columbiana, OH
1969	Peter Boyce	Melbourne, Australia
1970	Tom Jones	Oakland, CA
1971	Allen Meredith	Los Altos, CA
	Rick Tipton	Silver City, NV
1972	John Anderson	Newberg, OR
1973	John Anderson	Newberg, OR
	Ralph Bakkensen	Portland, OR
1974	Ken Kring	Santa Maria, CA
	Jim Royer	Campbell, CA

1975	Mike Hall	San Carlos, CA
1976	Tony Sandoval	Los Alamos, NM
1977	Steve Crowley	Madison, WI
	James Lofton	Los Angeles, CA
1978	James Lofton	Los Angeles, CA
1979	Gordon Banks	Los Angeles, CA
	Clay Bullwinkel	Burlingame, CA

IV. Top-Ten Stanford Marks with Jordan-Era Marks Highlighted[2]

All of us from the "Jordan-era" are well aware of the many changes in the sport that preclude definitive comparison of results over time. Track surfaces have changed, running events in the US have shifted from yards to meters, timing has changed from hand-held stopwatches to electronic devices, results were measured in tenths of a second and now in one-hundredths, javelins have changed, and the technology of vaulting poles has evolved continuously over the years. Thus, the various "old-basis" records too often are lost from current listings of school records.

The authors' sole objective here is to acknowledge and perpetuate the existence of these older marks, as recognized at the time. Track enthusiasts may debate forever how to properly integrate them; we just want to preserve them.

100-yard Dash

9.3	**Larry Questad**, 1963, 1965
9.4	Clyde Jeffrey, 1939
9.4	**Ken Curl**, 1972
9.5	**Eric Frische**, 1963
9.5	**Rick Tipton**, 1969
9.5	**Chuck Francis**, 1971

100-meter Dash

10.2	**Larry Questad**, 1964
10.3	**James Lofton**, 1978
10.3	**Darrin Nelson**, 1979
10.4	**Gordon Banks**, 1977
10.46	Jimmie Johnson, 1997
10.47	Stanley Wilson, 2001
10.48	**Marvin Holmes**, 1977
10.61	Leroy Sims, 2000
10.61	Milton Little, 2003
10.62	Damon Dunn, 1997

220-yard Dash

20.6	**Larry Questad**, 1963
20.7	Jack Weiershauser, 1937
20.8	Clyde Jeffrey, 1939 (straight)
21.0	**Ken Curl**, 1973
21.0	**James Lofton**, 1977
21.1	**Eric Frische**, 1963
21.1	**Gordon Banks**, 1977

200-meter Dash

20.5	**Larry Questad**, 1963
20.5	**James Lofton**, 1977
20.84	Clyde Jeffrey, 1939
20.95	Jimmy Johnson, 1997
21.10	Damon Dunn, 1996
21.24	**Gordon Banks**, 1977
21.31	Milton Little, 2003
21.34	**Darrin Nelson**, 1980
21.35	James Cramton, 1991
21.38	Rene Rodriguez, 1994

440-yard Dash

46.4	Ben Eastman, 1932
46.6	Ray Malott, 1938
46.9	**Jim Ward**, 1966
47.3	Bud Spencer, 1928
47.4	Charles Shaw, 1940
47.4	Craig Williamson, 1940
47.4	**Don Chesarek**, 1958
47.4	**Ken Fraser**, 1965

400-meter Dash

45.85	Rene Rodriguez, 1994
46.08	**Alan Sheats**, 1977
46.17	Jimmie Johnson, 1996
46.40	Ben Eastman, 1932
46.40	**James Lofton**, 1977

---

[2] Source: Stanford Media Relations website listing of top-ten performances by event, as last updated 8/11/03. Running events competed in "yards" have been added based on the Media Relations listing when such events were last competed. Where there is a difference in reported result between the then-current media guide and the current website listing, we used the then-current media guide.

46.71   James Cramton, 1991
46.86   Evan Kehy, 2002
46.99   Nick Sebes, 2003
47.0   Bud Spencer, 1928
47.52   Curtis Goehring, 2002

880-yard Run
1:47.3   **Ernie Cunliffe**, 1960
1:49.2   **Norm Lloyd**, 1958
1:49.4   **Pete Fairchild**, 1969
1:49.9   **Rich Klier**, 1962
1:50.2   **Tim Nicholson**, 1971
1:50.3   **Bill Pratt**, 1964
1:50.4   **Bob Miltz**, 1963
1:50.9   Ben Eastman, 1932

800-meter Run
1:46.20 Michael Stember, 2000
1:46.6   **Ernie Cunliffe**, 1960
1:46.83 Gabe Jennings, 2001
1:46.90 David Strang, 1990
1:47.92 Christian Skoog, 1986
1:47.96 Grant Robison, 2003
1:47.97 **John Schaer**, 1979
1:48.20 Bill Crowley, 1990
1:48.42 Ryan Carroll, 2001
1:48.78 Jason Lunn, 1997

Mile Run
3:55.16 Jeff Atkinson, 1986
3:59.11 Michael Stember, 1998
3:59.32 Gabe Jennings, 1998
3:59.6   **Duncan Macdonald**, 1970
3:59.69 Jonathon Riley, 2002
4:00.1   **Brian Mittelstaedt**, 1973
4:00.4   **Ernie Cunliffe**, 1960
4:01.5   **Harry McCalla**, 1963
4:02.3   **Paul Schlicke**, 1964
4:03.15 Grant Robison, 2002

1500-meter Run
3:35.11 Michael Stember, 2000
3:35.21 Gabe Jennings, 2000
3:35.75 Grant Robison, 2003
3:38.90 Jonathon Riley, 2000

3:39.26 Marc Olesen, 1988
3:39.27 Donald Sage, 2001
3:40.65 Andrew Powell, 2000
3:41.30 Mark Mastalir, 1991
3:41.32 Bill Crowley, 1990
3:41.68 Jeff Atkinson, 1985

2-mile Run
8:37.8   **Don Kardong**, 1971
8:45.2   **Greg Brock**, 1970
8:47.4   **Tony Sandoval**, 1976
8:49.4   **Arvid Kretz**, 1971
8:50.2   **Brian Mittelstaedt**, 1973

3000-meter Steeplechase
8:35.83 Jesse Thomas, 2002
8:38.19 David Frank, 1984
8:45.92 Fred Carter, 1992
8:48.52 Steve Miller, 1989
8:50.82 Mark Fadil, 1996
8:50.83 Ian Dobson, 2003
8:52.6   Bill Graham, 1982
8:53.6   **Bill Gail**, 1979
8:55.8   Rod Berry, 1981
8:56.0   Gary Stolz, 1992

3-mile Run
13:20.8 **Don Kardong**, 1971
13:25.8 **Tony Sandoval**, 1976
13:31.9 **Arvid Kretz**, 1971
13:36.4 **Greg Brock**, 1970
13:47.0 **Mark McConnell**, 1974
13:49.0 **Jeff Parietti**, 1976

5000-meter Run
13:27.31 Brad Hauser, 2000
13:29.15 Jonathon Riley, 2002
13:31.80 Louis Luchini, 2003
13:39.75 Brent Hauser, 1997
13:40.30 Grant Robison, 2002
13:44.60 Gabe Jennings, 2000
13:44.87 Jason Balkman, 1999
13:46.81 Seth Hejny, 2001
13:52.58 Nathan Nutter, 1999
13:52.67 Rob Reeder, 1997

6-mile Run
28:00.6 **Don Kardong**, 1971
28:03.8 **Tony Sandoval**, 1976
29:02.6 **Greg Brock**, 1970
29:10.6 **Jack Bellah**, 1974

10,000-meter Run
28:08.12 Brad Hauser, 1999
28:20.51 Ian Dobson, 2003
28:23.37 Brent Hauser, 2000
28:23.67 Adam Tenforde, 2003
28:32.21 Jason Balkman, 1999
28:32.62 Nathan Nutter, 1998
28:33.71 Jonathon Riley, 2001
28:40.12 Donald Sage, 2002
28:41.13 Louis Luchini, 2003
28:53.70 Thomas Murley, 2000

120-yard High Hurdles
13.7 **Rick Tipton**, 1971
13.8 **Steve Cortright**, 1963
13.9 **Chuck Cobb**, 1958
13.9 **John Foster**, 1975
14.0 **Dave Bagshaw**, 1973

110-meter High Hurdles*
13.94 **John Foster**, 1976
14.04 Bob Mathias, 1953
14.10 Justin Williams, 2003
14.14 **Rick Tipton**, 1969
14.15 Peter Kolotoutos, 1989
14.19 Michael Harte, 1999
14.22 Jay Thorson, 1986
14.27 Bill Graham, 1980
14.30 Rod Berry, 1980
14.30 Michael Melendez, 1980
* In 1960, Chuck Cobb ran 13.7 in the
U.S. Armed Services Championship while
stationed at the Stanford Navy ROTC unit
and training under Payton Jordan

440-yard Intermediate Hurdles
50.7 **Randy White**, 1971
51.3 **Matt Hogsett**, 1974
52.1 **Tom Long**, 1972
52.2 **Dave Bagshaw**, 1974
52.4 **Steve Cortright**, 1963

52.3 **Bud Walsh**, 1967
52.4 Jim Luttrell, 1955

400-meter Hurdles
50.4 **Randy White**, 1971
50.98 Jeff Allen, 1998
51.2 **Tom Shellworth**, 1977
51.3 **Matt Hogsett**, 1974
51.71 Garry Shumway, 1981
51.73 Shanghn Ryan, 1986
52.0 Garry Shumway, 1980
52.15 Tim Collins, 1988
52.63 Gerren Crochet, 2003
52.85 Kraig Sanders, 1986

440-yard Relay
39.7 **Frische, Rubin, McIntyre, Questad**, 1965
40.5 **Cox, Forbes, Ward, Questad**, 1966
40.7 **Sears, Forbes, Walsh, Cox**, 1967
40.8 **Frische, Rubin, Forbes, Questad**, 1965
40.8 **Sears, Guglielmetti, Walsh, Forbes**, 1967
40.8 **Holmes, Lofton, Sheats, Wingo**, 1975

400-meter Relay
39.84 **Nelson, Sheats, Banks, Lofton**, 1978
40.15 Little, Crochet, Sebes, Rushing, 2003
40.24 Little, Crochet, Rushing, Sebes, 2003
40.26 Goehring, Sebes, Kelty, Wilson, 2002
40.39 Goehring, Sebes, Kelty, Wilson, 2003
40.51 Bookman, Davis, Webb, Johnson, 1995
40.61 Goehring, Little, Sebes, Crochet, 2003
40.82 2001
41.04 Webb, Clark, Johnson, Rodriguez, 1994
41.04 Webb, Clark, Johnson, Rodriguez, 1994

Mile Relay

3:08.5	**Sheats, Shellworth, Banks, Lofton**, 1977
3:10.5	Shaw, Williamson, Clark, Jeffrey, 1940
3:10.5	**Frederickson, Rubin, McIntyre, Fraser**, 1965
3:10.8	**Wingo, Sheats, Hogsett, Lofton**, 1976
3:11.2	**Shellworth, Gerfen, Sheats, Lofton**, 1977
3:11.4	**Lassen, Cunliffe, Lloyd, Chesarek**, 1958
3:11.6	**Kauffman, Fairchild, Anderson, White**, 1971

1600-meter Relay

3:06.6	**McCarthy, Banks, Sheats, Lofton**, 1978
3:07.23	Little, Crochet, Goehring, Sebes, 2003
3: 07.4	**Sheats, Shellworth, Banks, Lofton**, 1977
3:07.77	Little, Crochet, Rushing, Sebes, 2003
3:09.17	Goehring, Crochet, Little, Sebes, 2003
3:09.36	Heath, Allen, Pigg, Johnson, 1996
3:09.65	Cramton, Skoog, Strang, Armstrong, 1988
3:09.96	Little, Kelty, Goehring, Sebes, 2002
3:10.56	Little, Goehring, Hassell, Kelty, 2002
3:10.58	Johnson, Heath, Clark, Rodriguez, 1994

Discus

198-7	Omer Inan, 2002
196-1	Glenn Schneider, 1988
193-2	**Dave Weill**, 1963
190-3	Dave Thomson, 1981
189-1	**Bob Stoecker**, 1966
187-2	Mark Ganek, 1999
182-6	**Steve Davis**, 1969
182-1	Pete Swanson, 1996
178-10	Nick Welihozkly, 2003
178-2	Pat Stowell, 1992, 1993

Shot Put

70-7	**Terry Albritton**, 1977
64-10 ¾	Garin Veris, 1982
60-7 ¼	Pete Swanson, 1995
60-1	Brian Boggess, 1989
59-11 ¾	**Jerry Winters**, 1960
58-8 ½	Andy Papathanassiou, 1989
58-5 ½	**T. C. Jones**, 1969
57-4 ⅜	Otis Chandler, 1950
57-0 ¼	Chris Sprague, 2000
56-10 ¼	Omer Inan, 2002

Javelin (old implement at 1980)

265-8	**Tom Colby**, 1969
243-6	Gary Bruner, 1980
241-10	**Art Batchelder**, 1962
239-7	Bob Kimball, 1953
235-9 ¾	Leo Long, 1954
235-3	**Gary Bruner**, 1979
233-4 ½	Bud Held, 1950
231-11	**George Porter**, 1965
230-5	**Steve Hopkins**, 1974
229-8 ½	**John Bugge**, 1955
229-1	**Dick Warwick**, 1968
228-4 ½	**Hank Roldan**, 1957

Javelin (1986 new implement)

234-0	Chad Wassink, 2001
233-11	Dave Pickett, 1988
205-9	Jason Goff, 2003
198-5	James Kostohyrz, 1991
191-7	John Roldan, 1995
189-5	Nick Rosen, 1988
187-3	Justin Strand, 1997
185-7	Josh Gleason, 1996

Long Jump

26-11 ¾	**James Lofton**, 1978
26-0 ¾	Marcus Hickerson, 1990
25-11	Milton Little, 2003
25-9 ½	**Dan Moore**, 1962
25-7 ½	**Darrin Nelson**, 1978
25-4 ¾	Gay Bryan, 1949
25-3	**Frank Herrmann**, 1957

25-2	**Bud Walsh**, 1967	16-11 ¾	**Jim Eshelman**, 1967
25-1	**Tom Anderson**, 1971	16-9 ¼	Chris Buddin, 1995
24-11 ½	**Craig Vaughan**, 1967	16-8 ¾	Adam Fusco, 1998
		16-7	**Casey Carrigan**, 1971

Triple Jump

52-3	**Allen Meredith**, 1970	16-6	**Bob Flint**, 1975
51-8 ½	**Ian Arnold**, 1968	16-0	Dave Pickett, 1985
51-1 ½	**Tom Massey**, 1969	15-8 ½	**Chuck Smith**, 1965
51-0	Jami Webb, 1994		
50-9 ½	Solomon Welch, 2003		

Hammer Throw

50-7	Brian Manning, 1994	240-10	Dave Popejoy, 1995
50-4	**Rod Utley**, 1973	237-3	Adam Connelly, 1999
50-0	Phil Cannon, 1986	233-5	Justin Strand, 1997
50-0	Henry Green, 1989	229-10	Brian Masterson, 1985
49-11 ¼	**Mike Hall**, 1974	225-1	Shaun Pickering, 1984
		222-5	Rick Buzz, 1980
		221-1	Nick Wolthozkly, 2003

High Jump

7-5 ¾	Brian Marshall, 1988	213-2	Dave Thonison, 1981
7-4 ½	Michael Ponikvar, 1999	211-0	Toby Norwood, 1995
7-3	**Peter Boyce**, 1968	208-5	Mark Ganck, 1999
7-3	Travis Clark, 1993		
7-1	John Hopkins, 1989		

Decathlon

7-0 ¼	Todd Beyerlein, 1998	7887	Bob Mathias, 1952
6-10	**Ed Hanks**, 1965	7529	Jay Thorson, 1986
6-10	**Skip Grodahl**, 1972	7428	Jason Goff, 2001
6-10	Chris Patrick, 1981	7287	Travis Clark, 1995
6-9 ¾	Ray Bergstrom, 2002	7228	Michael Heise, 1982
		7084	D. D. Harris, 1989
		7016	Timi Wusu, 2003

Pole Vault

18-9 ¼	Toby Stevenson, 2000	7013	Josh Gleason, 1996
17-8 ½	John Gash, 1987	6215	Chase Wimberly, 1999
17-0 ¾	Jamie Marek, 1993	5937	Nicholas Taylor, 2002

V. Stanford Jordan-Era Varsity Teammate Rosters

1957

Name	Event	Hometown	Major
Anixter, Ben	sprints	Kentfield	Elec. Eng
Bates, Len	sprints, hurdles	Mantica	Communications
Bondoc, Ron	HJ		Philosophy
Caddy, Terry	440		Geography
Carls, Bill	440, 880	Long Beach	Petro. Eng.
Chesarek, Don	440	San Francisco	Elec. Eng
Cobb, Chuck	hurdles	Fresno	Economics
Easter, Jim	440, 880	Cambridge, NB	Economics
Fehlen, Phil	HJ, hurdles	San Francisco	Philosophy
Franchetti, Mike	PV	Santa Rosa	Physics
Gast, Bob	PV	Saratoga, WY	Geography
Gonzales, Carlos	PV	Inglewood	Petro. Eng.
Graves, Maury	distance	Oakland	Bio. Science
Groat, Jack	sprints	Arcadia	Bio. Science
Hansen, Ken	LJ	Paso Robles	Economics
Herpick, Chuck	javelin		Social Science
Herrimann, Frank	sprints, LJ	San Jose	Civil Eng.
Hughes, Dick	PV	Lodi	Elec. Eng
Hyde, Robert	sprints	The Dalles, OR	Bio. Science
Ince, Charles	440	San Francisco	Architecture
Johnson, Hugh	javelin	Inglewood	Bio. Science
Kelly, Larry	HJ	San Jose	Economics
Love, Ralph	distance	Piedmont	Elec. Eng.
Lyons, Sam	PV	Makawao, HI	Social Science
Martin, Doug	distance	Glendora	Pol. Sci.
McKinnon, Don	880		Economics
Nelson, Bernie	hurdles, HJ	El Cajon	Bio. Science
Newman, Bob	hurdles	Burlingame	Education
Nieland, Kirk	javelin		Economics
Peters, Fred	discus		Geology
Peterson, Chuck	LJ		History
Plain, Chris	SP		Elec. Eng.
Richardson, Don	880	Mt. View	Economics
Roldan, Hank	javelin	Orosi	Education
Salcedo, Al	distance	Alhambra	Elec. Eng.
Schmidt, Archie	SP, discus	Taft	
Van Luchene, Bob	distance		Sociology
Willamson, Ray	SP, discus	Lafayette	Economics
Wood, Warren	distance		Elec. Eng.
Woollett, Joe	440, 880	Glendale	Architecture

1958

Name	Event	Hometown	Major
Anixter, Ben	sprints	Kentfield	Elec. Eng
Backstrand, Jim	javelin	Salem, OR	Pol. Sci.
Bates, Len	hurdles	Mantica	Journalism
Besse, Bob	javelin	Pomona	Physical Edu.
Campbell, Leon	440, mile relay	Pasadena	History
Chesarek, Don	440	San Francisco	Elec. Eng
Cobb, Chuck	hurdles	Fresno	Economics
Cunliffe, Ernie	880	Claremont	Physical Education
Coughlin, Steve	HJ		
DeWeese, Armand	discus, SP	Pacific Palisades	Civil Eng
Face, Skip	hurdles	Sunnyvale	Economics
Franchetti, Mike	PV	Santa Rosa	Physics
Gast, Bob	PV	Saratoga, WY	Geography
Graves, Maury	2-mi	Oakland	Bio. Science
Gillespie, Paul	HJ	Los Altos	Elec. Eng.
Hansen, Kent	LJ, jav	Paso Robles	Economics
Hendry, John			Economics
Hughes, Dick	PV	Lodi	Elec. Eng
Kelly, John	LJ	Glendale	Physics
Knapp, Bruce			Health Edu.
Lagerquist, Tom	discus	Woodside	Economics
Lassen, Dick	440, 880	Mesa, AZ	Economics
Limmer, Harlan	discus	Culver City	Physical Edu.
Lloyd, Norm	880, mile	Vancouver, BC	Pre-Law
Martin, Doug	distance	Glendora	Pre-Law
McKenney, Chuck			History
Merchant, Dave	PV	Pacific Palisades	Civil Eng.
Monzingo, Bob	880, 1 & 2-mi	San Diego	Elec. Eng.
Newman, Bob	hurdles		Education
Pease, Norm	sprints	Bend, OR	Biological Sciences
Peterson, John			
Pike, Gary			Psychology
Plain, Chris	SP		Elec. Eng.
Salcedo, Al	distance	Alhambra	Elec. Eng.
Smith, Dean	sprints	Omaha, NB	Mech. Eng
Stahler, John	PV		Bio. Sci.
Van Luchene, Bob	2-mi		Sociology
Willamson, Ray	SP, discus	Lafayette	Economics
Winters, Jerry	SP	Eureka	Economics

1959

Name	Event	Hometown	Major
Anixter, Ben	sprints	Kentfield	Elec. Eng.
Atkinson, Bob	SP	Woodside	Economics
Backstrand, Jim	javelin	Salem, OR	Pol. Sci.

Name	Event	Hometown	Major
Barrett, Craig	HJ	San Carlos	Engineering
Besse, Bob	javelin	Pomona	Physical Edu.
Chesarek, Don	440	San Francisco	Elec. Eng.
Cunliffe, Ernie	880	Claremont	Physical Education
DeWeese, Armand	discus, SP	Pacific Palisades	Civil Eng
Evans, Jeff	880	Cresson, PA	Psychology
Face, Skip	hurdles	Sunnyvale	Economics
Franchetti, Mike	PV	Santa Rosa	Physics
Gillespie, Paul	HJ	Los Altos	Elec. Eng.
Hauser, Kurt	sprints, 440	San Marino	History
Hughes, Dick	hurdles	Lodi	Elec. Eng.
Kelly, John	LJ	Glendale	Physics
Lagerquist, Tom	discus	Woodside	Economics
Lassen, Dick	440, 880	Mesa, AZ	Economics
Limmer, Harlan	discus	Culver City	Physical Edu.
Lloyd, Norm	440	Vancouver, BC	Pre-Law
Lundh, Bertil	880	Fredrikstad, Norway	Ind. Eng.
Martin, Doug	distance	Glendora	Pol. Sci.
Monzingo, Bob	880, 1 & 2-mi	San Diego	Elec. Eng.
Merchant, Dave	PV	Pacific Palisades	Civil Eng.
North, Jim	javelin	Medford, OR	Pol. Sci.
Nourse, John	HJ	Arcadia	Gen. Studies
Pease, Norm	sprints	Bend, OR	Biological Sciences
Saxton, Harry	HJ	Woodland Hills	Metl. Eng.
Smith, Dean	sprints	Omaha, NB	Mech. Eng.
Stahler, John	PV		Bio. Sci.
Townsend, Brooks	LJ	Oxnard	Gen. Studies
Wallace, Keith	mile	Orinda	English
Winters, Jerry	SP	Eureka	Economics

1960

Name	Event	Hometown	Major
Atkinson, Bob	SP, discus	Woodside	Economics
Backstrand, Jim	javelin	Salem, OR	Pol. Sci.
Barrett, Craig	LJ	San Carlos	Engineering
Barth, Chuck	LJ	Whittier	Elec. Eng.
Batchelder, Art	javelin	Lafayette	Pol. Sci.
Beaubier, Jeff	880	Fresno	
Bell, Don	discus, SP	Alameda	Education
Besse, Bob	440, 220	Pomona	Physical Edu.
Breschini, Len	440, 220	Salinas	History
Cunliffe, Ernie	880, mile	Claremont	Physical Edu.
Engebretsen, Rune	HJ	Concord	German Studies
Evans, Jeff	880	Cresson, PA	Psychology
Gillespie, Paul	HJ	Los Altos	Elec. Eng.
Heigold, Bob	HJ, discus, jav	Glendale	Chem. Eng.

122

Name	Event	Hometown	Major
Hungerland, Chris	220, 440	Los Angeles	Psychology
Hunter, Jack	discus	Elko, NV	Health Edu.
Kelly, John	LJ, TJ	Glendale	Physics
Klier, Rich	880	Oakland	Physical Edu.
Lassen, Dick	440, 880	Mesa, AZ	Economics
Lentz, Gib	PV	Sacramento	Pol. Sci.
Limmer, Harlan	discus	Culver City	Education
Lloyd, Norm	880, mile	Surrey, England	Pre-Law
Lundh, Bertil	880, mile	Fredrikstad, Norway	Ind. Eng.
Martin, Bob	hurdles	Los Angeles	Economics
McGuire, Bob	1 & 2-mi.	Whittier	Education
Merchant, Dave	PV	Salem, OR	Civil Eng.
Moore, Dan	LJ, hurdles	Salem, OR	Physical Edu.
Monzingo, Bob	1 & 2-mi.	San Diego	Elec. Eng.
Northway, John	1 & 2-mi.	Palo Alto	Architecture
Nourse, John	hurdles, HJ	Arcadia	Economics
Offenberg, Anders	LJ	Shien, Norway	Mech. Eng.
Parker, Rich	440, 880	S. Pasadena	Philosophy
Pease, Norm	sprints	Bend, OR	Biological Sciences
Robison, Billie	PV	Loleta	Mech. Eng.
Schmitt, Archie	discus, SP	Taft	
Schneider, Ron	hurdles	Menlo Park	Chemistry
Smith, Dean	100, 220, hurdles	Omaha, NB	Mech. Eng.
Stallings, Larry	javelin	Whittier	Pol. Sci.
Wallace, Keith	1 & 2-mi.	Orinda	English
Winters, Jerry	SP	Eureka	Economics

1961

Name	Event	Hometown	Major
Atkinson, Bob	SP, discus	Woodside	Economics
Barrett, Craig	LJ	San Carlos	Metal Eng.
Barth, Chuck	LJ	Whittier	Elec. Eng.
Batchelder, Art	javelin	Lafayette	Pol. Sci.
Bell, Don	discus	Alameda	Education
Breschini, Len	440, 220	Salinas	History
Buchler, Chuck	SP	Whittier	Medicine
Davis, Jim	440, 880	Philadelphia, PA	History
Downey, Sheridan	LJ, TJ, sprints	Oakland	Pre-Law
Emanuels, Ken	sprints	Seattle, WA	Pol. Sci.
Fischer, Larry	sprints	San Diego	Nuclear Eng.
Holgerson, Bob	880	Wichita, KS	Economics
Hungerland, Chris	440	Los Angeles	Psychology
Jessen, Chris	javelin	San Carlos	Medicine
Johnson, Bruce	2-mi.	Orinda	Pol. Sci.
Klier, Rich	hurdles, 880, mi.	Oakland	Physical Edu.
Lamoreaux, Phil	sprints	Napa	Business

Name	Event	Hometown	Major
McGinnes, Marc	javelin	Kennewick, WA	History
Marron, Ralph	PV	Albuquerque, NM	Physics
Moore, Dan	LJ, hurdles	Salem, OR	Physical Edu.
Northway, John	1 & 2-mi.	Palo Alto	Architecture
Nourse, John	HJ, hurdles	Arcadia	Economics
Nowinski, Robin	2-mi.	Coronado	Civil Eng.
Parker, Rich	440, 880	S. Pasadena	Philosophy
Stack, Chris	javelin	Chicago, IL	Gen. Studies
Taylor, Bob	sprints	Los Angeles	Mech. Eng.
Tousch, Bill	880, mi.	Riverside	Mech. Eng.
Wallace, Frank	1 & 2-mi.	Carmel	Engineering
Wandrey, Bill	hurdles	Evanston, IL	Medicine
Weill, Dave	discus	Walnut Creek	Elec. Eng.
White, Phil	PV	Carmel	Engineering
Wright, Ted	javelin	San Mateo	Elec. Eng.
Wyeth, Harry	hurdles	Santa Barbara	Gen. Studies

1962

Name	Event	Hometown	Major
Arch, Steve	SP, discus	Reno, NV	Biology
Babbs, Chris	sprints	Denver, CO	Medicine
Barth, Chuck	LJ	Whittier	Elec. Eng,
Batchelder, Art	javelin	Lafayette	Pol. Sci.
Bell, Don	discus, HJ, LH	Alameda	Education
Chesarek, Rich	220, 440	San Francisco	Elec. Eng.
Cortright, Steve	hurdles, TJ	Long Beach	Art
Davis, Jim	880	Philadelphia, PA	History
Downey, Sheridan	LJ, TJ	Oakland	Psychology
Emanuels, Ken	440	Medina, WA	Int'l Rel.
Fischer, Larry	100, 220	San Diego	Mech. Eng.
Fontius, John	HJ	Newport Beach	Physical Edu.
Gilmer, Graham	javelin	Orange	Pre-Med
Grant, Frank	LJ, PV	Hoopa	Physics
Hastings, Chick	javelin	Long Beach	Gen. Studies
Haynie, John	LJ	Gr. Junction, CO	Math
Johnson, Jeff	1 & 2-mi	Los Altos	Anthropology
Klier, Rich	440, 880, mi	Oakland	Physical Edu.
Lamoreaux, Phil	100, 220, 440	Napa	Economics
McCalla, Harry	1 & 2-mi	Berkeley	Gen. Studies
Miltz, Bob	440 to 2-mi	Alhambra	History
Minyard, Handsel	LJ	Phoenix, AZ	Gen. Studies
Moore, Dan	LJ	Salem, OR	Physical Edu.
Northway, John	LJ	Palo Alto	Architecture
Parker, Rich	440, 880	S. Pasadena	Philosophy
Phillips, Truman	HJ, hurdles	Terre Haute, IN	Mech. Eng.
Pilz, George	2-mi	Clarksburg	Biology

Name	Event	Hometown	Major
Pratt, Bill	880, mile	Wenatchee, WA	Int'l Rel.
Raaka, Clayton	HJ	La Mesa	Gen. Studies
Rhoads, Roger	PV	Pebble Beach	Economics
Ruble, Robin	880, mile	Los Altos	Education
Shafer, Larry	1 & 2-mi	Denver, CO	Physics
Sisler, Jim	LJ, hurdles	Orinda	Pol. Sci.
Stack, Chris	javelin	Chicago, IL	History
Stone, Dave	880	Berkeley	Social Sci.
Taylor, Bob	220, 440	Los Angeles	Mech. Eng.
Walker, Gary	100, 220, 440	Santa Ana	Economics
Wandrey, Bill	hurdles	Evanston, IL	Economics
Weill, Dave	discus	Walnut Creek	Elec. Eng.
Wordell, Steve	javelin	Bijou	Speech & Drama
Yetter, Stan	PV	Manhattan Beach	Math

1963

Name	Event	Hometown	Major
Amos, Eugene (Skip)	440	Long Beach	Elec. Eng.
Andrews, Harlan	880, mile, 2-mi	Eugene, OR	Engineering
Arch, Steve	SP	Reno, NV	Biology
Arnaudo, Phil	hurdles	Mt. View	Biology
Beck, John	mile	Portland, OR	Gen. Studies
Breschini, Len	100,220, 440	Salinas	Pol. Sci.
Bruce, Doug	PV	Fairbanks, AK	Physics
Chapman, Allan	880, mile	Los Altos Hills	English
Chapple, Jack	SP	Coronado	Gen. Study
Chesarek, Richard	220, 440	San Francisco	Elec. Eng.
Cortright, Steve	hurdles, TJ	Long Beach	Art
Downey, Sheridan	LJ, TJ	Oakland	Psychology
Emanuels, Ken	440	Medina, WA	Int'l Rel.
Fraser, Ken	220, 440	Pasadena	Economics
Frische, Eric	100, 220	Glen Head, NY	Biology
Fontius, John	HJ	Newport Bch	Phys. Ed.
Gilmer, Graham	javelin	Orange	Biology
Gilstrap, William	javelin	Albuquerque, NM	Pre-Law
Groeling, John	440, 330IH	Bellflower	Psychology
Hastings, Chick	javelin	Long Beach	History
Johnson, Bruce	mile, 2 mi	Orinda	Pol. Sci.
Johnson, James	880, mile	Jamaica, NY	Chem. Eng.
Kirkland, Weym	mile, 2&3-mi	Winnetka, IL	Gen. Studies
Lamoreaux, Phil	100, 220, 440	Napa	Economics
Mallen, Ron	discus	Berkeley	Chem. Eng.
Marik, Jay	HJ	Glendale	Biology
McCalla, Harry	mile, 2&3-mi	Berkeley	Pol. Sci.
McIntyre, Bob	sprints, LJ	Medford, OR	Biology
Miltz, Bob	440 to 2-mi	Alhambra	History

Name	Event	Hometown	Major
Moore, Dan	LJ	Salem, OR	Phys. Ed.
Peterson, Lorne	SP, discus	N. Surry, BC, Can.	Engineering
Peterson, Russell	LJ, 440	Arlington, VA	Pre-Med
Pilz, George	1&2-mi	Clarksburg	Biology
Pratt, Bill	880, 1&3-mi	Wenatchee, WA	Biology
Prono, Dan	javelin	Glendale	Engineering
Questad, Larry	100, 220	Livingston, MT	Mech. Eng.
Raaka, Clayton	HJ	La Mesa	Biology
Rees, David	1&2-mi	Vida, OR	Chem. Eng.
Ruble, Robin	880, mile	Los Altos	Education
Scherer, Rick	hurdles	Long Beach	Civil Eng.
Schlicke, Paul	880 to 3-mi	Spokane, WA	Pre-Med
Scott, Jack	sprints	Syracuse, NY	Psychology
Taylor, Bob	220 to 2-mi	Los Angeles	Mech. Eng.
Treese, Clifford	2-mi	Seattle, WA	Am. Studies
Twitchell, Dennis	SP	Santa Maria	Pol. Sci.
Walker, Gary	440, 330 IH	Santa Ana	Pol. Sci.
Weill, David	discus	Walnut Creek	Elec. Eng.
White, Philip	PV	Carmel	Mech. Eng.

1964

Name	Event	Hometown	Major
Amos, Eugene (Skip)	440	Long Beach	Ind. Eng.
Andrews, Harlan	880, mile	Eugene, OR	Engineering
Arch, Steve	SP	Reno, NV	Biology
Arend, Larry	LJ, hurdles	Grand Jun., CO	Math
Arnaudo, Phil	hurdles	Mt. View	Pol. Sci.
Bruce, Doug	PV	Fairbanks, AK	Physics
Chapman, Allan	880, mile	Huntington, NY	English
Chesarek, Richard	220, 440	San Francisco	Elec. Eng.
Cortright, Steve	hurdles, TJ	Long Beach	Art
Curfman, Larry	440	Wichita, KS	Gen. Studies
Deubner, Dave	1, 2, 3-mi	Orinda	Physics
Fitzmorris, Tyce	100, 220	San Jose	Pol. Sci.
Fraser, Ken	220, 440	Pasadena	History
Frische, Eric	100, 220	Glen Head, NY	Biology
Friedrich, Jim	PV	Sherman Oaks	History
Gilmer, Graham	javelin	Orange	Biology
Goode, John	LJ, TJ, HJ, jav	Fowler	Gen. Studies
Hammen, Richard	100, 220	Missoula, MT	Chemistry
Hill, Martin	1 & 2-mi	San Joaquin	Chemistry
Johnson, Bruce	1 & 2-mi	Orinda	Pol. Sci.
Kirkland, Weym	1, 2, 3-mi	Winnetka, IL	English
McCalla, Harry	mile, SC	Berkeley	Pol. Sci.
McIntyre, Bob	100, 220, 440	Medford, OR	Biology
Miltz, Bob	440, 880, mi	Alhambra	History

Name	Event	Hometown	Major
Mullen, Ron	discus	Berkeley	Chem. Eng.
Peterson, Lorne	SP, discus	N. Surrey, B.C.	Economics
Porter, George	javelin	Shreveport, PA	Pre-Med
Pratt, Bill	880, mile	Wenatchee, WA	Pre-Med
Prono, Dan	javelin	Glendale	Engineering
Robertson, Jim	HJ	Pasadena	Gen. Studies
Raaka, Clayton	HJ	La Mesa	Biology
Ruble, Robin	880, mile	Los Altos	Education
Scherer, Rick	hurdles	Long Beach	Civil Eng.
Schlicke, Paul	1, 2, 3-mi	Spokane, WA	Pre-Med
Shilts, John	330IH	Venice	History
Smith, Chuck	PV	Torrance	Mech. Eng.
Stoecker, Bob	discus, jav	Los Altos	Architecture
Walker, Gary	440, 330 IH	Santa Ana	Pol. Sci.
Wilkins, Tyler	SP, discus	Los Altos	Mech. Eng.
Wool, Mickey	discus, SP	San Jose	Mech. Eng.

1965

Name	Event	Hometown	Major
Andrews, Harlan	880, mile	Eugene, OR	Elec. Eng.
Arnaudo, Phil	hurdles	Mt. View	Pol. Sci.
Bardin, Dick	440	Arcadia	Civil Eng.
Barkley, Dick	PV	Palo Alto	Engineering
Deubner, Dave	880, 1&2-mi	Orinda	Physics
Eshelman, Jim	PV	Palo Alto	Math
Forbes, Donn	sprints	Levenworth, KS	Gen. Engineering
Ford, Greg	hurdles	Concord	Gen. Studies
Fraser, Ken	220, 440	Pasadena	History
Fredrickson, Terry	100 to 880	Northfield, MN	History
Frische, Eric	sprints	Glen Head, NY	Biology
Goode, John	HJ, LJ, TJ, jav	Fowler	Economics
Havskjold, Glenn	sprints, LJ	Havre, MT	Mech. Eng.
Hill, Martin	1&2-mi	San Joaquin	Chemistry
Hyvonen, Randy	880, mi	Red Lodge, MT	German
Kirkland, Weym	1&2-mi	Winnetka, IL	English
McIntyre, Bob	sprints, LJ	Medford, OR	Biology
Marik, Jay	HJ	Glendale	Biology
Miller, Art	sprints	Pacheco	English
O'Brian, Jack	440, 880	Ventura	Biology
Peterson, Lorne	SP, discus	N. Surry, B.C.	Philosophy
Porter, George	javelin	Shreveport, LA	Anthropology
Prono, Dan	javelin	Glendale	Elec. Eng.
Questad, Larry	sprints	Livingston, MT	Mech. Eng.
Robertson, Jim	HJ	Pasadena	Economics
Rubin, Dale	sprints	Oakland	Psychology
Scherer, Rick	hurdles	Long Beach	Civil Eng.

Name	Event	Hometown	Major
Schlicke, Paul	1&2-mi	Spokane, WA	English
Slaughter, Don	javelin	Fresno	Gen. Studies
Smith, Chuck	PV	Torrance	Mech. Eng.
Stoecker, Bob	discus, SP, jav	Los Altos	Architecture
Walsh, Bud	hurd, LJ, TJ, HJ	Coos Bay, OR	Gen. Studies
Wilhelm, Bruce	SP, discus	Los Altos	Gen. Studies
Wilkins, Tyler	SP, discus	Los Altos	Mech. Eng.
Wool, Mickey	discus	San Jose	Mech. Eng.

1966

Name	Event	Hometown	Major
Arnold, Ian	TJ	Don Mills, Ont.	History
Barkley, Richard	PV	Palo Alto	Mech. Eng.
Cox, Roger	sprints	Redlands	Pol. Sci.
Coy, Steve	LJ, TJ	Los Altos	Architecture
Deubner, Dave	880, 1 & 2-mi	Orinda	English
Eshelman, Jim	PV	Palo Alto	Math
Forbes, Donn	sprints	Levenworth, KS	Pol. Sci.
Frederickson, Terry	440	Northfield, MN	History
Fyall, Bill	SP	Seattle, WA	Engineering
Havskjold, Glenn	440	Havre, MT	Mech. Eng.
Hughes, Mike	440	Tucson, AZ	Gen. Studies
Hyvonen, Randy	880, mile	Red Lodge, MT	English
Jacobs, Mike	880	Hillsborough	Economics
Johnson, Bruce	2-mi, Sc	Orinda	Pol. Sci.
Kelley, Bob	2-mi	Spokane, WA	History
Letterer, Jim	1 & 2-mi	Berkeley, IL	Elec. Eng.
Lund, Henrik	880	Oslo, Norway	Civil Eng.
Martin, Del	220, 440	Portland, OR	English
Means, Grady	hurdles	North Hollywood	Biology
Miller, Art	LJ, TJ	Pacheco	English
Mitchell, Bruce	SP	Palo Alto	Civil Eng.
Newton, Carter	javelin	Vandenberg AFB	Engineering
O'Brien, Jack	440, 880	Ventura	Biology
Porter, George	javelin	Ft. Worth, TX	Anthropology
Questad, Larry	sprints	Livingston, MT	Mech. Eng.
Schembra, Chuck	discus	San Leandro	Gen. Studies
Sears, Andy	sprints	Belmont	Gen. Studies
Slaughter, Don	javelin	Fresno	Biology
Smart, Chuck	SP, javelin	Los Altos	Gen. Studies
Smith, Chuck	PV	Torrance	Mech. Eng.
Stoecker, Bob	discus, SP, jav	Los Altos	Architecture
Suomi, Steve	HJ	Madison, WI	Gen. Studies
Taplin, Russ	sprints	Modesto	Gen. Studies
Vaughan, Craig	LJ	Pasadena	History
Walsh, Bud	LJ, HJ, hurdles	Coos Bay, OR	History

Name	Event	Hometown	Major
Ward, Jim	sprints	Columbiana, OH	Economics
Warwick, Dick	javelin	Oakesdale, WA	Gen. Studies
Whittle, Alex	880, 1 & 2-mi	Los Altos	Mech. Eng.
Willett, Boyd	javelin	Denver, CO	Engineering
Williamson, John	hurdles	Prairie Village, KS	Biology
Wool, Mickey	discus	San Jose	Mech. Eng.

1967

Name	Event	Hometown	Major
Anchondo, Bob	2-mi	El Paso, TX	Gen. Studies
Arnold, Ian	TJ	Don Mills, Ont.	Economics
Boyce, Peter	HJ	Melbourne, Aust.	Engineering
Cox, Roger	sprints	Redlands	Pol. Sci.
Delaney, Bill	sprints	Palo Alto	Communications
Donley, Mike	440, 880, mi	Bend, OR	Gen. Studies
Douglass, Richard	880	Compton	Physics
Eshelman, Jim	PV	Palo Alto	Math
Forbes, Donn	sprints	Levenworth, KS	English
Fyall, Bill	SP	Seattle, WA	Mech. Eng.
Giddens, Dan	HJ	Ventura	Pre-Med
Grimm, Tom	discus	San Carlos	Mech. Eng.
Guglielmetti, Gary	sprints	San Diego	Psychology
Halligan, Bill	HJ	Fullerton	Biology
Harrington, Dave	SP, discus	Fairfield	Gen. Studies
Jacobs, Mike	880	Hillsborough	Economics
Jones, David	440	Topeka, KS	Gen. Studies
Kommers, Tom	hurdles	Portland, OR	Gen. Studies
Larson, Larry	440	Kelseyville	Gen. Studies
Lemons, Mike	PV	Riverside	Chemistry
Letterer, Jim	1 & 2-mi	Berkeley, IL	Elec. Eng.
Marlar, Jim	hurdles	Phoenix, AZ	History
Martin, Lance	javelin	Olympia, WA	Economics
Newton, Carter	javelin	Vandenberg AFB	Engineering
O'Brien, Jack	880	Ventura	Biology
Pyles, John	hurdles	Long Beach	Chem. Eng.
Sanford, Allen	1 & 2-mi	Tustin	Gen. Studies
Schembra, Chuck	discus	San Leandro	Mech. Eng.
Scott, Jack	PV	Paoli, PA	Pol. Sci.
Sears, Andy	sprints	Belmont	History
Slaughter, Don	javelin, TJ	Fresno	Biology
Smart, Chuck	SP, discus	Mt. View	Math
Smith, Scott	SP, discus	Walnut Creek	Economics
Spearman, Ted	SP	Yakima, WA	Philosophy
Stephens, Lloyd	880	San Jose	History
Sturm, Rick	440	Hoquiam, WA	Gen. Studies
Taplin, Russ	440	Modesto	History

Name	Event	Hometown	Major
Vaughan, Craig	LJ	Pasadena	Ancient History
Walsh, Bud	LJ, hurdles	Coos Bay, OR	Pol. Sci.
Ward, Jim	440, sprints	Columbiana, OH	Economics
Warwick, Dick	javelin	Oakesdale, WA	English
Woodruff, Dan	220, 440	Washington, DC	Gen. Studies

1968

Name	Event	Hometown	Major
Anchondo, Bob	mile, 2-mi	El Paso, TX	Pol. Sci.
Arnold, Ian	TJ, LJ	Don Mills, Ont.	Economics
Boyce, Peter	HJ	Melbourne, Aust.	Civil Eng.
Brock, Greg	880, 1&2-mi.	Sacramento	Psychology
Colby, Thomas	javelin	Amherst, MA	Psychology
Cox, Roger	sprints	Redlands	Pol. Sci.
Coy, Steve	TJ, LJ	Los Altos	Economics
Donart, Jim	sprints	Anaheim	Gen. Studies
Faris, Rich	hurdles, sprints	Pomona	Civil Eng.
Flannery, Steve	PV	Downey	Engineering
Gibson, Chris	LJ	Long Beach	Gen. Studies
Griffith, Bill	hurdles, 440	Glendale	Mathematics
Harper, Dave	HJ	Piedmont	Gen. Studies
Harrington, Dave	SP, discus	Fairfield	Psychology
Jacobs, Michael	880, 440	Burlingame	Economics
Jones, Steve	1 & 2-mi.	Spokane, WA	Gen. Studies
Kaplan, Paul	880, mile	Redondo Beach	Pre-Med
Karpinos, Steve	1 & 2-mi.	Silver Springs, MD	Gen. Studies
Kommers, Tom	hurdles	Portland, OR	English
Larson, Larry	440	Kelseyville	Pol. Sci.
Letterer, Jim	1 & 2-mi.	Berkeley, IL	Elec. Eng.
Massey, Tom	TJ, HJ, hurd.	Long Beach	Psychology
Mallery, Jim	LJ	Seattle, WA	Communications
Means, Grady	440, hurdles	Newbury Park	Mech. Eng.
Menz, Chuck	1 & 2-mi.	Cupertino	Elec. Eng.
Mogno, Leonard	SP	Los Angeles	Psychology
Norberg, Hank	discus	Palo Alto	History
Ostrander, Clint	PV	Woodland Hills	Engineering
Porter, Jerry	javelin	Manhattan Beach	Gen. Studies
Redwine, David	1 & 2-mi.	Ft. Worth, TX	Biology
Saenz, Mike	hurdles	Sunnyvale	Civil Eng.
Sears, Andy	sprints	Belmont	History
Still, Pete	880, 440	Thousand Oaks	Biology
Taplin, Russ	440, 220	Modesto	History
Thomas, Brook	mile, 880	Catonsville, MD	English
Vaughan, Craig	LJ, TJ	Pasadena	History
Ward, Jim	440, 220	Columbiana, OH	Economics
Warwick, Dick	javelin	Oakesdale, WA	English

Name	Event	Hometown	Major
Washington, Gene	sprints	Long Beach	History
Williams, Howie	LJ, TJ, 100	Tarzana	Gen. Studies
Woodruff, Dan	220, 440	Washington, DC	Psychology
Yelderman, Mark	880	Rosenberg, TX	Mech. Eng.

1969

Name	Event	Hometown	Major
Anchondo, Bob	mile, 2-mi.	El Paso, TX	Pol. Sci.
Barber, Glenn	440, 880	Silver Springs, MD	Pol. Sci.
Boyce, Peter	HJ	Melbourne, Aust.	Civil Eng.
Brock, Greg	2, 3, 6-mi.	Sacramento	Psychology
Brown, Bubba	LJ	Oxnard	History
Buchler, George	SP	Whittier	Pol. Sci.
Colby, Thomas	javelin	Amherst, MA	Psychology
Crosby, Peter	discus	San Pedro	Economics
Davis, Steve	discus, SP	Los Altos	Pol. Sci.
Delurgio, Nick	220, 440	Glendale	Psychology
Evers, Bob	440	Palo Alto	Economics
Fairchild, Pete	440, 880	Sacramento	Pre-Med
Faris, Rich	220, 440	Pomona	Civil Eng.
Flannery, Steve	PV	Downey	Mech. Eng.
Ford, Greg	hurdles	Concord	Biology
Francis, Chuck	sprints	Toronto, Canada	Pol. Sci.
Gibson, Chris	LJ	Long Beach	Gen. Studies
Griffith, Bill	hurdles	Glendale	Mathematics
Hansen, George	javelin	Portland, OR	Gen. Studies
Harper, Dave	HJ	Piedmont	Economics
Hoftiezer, Jim	SP, discus	Peoria, IL	Pre-Med
Jones, Steve	2 & 3-mi.	Vashow, WA	Gen. Studies
Kauffman, Jim	440, LJ	Millbrae	English
Kommers, Tom	hurdles	Honolulu, HI	English
Larson, Larry	440	Kelseyville	Pol. Sci.
Macdonald, Duncan	880, mile	Kailua, HI	Gen. Studies
McNair, Kevin	sprints	San Mateo	Gen. Studies
Mallery, Jim	LJ	Seattle, WA	Pol. Sci.
Massey, Tom	TJ, HJ	Long Beach	Psychology
Martin, Lance	javelin	Olympia, WA	Communications/Econ.
Menz, Chuck	2, 3-mi., SC	Cupertino	Elec. Eng.
Norberg, Hank	discus	Palo Alto	Psychology
Nourse, Steve	javelin	Lake Oswego, OR	Mech. Eng.
Ostrander, Clint	PV	Woodland Hills	Mech. Eng.
Peterson, Todd	PV	Los Altos	Gen. Studies
Porter, Jerry	javelin	Minot, ND	Psychology
Sanford, Allen	1 & 2-mi.	Santa Ana	Pol. Sci.
Snyder, Walt	HJ	Reedley	Gen. Studies
Spanner, Bob	sprints	Woodland Hills	Econ./Psychology

Name	Event	Hometown	Major
Storek, Fred	sprints	Menlo Park	Economics
Sweetwyne, Kermit	880	Oakland	French
Thomas, Brook	880, 1 & 2-mi., SC	Baltimore, MD	English
Tipton, Rick	hurdles, 100	Silver City, NV	Gen. Studies
Wagar, Roger	sprints, LJ	San Diego	History
Washington, Demea	100, 220	Kensington	Gen. Studies
Weed, Ken	PV	Palo Alto	Gen. Studies
White, Randy	hurdles, 440	Burlingame	Elec. Eng.

1970

Name	Event	Hometown	Major
Adams, Doug	discus	Brentwood	Gen. Studies
Bach, Steve	javelin	Portland, OR	Math
Brock, Greg	2 & 3-mi	Sacramento	Psychology
Carrigan, Mike	PV	Orting, WA	undeclared
Davis, Steve	SP, discus	Los Altos	Pol. Sci.
Dews, Bob	HJ	Colo. Sp., CO	Gen. Studies
Donart, Jim	100, 220, LJ	Anaheim	Psychology
Ertl, Rett	880	Boulder, CO	Liberal Arts
Fairchild, Peter	880	Sacramento	Pre-Med
Flannery, Steve	PV	Downey	Engineering
Ford, Greg	hurdles	Concord	Biology
Francis, Chuck	sprints	Toronto, Canada	Pol. Sci.
Greenlaw, Dave	mile	Renton WA	Physics
Griffith, Bill	120HH	Glendale	Math
Haight, Mark	hurdles	Evanston, IL	Gen. Studies
Harper, Dave	HJ	Piedmont	Economics
Hession, Pat	440IH	Carmichael	Chem. Eng.
Jones, Steve	SC	Vashon, WA	Economics
Jones, Tom	SP	Oakland	Economics
Kardong, Don	2 & 3-mi	Bellevue, WA	Psychology
Kauffman, Jim	440, LJ	Millbrae	Engineering
Kretz, Arvid	2 & 3-mi	Millbrae	Music
Lawson, Jack	2-mi, SC	Modesto	Pol. Sci.
Lindley, Robert	HJ	Santa Ana	Gen. Studies
McCormmach, Bruce	mile, 880	Portland, OR	Gen. Studies
McElwain, Doug	hurdles	Piedmont	Economics
McNair, Kevin	100, 220	Mt. View	Gen. Studies
Macdonald, Duncan	880, mile	Kailua, HI	Gen. Studies
Mallery, Jim	TJ, LJ	Seattle, WA	Pol. Sci.
Menz, Chuck	2-mi, SC	Cupertino	Elect. Eng.
Meredith, Allen	TJ, LJ	Los Altos	French
Nicholson, Tim	880	Anaheim	Elec. Eng.
Ostrander, Clint	PV	Woodland Hls.	Mech. Eng.
Peterson, Todd	PV	Los Altos	Gen. Studies
Porter, Jerry	javelin	Minot, ND	Psychology

Name	Event	Hometown	Major
Stillinger, Scott	PV	Pomona	Engineering
Storek, Fred	100, 220	Menlo Park	Economics
Sweetwyne, Kermit	880	Oakland	Linguistics
Tenny, Doug	LJ, TJ	Walnut Creek	Gen. Studies
Thomas, Brook	2-mi, SC	Baltimore, MD	English
Tipton, Rick	100, 120HH	Silver City, NV	Psychology
Virga, Joe	SP	No. Highlands	Pol. Sci.
Watson, George	2-mi	Torrance	Math
Weed, Ken	PV	Palo Alto	Psychology
White, Randy	440, hurdles	Burlingame	Elec. Eng.
Whiteling, Dave	880	Monterey Pk.	History

1971

Name	Event	Hometown	Major
Adams, Doug	discus	Brentwood	Pol. Sci.
Anderson, John	hurdles	Newberg, OR	Mech. Eng.
Anderson, Thomas	LJ, HJ	Los Altos Hills	Mech. Eng.
Bakkensen, Ralph	SP, discus	Portland, OR	Gen. Studies
Carrigan, Casey	PV	Orting, WA	Pol. Sci.
Davis, Steve	SP, discus	Los Altos	Pol. Sci.
Dews, Robert	HJ	Colo. Sp., CO	Gen. Studies
Dougherty, Stephen	SP, discus	La Mesa	Gen. Studies
Dreissigacker, Peter	discus	Orange, CT	Product Design
Dyson, Albert	sprints, LJ	Wash., DC	Pol. Sci.
Ertl, Rett	880	Boulder, CO	Russian
Fairchild, Peter	880	Sacramento	Economics
Francis, Charles	sprints	Toronto, Canada	Pol. Sci.
Geisler, Rick	distance	Camarillo	History
Haight, Mark	hurdles	Battle Creek, MI	Gen. Studies
Harmatz, Paul	PV	Oakridge, TN	Pre-Med
Jordan, Tom	880	Urbana, IL	History
Kardong, Don	distance	Bellevue, WA	Psychology
Kretz, Arvid	distance	Milbrae	Music
Lahde, Bernhard	2 & 3-mi	Los Altos	Pre-Med
Larson, David	HJ	Danville	Gen. Studies
Long, Thomas	hurdles	Sacramento	Env. Eng.
Macdonald, Duncan	880, mile	Kailua, HI	Bio. Sci.
McAvity, Thomas	hammer	Greenwich, CT	English
McElwain, Douglas	440IH	Piedmont	Economics
McNair, Kevin	100, 220	West Covina	English
Meredith, Allen	TJ	Los Altos	Economics
Mueller, Larry	880	Syosset, NY	Gen. Studies
Nicholson, Tim	880	Anaheim	Elec. Eng.
Peterson, Todd	PV	Los Altos	Psychology
Reed, John	440IH	LaCanada	Biology
Roberts, Frank	440	Claremont	Psychology

Name	Event	Hometown	Major
Tenney, Doug	LJ, TJ	Walnut Creek	Philosophy
Tipton, Rick	100, 120HH	Silver City, NV	Psychology
Tirado, Leo	mile	Morgan Hills	Gen. Studies
Utley, Rodney	TJ	San Jose	Human Bio.
White, Randy	440, 440IH	Burlingame	Elec. Eng.
Whiteing, David	880	Monterey Park	History

1972

Name	Event	Hometown	Major
Adams, Doug	discus	Brentwood	Pol. Sci.
Anderson, John	hurdles	Newberg, OR	Mech. Eng.
Anderson, Thomas	LJ, HJ	Los Altos Hills	Civil. Eng.
Bakkensen, Ralph	SP, discus	Portland, OR	Economics
Barmeyer, Robert	100, 220	Long Beach	Pre-Med
Cautley, Daniel	1 & 2-mi	Madison, WI	Gen. Studies
Curl, Kenneth	100, 220, relays	Houston, TX	Human Bio.
Daniel, David	mile, SC	Redwood City	History
Dougherty, Stephen	SP, discus, jav	La Mesa	Anthropology
Dreissigacker, Peter	discus, javelin	Orange, CT	Product Design
Garcia, Rod	javelin	La Mirada	Gen. Studies
Haight, Mark	hurdles	Battle Creek, MI	English
Hayman, Robert	3K, SC	San Francisco	Gen. Studies
Henry, Bruce	440, 220	Dayton, OH	Engineering
Ho, Melvin	LJ, TJ	Sunnyvale	Civil Eng.
Hopkins, Stephen	javelin	Portland, OR	Engineering
Hubbard, Philip	PV	Kansas City, MO	Engineering
Hustwick, David	880	Laguna Beach	Economics
Kessel, John	440, 220	Los Altos	History
Kretz, Arvid	distance	Milbrae	Music
Lahde, Bernhard	2 & 3-mi	Los Altos	Pre-Med
Larson, David	HJ	Danville	Psychology
Larson, Richard	javelin	Eugene, OR	Gen. Studies
Lindsay, Thomas	PV	Carmichael	Human Bio.
Long, Thomas	hurdles	Sacramento	Psychology
McAvity, Thomas	hammer	Greenwich, CT	English
McElwain, Douglas	220	Piedmont	Economics
McFadden, Leslie	880, mile	Vista	Anthropology
Mittelstaedt, Brian	880, mile	Tacoma, WA	Biology
On, Roger	880	San Francisco	Chemistry
Raines, William	LJ, 100	Los Alamitos	Biology
Royer, James	discus	San Jose	Art
Schuchard, Robert	SC	Palos Verdes Est.	Gen. Studies
Underwood, Decker	880, 1 & 2-mi	Redondo Beach	Gen. Studies
Utley, Rodney	TJ	San Jose	Human Bio.
Whiteing, David	880	Monterey Park	History
Wilson, Brian	discus	Hawthorne	Math

1973

Name	Event	Hometown	Major
Anderson, John	hurdles	Newberg, OR	Mech. Eng.
Anderson, Thomas	LJ, HJ	Los Altos Hills	Civil. Eng.
Bagshaw, David	120HH, mile	Stanford	Mech. Eng.
Bakkensen, Ralph	SP, discus	Portland, OR	Economics
Cautley, Daniel	1 & 2-mi	Madison, WI	Mech. Eng.
Curl, Kenneth	100, 220, relays	Houston, TX	Human Bio.
Dreissigacker, Peter	discus, javelin	Orange, CT	Product Design
Hall, Michael	TJ	San Carlos	Elec. Eng.
Henry, Bruce	440, 880	Dayton, OH	Econ./Civil Eng.
Ho, Melvin	LJ, TJ	Sunnyvale	Civil Eng.
Hopkins, Stephen	javelin	Portland, OR	Civil Eng.
Howard, James	discus	Portland, OR	Gen. Studies
Hubbard, Philip	PV	Kansas City, MO	Communications
Hustwick, David	880	Laguna Beach	Economics
Ingaham, Davie	mile	Evanston, IL	Gen. Studies
Jackson, Vernell	880, relay	Bakersfield	Psychology
Kessel, John	440, relay	Los Altos	History
Kring, Kenny	dec, PV, 440IH	Eugene, OR	History
Larson, Richard	javelin	Eugene, OR	History
Lindsay, Kelly	PV	Carmichael	Biology
Long, Thomas	hurdles	Sacramento	Psychology
McAvity, Thomas	hammer	Greenwich, CT	English
McConnell, Mark	2 &3-mi	Santa Cruz	Gen. Studies
McFadden, Leslie	880, mile	Vista	Anthropology
Mittelstaedt, Brian	880, mile	Tacoma, WA	Biology
Royer, James	discus	Atascadero	Art
Schoenrock, Kurt	2-mi, SC	Carmichael	History
Utley, Rodney	TJ	San Jose	Human Bio.

1974

Name	Event	Hometown	Major
Bagshaw, David	hurdles, relays	Stanford	Mech. Eng.
Bellah, Jack	2,3-mi, SC	Los Gatos	Biology
Bordoni, James	880	Vallejo	Biology
Curl, Kenneth	100, 220, relays	Houston, TX	Pol. Sci.
Densmore, Gregg	120 HH	Chico	Pre-Med
Hall, Michael	LJ, TJ	San Carlos	Elec. Eng.
Harwood, Charles	PV	Portola Valley	Econ.
Hayman, Robert	SC	San Francisco	Biology
Henry, R. Bruce	440, relays	Dayton, OH	Economics
Hogsett, Mathew	440 IH, relays	Newport Beach	History
Hopkins, Steven	javelin	Portland, OR	Civil Eng.
Jackson, Vernell	880	Bakersfield	Psych.
Kessel, John	440, relays	Los Altos	History
Kring, Kenny	LJ, PV, Dec	Santa Maria	Psych

Name	Event	Hometown	Major
Laney, Robert	HJ	Eugene, OR	Pol. Sci.
Larson, Richard	javelin	Eugene, OR	History
McConnell, Mark	1, 2, 3-mi	Santa Cruz	Economics
Rossner, Otto	100, 220, relays	Concord	Aeronautics
Royer, James	discus	Campbell	Art
Sandoval, Anthony	1, 2, 3, 6-mi	Los Alamos, NM	Engineering
Scheible, Ben	880	Rocklin	Pol. Sci.
Toliver, Derek	TJ	San Francisco	Economics
Wolfe, Bruce	880	Piedmont	Civil Eng.

1975

Name	Event	Hometown	Major
Bagshaw, David	hurdles	Stanford	Mech. Eng.
Bellah, Jack	1,2,6-mi	Los Gatos	Biology
Berry, George	440, 880	Sterling Jct, MA	Pol. Sci.
Bordoni, James	880	Vallejo	Biology
Crowley, Stephen	mile	Madison, WI	Bio. Science
Cummings, Alan	mile	Whittier	Chem. Eng.
Densmore, Gregg	120HH	Chico	Biology
Ellis, Thomas	decathlon	Bellevue, WA	undeclared
Flint, Robert	PV	Del Rey	Pol. Sci.
Foster, John	hurdles, HJ	Los Altos	Psychology
Geiken, Stacy	2-mi, SC	Palo Alto	undeclared
Gonzalez, Manuel	100, 220	Los Angeles	Human Biology
Greer, Roger	discus	Visalia	Economics
Hadley, Mark	880	Napa	Pre-Med
Hall, Michael	TJ, LJ	San Carlos	Elec. Eng.
Harwood, Charles	PV	Portola Valley	Economics
Hayflick, Joel	HJ	Stanford	undeclared
Hill, Mark	discus	Santa Clara	undeclared
Hogsett, Matt	440, 440IH	Newport Beach	History
Holmes, Marvin	100, 200	Monrovia	Mech. Eng.
Holman, Jon	440	Gig Harbor, WA	Ind. Eng.
Johnk, Carl	120HH, dec	Menlo Park	undeclared
Jones, Scott	440	Northbrook, IL	Engineering
Karakozoff, Alexander	SP, discus	San Francisco	Economics
Kolesnikow, Andrew	120HH	Burlingame	Human Biology
Langford, Jon	javelin	Atwater	Psychology
Lofton, James	LJ, 440, HJ	Los Angeles	undeclared
Macrorie, John	javelin, LJ	Fullerton	Pol. Sci.
Makous, Monte	javelin	Merion, PA	Chemistry
Martin, Forrest	100, 440 relay	Pasadena	Biochemistry
Mason, Reginald	440IH, mi relay	Los Angeles	Bio. Science
Mayes, Orlando	100, 220	San Bernardino	undeclared
McConnell, Mark	1-3-mi	Santa Cruz	Economics
McLean, Douglas	SC, 6-mi	Moraga	Ind. Eng.

Name	Event	Hometown	Major
Merlo, Richard	discus	Sanger	Human Biology
Morgan, James	2-mi	Princeton, NJ	undeclared
Norton, Jeffrey	mile	Los Altos	Human Biology
Olenchalk, John	SP	Antioch	Human Biology
Parietti, Jeffrey	1,2-mi	Mercy Is., WA	undeclared
Pitchford, Thomas	880, mile	Los Angeles	Human Biology
Reynolds, Wes.	hammer	Lebanon, OR	Economics
Rossner, Otto	100, 220	Concord	Aero. Eng.
Sandoval, Anthony	1-6-mi	Los Alamos, NM	Mech. Eng.
Scheible, Ben	880	Rochlin	Pol. Sci.
Schreiber, David	100	Beverly Hills	Space Medicine
Seaman, Matthew	440, 880	Pasadena	Chemistry
Sexton, Mark	PV	Westlake Village	Engineering
Sheats, Alan	440, 220, 100	Altadena	Pre-Dental
Smith, Kimble	440, 880	Oakland	Elec. Eng.
Tucker, Randall	HJ	Honolulu, HI	undeclared
Wingo, Scott	440, mi relay	Santa Paula	Human Biology
Witt, Peter	mile, SC	Carmichael	Engineering

1976

Name	Event	Hometown	Major
Bellah, Jack	1,2,6-mi	Los Gatos	Biology
Berry, George	880	W. Boylston, MA	Pol. Sci.
Bullwinkel, Clay	LJ, TJ	Burlingame	undeclared
Celms, Harold	880-2-mi	Tacoma, WA	Economics
Crowley, Stephen	mile	Madison, WI	Bio. Science
Densmore, Gregg	120HH	Chico	Biology
Doyle, Kent	HJ	Granada Hills	undeclared
Ellis, Thomas	decathlon	Bellevue, WA	undeclared
Emory, Jerry	1-2-mi	Palo Alto	undeclared
Flint, Robert	PV	Del Rey	Math Science
Ford, George	discus	Los Altos	Physics
Foster, John	hurdles, HJ	Los Altos	Psychology
Geiken, Stacy	1-3-mi, SC	Palo Alto	undeclared
Greenwood, Doug	SP, discus	Rosemont, PA	Mech. Eng
Hadley, Mark	880	Napa	Pre-Med
Hill, Mark	discus	Santa Clara	Psychology
Hogsett, Matt	440, 440IH	Newport Beach	History
Holmes, Marvin	100, 200	Monrovia	Civil. Eng.
Hulburd, Chris	mile	Saratoga	Pre-Med
Joerger, Kurt	880	Hillsborough	Civil Eng
Johnk, Carl	decathlon, LJ	Menlo Park	Chem. Eng.
Jones, Scott	440	Northbrook, IL	Elec. Eng.
Kissin, Roy	1-6-mi	Danville	undeclared
Lofton, James	LJ, TJ, 440	Los Angeles	Ind. Eng.
Macrorie, John	javelin	Fullerton	Pol. Sci.

Name	Event	Hometown	Major
McCarthy, Paul	440, 880	San Francisco	undeclared
McLean, Douglas	SC, 6-mi	La Jolla	Ind. Eng.
Merlo, Richard	SP, discus	Sanger	Human Biology
Merrill, Robert	PV	Burlingame	undeclared
Novotny, Jerry	100, 220	Houston, TX	Pre-Med
Olenchalk, John	SP, discus	Antioch	Human Biology
Parietti, Jeffrey	1,3-mi	Mercy Is., WA	Journalism
Pitchford, Thomas	880	Los Angeles	Human Biology
Sanchez, John	440IH	Lakewood	undeclared
Sandoval, Anthony	1-6-mi	Los Alamos, NM	Mech. Eng.
Sheats, Alan	220, 440	Altadena	Human Biology
Slinkard, Brad	SP, discus	Lakewood	undeclared
Wingo, Scott	440	Santa Paula	Human Biology

1977

Name	Event	Hometown	Major
Albritton, Terry	SP, discus	Newport Beach	Communications
Allen, David	distances	LaGrange, IL	Humanities
Banks, Gordon	100, 200	Los Angeles	undeclared
Boutin, Frank	distances	Sacramento	Human Biology
Brown, Ricky	javelin	New Orleans, LA	undeclared
Bullwinkel, Clay	TJ	Burlingame	Economics
Buss, Rick	discus, SP	Green Bay, WI	Pre-Med
Celms, Harold	distances	Tacoma, WA	Economics
Corey, Craig	distances	Hillsborough	Ind. Eng.
Crowley, Stephen	mile	Madison, WI	Bio. Science
Doyle, Kent	HJ	Reseda	Economics
Ellis, Thomas	javelin	Seattle, WA	Biology
Emory, Jerry	distances	Palo Alto	undeclared
Gail, Bill	distances	Sudbury, MA	Physics
Geiken, Stacy	SC	Palo Alto	Journalism
Gerfen, Earl	400, LJ	St. Louis, MO	undeclared
Greenwood, Doug	SP, discus	Rosemont, PA	undeclared
Hadley, Mark	800	Napa	Pre-Med
Haldeman, Bill	distances	Malibu	undeclared
Hickman, Bill	800	Kentfield	Elec. Eng.
Hill, Mark J.	discus	Santa Clara	Psychology
Hirschberg, Eric	400IH	Harrington Pk, NJ	Pol. Sci.
Holmes, Marvin	100, 200	Los Angeles	Civil. Eng.
Joerger, Robert	800	Hillsborough	Civil Eng
Johnk, Carl	decathlon	Menlo Park	Chem. Eng.
Kissin, Roy	distances	Danville	Classics/English
Littleboy, John	HJ	Palo Alto	Art
Lofton, James	LJ, 200, 400	Los Angeles	Ind. Eng.
McCarthy, Paul	400, 800	San Francisco	Economics

Name	Event	Hometown	Major
Merrill, Robert	PV	Burlingame	undeclared
Monmouth, Mike	hurdles	Houston, TX	Biology
Morgan, Daryle	TJ	El Cerrito	undeclared
Norton, Jeff	distances	Los Altos	Human Biology
Novotny, Jerry	100	Houston, TX	undeclared
Parietti, Jeffrey	distances	Mercy Is., WA	Journalism
Sheats, Alan	200, 400	Altadena	Human Biology
Shellworth, Tom	hurdles, 800	Atherton	Communications
Wells, David	800	Eureka	Economics

1978

Name	Event	Hometown	Major
Ballinger, Doug	PV	Kentfield	undeclared
Banks, Gordon	100, 200, 400	Los Angeles	Pol. Sci.
Brown, Kelvin	LJ, TJ	Washington, DC	Ind. Eng.
Brown, Rick	javelin	New Orleans, LA	Human Bio/Econ.
Bullwinkel, Clay	LJ, TJ	Burlingame	Economics
Burch, Fred	SP	Torrance	Human Biology
Buss, Rick	discus	Green Bay, WI	Human Biology
Cerf, Larry	HJ	Edina, MN	Economics
Celms, Harold	distances	Tacoma, WA	Economics
Corey, Craig	SC	Hillsborough	Ind. Eng
Critchfield, Mike	HJ	Los Altos Hills	Engineering
Ellis, Thomas	javelin	Seattle, WA	Biology
Gail, Bill	distances	Sudbury, MA	undeclared
Gaul, Pete	5K	Fair Oaks	Math/Chem
Geiken, Stacy	5K	Palo Alto	Journalism
Greenwood, Doug	SP, discus	Rosemont, PA	Elec. Eng.
Hadley, Mark	800	Napa	Pre-Med
Haldeman, Bill	SC, 5K	Malibu	Pre-Med/Chem
Hill, Mark	discus	Santa Clara	Psychology
Hirschberg, Eric	dec, 400IH	E. Orleans, MA	Int'l Rel.
Johnk, Carl	dec, 110HH	Menlo Park	Chem. Eng.
Kissin, Roy	1500, 5K	Danville	Classics/English
Littleboy, John	HJ	Palo Alto	Studio Art
Lobsinger, Tom	800, 1500, 5K	Waterloo, Ont	undeclared
Lofton, James	LJ, 200, 400	Los Angeles	Ind. Eng.
Mahoney, Phil	discus	Cambridge, MA	Economics
Margerum, Ken	110HH, 100, TJ	Fountain Valley	undeclared
Mayhew, Mike	mile	Kanoehe, HI	Economics
McCarthy, Paul	400, 800	San Francisco	Pol. Sci.
Monmouth, Mike	hurdles	Houston, TX	Biology
Nelson, Darrin	100, 200	Los Angeles	undeclared
O'Neil, Tom	1500, 5K	Sacramento	undeclared
Pear, Matt	SP	Los Altos	undeclared
Raftery, Rich	5K	Dixon	undeclared

Name	Event	Hometown	Major
Sheats, Alan	100, 200, 400	Altadena	Human Biology
Shellworth, Tom	hurdles	Atherton	Communications
Stillman, Mark	800, 1500	San Jose	Mech. Eng.
Thomson, David	discus, HT	Los Olivos	undeclared
Weidmann, Chuck	SP, HT	San Jose	Chem. Eng.
Wells, David	800	Eureka	Economics

1979

Name	Event	Hometown	Major
Austin, Dave	5K	Garden Grove	Math
Awbrey, Craig	discus	Atherton	Human Biology
Banks, Gordon	100, 200, 400	Los Angeles	Pol. Sci.
Berry, Rod	1500, 5K, 10K	Kentfield	Economics
Bolton, Tim	5K, SC	Marysville	Physics
Brown, Rick	javelin	New Orleans, LA	
Bruner, Gary	jav, PV, dec	Palm Desert	Economics
Bullwinkel, Clay	LJ, TJ	Burlingame	Economics
Buss, Rick	discus, HT	Green Bay, WI	Bio. Sci.
Celms, Harold	SC, 5K	Tacoma, WA	Economics
Corey, Craig	5K, 10K	Hillsborough	Ind. Eng.
Dawson, Steve	400, 400IH	Newport Beach	Int'l. Rel.
Douglas, Michael	discus	Sedona, AZ	
Doyle, Kent	HJ	Sepulveda	Economic
Gail, Bill	SC, 5K	Sudbury, MA	Physics
Gervais, Rick	100, 200	Bend, OR	Ind. Eng.
Greenwood, Doug	SP, discus	King of Prussia, PA	Elec. Eng.
Grolle, Fred	TJ, LJ	Los Altos	Ind. Eng.
Haldeman, Bill	SC, 5K	Malibu	Geology
Harris, Larry	100, 200	Kansas City, KS	Communications
Harris, John	javelin	Irving, TX	Human Bio.
Hirschberg, Eric	400IH	East Orleans, MA	Int'l Rel.
Holliday, Brian	SP, discus	Potomac, MD	
Jones, Irvin	100, 200	Northfield, MN	
Kissin, Roy	5K, 10K	Danville	English
Lobsinger, Tom	1500, 5K	Waterloo, Ont.	Human Bio.
Maiocco, Robert	400, 200	Brentwood	Economics
Margerum, Ken	hurdles, TJ	Fountain Valley	Communications
McCarthy, Paul	400, 800	San Francisco	Pol. Sci.
Milner, Mark	TJ, LJ	Glendale	Economics
Nelson, Darrin	100, 200, LJ	Los Angeles	Ind. Design Maj. (H&S)
O'Neil, Tom	5K, 10K	Rocklin	Economics
Roessler, Kurt	TJ, 400IH	Havertown, PA	Pol. Sci.
Schaer, John	800, 1500	Corvallis, OR	Bio. Sci.
Shumway, Garry	hurdles	Los Angeles	
Stillman, Mark	800, 1500	San Jose	Mech. Eng.
St. Geme, Joe	400IH	Rancho Palos Verdes	Bio. Sci.

Name	Event	Hometown	Major
Thomson, Dave	discus, HT	Los Olivos	Economics
Varnado, Art	800	Annandale, VA	Ind. Eng.
Warwick, Greg	discus	Red Bluff	English
Weidmann, Chuck	HT, SP	San Jose	Chem. Eng.
White, Jere	discus, SP	Bakersfield	Chem. Eng.
Winterer, Sean	HJ, 400IH	Clayfield, Australia	

VI. Teammate Write-ups

Following is a recap of teammate write-up by year.

1957: Phil Felnen; Hank Roldan
1958: Chuck Cobb; Maury Graves
1959: Ben Anixter; Don Chesarek; Ernie Cunliffe
1960: John "Jake" Kelly; Harlan "Jolly" Limmer; Norm Lloyd; Bertil Lundh;
      Norm Pease
1961: Craig Barrett; Don Bell; Paul Schlicke
1962: Art Batchelder; Len Breschini; Chris Hungerland; Dan Moore
1963: Phil Lamoreau; Dave Weill
1964: Steve Arch
1965: Eric Frische; Harry McCalla; Bob McIntyre; Larry Questad; Weymouth Kirkland
1966: Harlan Andrews; George Porter; Chuck Smith
1967: Jim Eshelman; Glenn Havskjold; Jack Scott; Bob Stoecker; Bud Walsh
1968: Roger Cox; Mike Jacobs; Jim Letterer; Grady Means; Russ Taplin;
      Craig Vaughan; Jim Ward; Dick Warwick
1969: Peter Boyce; Tom Colby; Brook Thomas
1970: Steve Flannery; Clint Ostrander
1971: Charlie Francis; Don Kardong; Jim Kauffman; Rick Tipton
1972: Duncan Macdonald
1973: John Andersen
1974: none
1975: Jim Bordoni; Kenny Kring; Derek Toliver
1976: John Foster; Matt Hogsett; David Schreiber
1977: John Olenchalk; Jeff Parietti
1978: Stacy Geiken; Mark Hadley; James Lofton
1979: Clay Bullwinkel; Roy Kissin; Mark Stillman
1980: Gordon Banks
1981: Darrin Nelson
1982: Robert Maiocco; Garry Schumway

Deceased Teammates

Phil Fehlen

I was a journeyman high jumper and team captain who managed to win the conference meet in my senior year and set the school record at 6' 8 ½".

Coach Jordan brought prestige and attention to our sport by giving the team its own dressing room, establishing a records wall, changing the uniform, and building strong press relations. There was some rebellion to his methods; there was strong loyalty to the past. It was my philosophy at the time and may still be that after awhile the athlete made his own decisions and won or lost according to his own will and effort and that the coach after awhile became a mentor defined as a wise and experienced advisor instead of director of every aspect of your training program. In other words, the freshman evolved from needing direction and step-by-step guidance into his own man, depending on his coach for the insights of experience and broad knowledge but free to follow his own course. Armed with that view and a not insignificant ego, I clashed with Coach Jordan over who was in charge. I am afraid I caused him more consternation than I would have wished. At the end of my senior year he confided that he was not going through what he had with me any more - and from what I heard he didn't. Years later at the dedication of the new track he introduced me as the man "who told him how they did things on the Farm."

Years later I competed in the Masters program. Jordan and I met working out at Stanford stadium and developed a warm friendship. He coached me but only on request.

As I see it, he was one of the great athletes of his time, with grace and integrity not seen in modern track and field. He made a major contribution to Stanford, which was not reciprocated. His management of the classic USA-USSR meet at Stanford alone makes him worthy of the highest acclaim by Stanford. Alas, not yet forthcoming.

Hank Roldan

From across the vast Pacific my dad journeyed to America bearing his Filipino heritage and Spanish surname. While struggling to earn his wages in the fields, he met my mom who was the daughter of Mexican migrant workers. Dad had an eighth-grade education; mom had a third-grade. I was the first born and first to attend college.

At Orosi High School I competed in all sports and during my senior year was voted all-league in four sports. Now, one of my now cherished memories is scoring more points at our district meet than another young fellow by the name of Rafer Johnson. Little did I know I would hear more of him in the future!

Stanford

I attended Stanford from 1953-59, earning my BA in 1957 and my MA in 1959. I also worked part-time at the Stanford training quarters, Rosotti's Alpine Beer Garden in Woodside, and the Bethlehem Steel plant in South San Francisco. I was recruited to play football and compete in track. I visited other universities but preferred the open space surrounding "the farm" and the coaches were congenial and reassuring. It was quite an adjustment for this small-town kid, but I got more comfortable day-by-day.

Freshman football proved to be OK. We really had only a two-game season, playing the Cal freshmen twice. I was the starting halfback and John Brodie was our quarterback. I won the award for scoring the most touchdowns, but again we played just one team, twice. Since I missed spring football practice I was having a hard time maintaining my competitiveness. So after a year and a half, I decided it was time to concentrate full-time on the javelin. But, I did continue my part-time work as an athletic trainer. I came back and played football my senior year. With my extensive experience working as a trainer, I gained national newspaper coverage when I took off my helmet and attended to one of our injured players on the turf.

Back to track. Due to an injury I decided to shy away from the 440 and long jump my freshman year. The javelin looked like it made sense under the circumstances, although I found that a great throw required the same leg strength as a center fielder making a throw to home plate. But, this was the beginning of my collegiate javelin career. By my sophomore year I was the best javelin thrower on the team and had recovered, so I also could run the hurdles and long jump. Junior year was a bit frustrating due to an arm injury but I still managed to place eighth at the NCAA Championships.

Payton Jordan Comes to Stanford my Senior Year
Coach Jordan was very active in his coaching style. He could be at two places at one time. He would go from event to event, encouraging and coaching us with his contagious enthusiasm and energy. He even would participate in our starting drills and beat most of us out of the blocks. He always made me feel important and appreciated, and this made me want to work even harder to improve my skills. It was a great season our senior year. We placed third as a team in the NCAA Championships and I managed a third place in the javelin.

At 5'9" and 168 lbs. I guess I should feel satisfied with my athletic accomplishments. But, these don't compare with the value I place on the lasting friendship that Coach Jordan and I have developed all these years. He is a special and unique person, and I have been blessed to know him. Other than my dad, Coach Jordan has influenced me more than any other individual in my character development as a coach and person. My dad gave me love and direction; Coach gave me confidence, motivation, determination, and friendship.

Post-Stanford
After completing my masters degree, I obtained a teaching and coaching job at Clovis High School with Jordan's help. Three years later I moved on to Mt. Whitney High School in Visalia, CA, where I worked for the next 34 years and coached track. My wonderful and loving wife Mary and I have been married for over 35 years. She taught French at Mt. Whitney before we married. We have four now-adult children and seven grandchildren. All the children turned out to be outstanding athletes with two competing in college at the Division 1 level. Kathi was the CA state champion in the 800 meters, then went on to compete for UCLA. John went on to compete for Stanford. How exciting it was for me to see him win the javelin competition in the 1995 Big Meet with Cal!

Chuck Cobb

Pre-Stanford Years

I attended Fresno High School where I competed in football, basketball and track and field. I was a wide receiver and one of the captains of the team in football, a forward in basketball and a high jumper and hurdler in track and field. My best sport was probably football, but I was also a 14.1 high hurdler and a 6'2" high jumper.

Stanford Undergraduate Years

Freshman year, Jack Weiershauser, the Stanford Track and Field Coach at that time, talked me out of playing football to concentrate on track and field. I was not an outstanding track performer during my freshman year, but I won most of my hurdle races and also scored a few points in the high jump and long jump. I was better known, then, for my partying exploits at the Phi Delt fraternity than I was for any athletic achievements.

The first real success that I had in track at Stanford was during my sophomore year against the University of Southern California in the Los Angeles Coliseum, the site of both the 1932 and 1984 Olympics. My USC opponent in the low hurdles was a great athlete named Whilhelm who had set a national junior college record in the low hurdles the year before. It was an imposing environment for an 18 year old: a) the LA Coliseum holds 105,000 people and is one of the most impressive athletic sites in the world; and b) I was a young, slow and not-very-athletic kid from Fresno that had just flown on his first airplane the day before. (That's right! I had never been on an airplane nor had I been in such a large stadium until that USC meet in my sophomore year.) I beat Wilhelm, and *The Los Angeles Times* had a big picture and a big story of my victory the next day. For the first time I had concluded that I was prepared to take this "track thing" seriously because the personal satisfaction was greatly in excess of the hard work.

Coach Jordan arrived at Stanford in the summer of 1956, which was the start of my junior year. I was again intent on playing football but was convinced by Coach Jordan that I had a better career as a hurdler than a football player. I was at first a little skeptical of Coach Jordan's inspirational talks where he was trying to convince me that I could become one of the best hurdlers in the world. I was also a little skeptical of Coach Jordan's signs in the locker room and his other inspirational messages. Within a few months, I totally accepted his philosophy of excellence with all the required commitments of discipline, training and other preparations needed for peak performance. Like a great evangelist, Coach Jordan converted me.

My junior year was modestly successful — more successful than my freshman and sophomore years, but not on a par with my senior year. The "Jordan Magic" was just beginning to work during his first year at Stanford. In the fall of my junior year, I also met my Stanford wife of over 45 years, Ambassador Sue McCourt Cobb, the current U.S. Ambassador to Jamaica. Ambassador Sue was a disciplinarian just like Coach Jordan and she was also a successful competitive athlete in skiing, tennis, basketball and field hockey. She accelerated my conversion to "Jordan-ism." In 1988, she attempted to be the first American woman to summit Mt. Everest and wrote a best-selling book entitled *The Edge of Everest*.

During my junior year, I ran non-winning times of 13.9 in the high hurdles and 22.9 in the low hurdles, which bettered both Stanford records. I placed second in both events in the Pacific Coast Conference Championships and third at the NCAA. All of us were pleased that the Stanford team was second in the 1957 NCAA team competition. The year 1957 provided a very good start for Coach Jordan during his first year at Stanford.

Senior year proved more successful. The "Jordan Magic" and discipline were now fully working. My highlight was against USC. The Brooklyn Dodgers had just moved to Los Angeles and the new LA Dodgers did not yet have a stadium so they played baseball in the LA Coliseum. Therefore, because the baseball configuration required that they remove the running track, the USC/Stanford track meet was moved to Occidental College — Coach Jordan's former home. I won both the high hurdles and the low hurdles that day at "Oxy" and set a school record in the highs. In addition, my 13.9 time bettered the USC/Stanford meet record time of 14.0 held by two previous world record holders from USC - Dick Attlesey, who set the world record of 13.5 in the late '40s; and Jack Davis, who set the world record of 13.4 in 1956. I particularly got a thrill out of beating Jack Davis' meet record because he soundly beat me the day he set the world record of 13.4 in Bakersfield in the Olympic Trials in 1956. My 13.9 that April day in 1958 was the best time in the world up to that date in 1958. Later in 1958, others ran faster, but I think I ended 1958 as one of the top ten hurdlers in the world.

During my senior year in 1958, which was Coach Jordan's second year at Stanford, I had now not only totally "bought in" to Coach Jordan's program and regime, but I was now one of its top advocates. I was honored that my teammates elected me captain, but I am not sure if I would have been elected without Coach Jordan as my campaign manager. I was also pleased that I was the high point man for the team for the year, and Don Chesarek, Dean Smith and Ernie Cunliffe and I set the Stanford record for the sprint medley relay at 3:21.9, which I understand is a Stanford record that still stands over 45 years later. I was also awarded an "All American Certificate" by the NCAA.

The biggest disappointment in my senior year was that I got pneumonia near the end of the season on the day before the Cal meet. I was out for several weeks and never did quite recover for the NCAA Championships. While I was the favorite to win the high hurdles in the NCAA because of my best time in the world earlier in the year and the two guys that had beaten me the year before had both graduated, I placed a disappointing 6th at the NCAA because of the illness.

Stanford Graduate Years
After I graduated, I married Sue McCourt and had the pleasure to spend most of the next two years on the Stanford campus training with Coach Jordan for the 1960 Olympics. I was a naval officer and the U.S. Navy provided the opportunity for all Olympic athletes to train for international competitions like the Olympics. I was assigned to the Stanford NROTC unit in order to train with Coach Jordan. The Coach Jordan regime during these years was even more intense for me because there was no school or extracurricular activities to interfere with training.

146

During these two post-graduate years, I competed all over the world with extensive tours of Japan and the Scandinavian countries. My best winning times without wind were 13.7 for the 110-meter high hurdles in the U.S. Armed Services Championship in 1960 and 22.8 in the lows. I understand both times remain the best for a Stanford athlete. With fast tracks, better equipment and improved training facilities, you would think the Stanford hurdlers of today could improve on these times of over 45 years ago, but they don't have the "magic" of Payton Jordan coaching them.

My biggest disappointment in these two years was not being able to compete in the 1960 Olympics in Rome. In 1960, I found myself one of the best five hurdlers in the world but only the fourth best hurdler in the United States. My fourth place finish in the final U.S. Olympic Trials in Stanford Stadium got me on the U.S. team as the Alternate in the 110-meter high hurdles, but I was unable to compete in Rome. Coach Jordan had 60,000 fans in the Stanford Stadium stands pulling for me as a hometown crowd in the 1960 U.S. Olympic Trials, but earning the Alternate slot in the 110-meter high hurdles was the best I could do that day.

In the fall of 1960, I retired from track at the ripe old age of 24 to go back to the Stanford Business School. During these next two years, I was first team wing on the rugby team and Stanford won the Monterey Peninsula Rugby Championship. We had one of the best rugby teams in the United States. I finally got a chance to play some form of Stanford football, and it was a very enjoyable experience.

Post Stanford Years
After my eight years on the Stanford campus (four undergraduate, two training for the Olympics and two at business school), Payton Jordan sent me out into the real world. I have used the values and the discipline instilled by Coach Jordan in many venues over the years. I have been the chairman, CEO or COO of several large corporations (Arvida, Disney Development, Pan Am, Penn Central), been on the boards of directors of about 15 different companies - seven of which were public companies; been an Under Secretary of Commerce for President Reagan, been an Ambassador for President George H. W. Bush; been the chairman of the Board of Trustees of the University of Miami and been involved in many civic, church and charitable activities. The Payton Jordan leadership skills have also served me well with my family, consisting of a fabulous wife, two great sons and seven wonderful grandchildren. Over and over again I have implemented the lessons learned from Payton Jordan in my life since Stanford. His impact on me was profound.

Maury Graves
My track career began in the 10th grade at Oakland High School. Here my career was established in my first race as a J.V. out-running the Varsity team by seven seconds. Coach Ludeke entered me in the mile and that suited me well. Oakland High, in 1952, did not have cross-country or the 2-mile. So, I was limited to the mile in high school. As a senior in 1954, my time for the mile was 4:28.3.

Coach Ludeke recommended to Coach Weiershauser that Stanford accept me primarily as a 2-miler. With acceptance at Stanford I was granted a track scholarship (tuition only).

147

The scholarship was guaranteed, so long as I maintained satisfactory grades and continued to compete in cross-country and track. My twin brother, Larry, was granted an academic scholarship. Neither of us would have been able to attend Stanford without these scholarships.

By the end of my sophomore year at Stanford, my times were: 2-mile (9:08.9) and mile (4:15.5). Junior year, however, saw a change in my curriculum to pre-med biology. Since I had only three biology classes in my first two years, I had a lot of lab classes to complete. In one quarter I had seven labs per week with 18 credits. Practice suffered and my times leveled off. In fact, they were all over the board. In my senior year (1958) I did run 9:04.9 2-mile, a school record.

Coach Jordan arrived in 1956, my junior year. He was most understanding of my class schedule and mono-like health problems (weight loss under 153 lbs, extreme fatigue). Both of the above contributed to my erratic track performance. In addition, Coach Jordan came to my rescue when a zealous professor was persuaded to allow me to take a mid-term exam in a hotel room in Oregon with Coach Jordan as my proctor at the exact same time as the other students took the exam on campus. Two hours later, I was on the track competing in the PAC-8 meet. My recollection is that I did poorly on the exam, and poorly in the meet. But, I will never forget Coach Jordan going to "bat" for me.

My track career ended in 1958 with graduation and subsequent acceptance into Marquette Medical School, Milwaukee, WI. There, I met my wife of 44 years, Barbara. Following graduation, 1962, I completed a general internship and then a pediatric residency at Milwaukee Children's Hospital. I joined the Medical Arts Clinic pediatric team in Appleton, WI, 1965. Shortly thereafter, I was drafted into the military and was stationed at Fort Leavenworth, KS from 1966-1968. Fort Leavenworth was the Army Command College for Officers. While there, my duties included pediatrics care for Army families, emergency room duty, and as duty officer at the Leavenworth Prison.

Upon completion of military duty, I returned to Appleton, WI and continued a pediatric practice for the next 32 years.

At present, I am retired and have been blessed with four children (2 sons and 2 daughters). And now we have 5 granddaughters.

I've always appreciated my education at Stanford, and the caring and understanding of the Stanford coaching staff and particularly that of Coach Jordan!

1959

Ben Anixter

My story goes back to my childhood when as kids of seven or eight years old, we played games on the streets and parks of San Francisco. I was a diminutive child always smaller than the other kids. However, I found that when we played games I was able to not only keep up but also run faster than the other kids.

I learned that my father had been a sprinter at Lowell High. When I entered junior high (7th grade) at Roosevelt Junior High I went out for the track team. Remarkably, I had good success at the 50 and 75-yard dash, the 220-yard relay (each of the four runners ran 55 yds.), and the long jump. The culmination of the year for me was taking third place in the San Francisco all-city meet running 7.1 seconds for the 50-yd. dash.

As an aside, Kezar stadium where we ran, was a "cinder" track. There were no such things as starting blocks. You would dig holes to put your feet into for the start as in the pictures in the movie "Chariots of Fire." And the spikes that we used were about 7/8 inches long, necessary to get purchase in the track.

We moved to Marin County and the next time my track "career" picks up is in my freshman year at Sir Francis Drake High School. I was 90 pounds and 4' 10" as a freshman. I ran four years at Drake and loved it. I ran in the "C" division for two years and the "B" division for the other two. A combination of height, weight, and age determined what division you were in. I loved the competition and running made me feel great. I had great success in high school. I ran the 75 and 150-yard dashes, the 440-yard relay and occasionally threw the discus. Again the tracks were dirt and not until the last two years was the innovation of starting blocks available.

As a freshman I ran 8.6 seconds for the 75. By the time I was a senior, at 5' 4" and 125 pounds, I had improved to 7.9s for the 75 and 15.5s for the 150. I had done well in the league meets, had lots of fun, won individual league championships, and learned that I loved to run. Believe it or not I threw the "lightweight" discus 126 feet, placing in the league meet. I held the school records for my events for a long time but lost track of the records.

On to Stanford!

I had no idea how meaningful the next four years would be. I was a walk-on in the spring of 1956. Jack Weiershauser was the varsity coach and Floyd Strain was the freshman coach. I met impressive guys out on the practice field: Frank Herrmann, Chuck Cobb, Bernie Nelson, Maury Graves, to mention only a few from the varsity. They were inspirational in their work ethic. I also met the guys in the freshman class whom I would run with for four years: Don Cheserek (440), Ernie Cunliffe (880/mile) to mention only two. The level of training was also more intense than in high school. Then in 1957 others came that added to our team. John Kelly (long jump), Dean Smith (sprints), Norm Pease (sprints), Norm Lloyd (middle-distance), Mike Franchetti (pole vault), and many others. And Payton Jordan was our new coach.

Payton was inspirational and innovative. And he wasn't beneath coming out on the track to mix it up with us sprinters. We all thrived under his tutelage. As a team we became more competitive. Norm Lloyd, Ernie Cunliffe, Don Cheserek (Chez to us all), and others became stars. The sprint squad of Dean Smith, Norm Pease, and me ran faster than we thought we could and had fun.

As a freshman my marks were 10.4 (100 yds.) and 23.0 (220). By the time my eligibility was over in 1959, I had run 9.7 (100yds.), 21.6 (220), and 41.4 (440-yd. relay with Norm, Dean, and Len Bates).

During these college years Payton was a role model extraordinaire. His positive attitude was infectious. He taught me what sportsmanship is and how it works and why it is important. His attitude brought out the best in all of us. I worked hard and enjoyed the good physical and the mental feeling of accomplishment. He taught us perseverance. These lessons carried over to my non-sports life at Stanford and beyond. What a coach!

After graduation I went to work in Silicon Valley. I was very busy; my physical training stopped. I found myself out of shape and not liking it. However, I still kept up with the track world being an avid spectator. Coach Jordan again set the example for me to return to running. At a meet, the Masters 100yd race featured coach Jordan. I started running again at age 31 in 1968 starting with "long distance" but quickly returned to what I liked—sprinting. I entered my first Masters race at 33. I ran and competed in the Masters until my knee, which was injured at age 18, didn't allow me to run anymore. My post college running career ended at age 61, not a bad career starting at 12 years old and lasting 49 years. I saw coach at many meets and practices during those years. He was an inspiration. We had lots of fun.

I had excellent success as a Masters sprinter winning many races, meeting and competing with some nice guys. My marks were good. I ran 10.9 for 100m, 22.8 for 200m at age 37, and was under 12 and 25 seconds at age 50. I learned a lot about technique during those years and was a better runner as time went on.

One aspect surprised me. I thought that as a mature adult I wouldn't get nervous before a race. I found, however, the familiar adrenalin rush as my first Masters race approached. I guess you never lose the edge. I love to run.

At age 61, in 1997, I learned sprinting using roller-blades (in-line skates). I still sprint, using my skates on a track, keep times and records in a diary, and look forward to each workout.

Jordan is simply the best. He has positively influenced my life since I met him in college in 1957. He is upbeat, encouraging, and inspirational - a national treasure. His precepts reach out to myriads of young men and women. They don't make people like Payton Jordan very often. We who know him are very fortunate.

Don Chesarek

Memorable Experiences
The end of my junior year I was plagued by leg cramps, which ended my season early. Payton told me that I was probably deficient in calcium...so in my senior year, I went on a high calcium diet...pills...lots of milk, a large bowl of cottage cheese with fruit for lunch every day...no cramping the entire senior year. I was a member of the 2-mile distance medley relay team that went undefeated.

We thought we had a chance at the University record in the 2-mile relay at the Coliseum relays being pushed by a team from Penn State...second leg was too slow and we had a very close race all the way. We won by about 6 feet. *L A Times* got a great picture of the final exchange ...we were neck-and-neck with Penn State. There was a furious battle at the 660 mark but Ernie [Cunliffe] held off the Penn State runner over the final 220.

Modesto was the last Relay meet of the year. The USC team wanted to know what event we were running that night....distance medley...so they ran the 2-mile relay and won. We won the distance medley...each member of the team received a transistor radio as a first place prize. At that time transistor radios were just being produced. I still have the radio and it still works as well today as it did when we won it.

Post-Stanford
Continued education to obtain a Masters Degree in Electrical Engineering from Stanford. Spent 2 years in the US Navy. Joined IBM in San Jose in 1962. Returned to Stanford to obtain a PhD in Electrical Engineering. Currently in an IBM executive position: Distinguished Engineer.

Payton Jordan combined with Stanford to instill a continuing drive for excellence that runs through everything that I do.

Ernie Cunliffe

Ernie Cunliffe is no doubt one of the greatest runners in Stanford history. Ernie was a world record holder, Olympian, two-time All-American, and elected to the Stanford Athletic Hall of Fame. His Stanford record in the 880-yard run remains. His record in the 800 meters (1:46.6) stood for 40 years and has been bettered by only one person, Michael Stember, who ran 1:46.2 in 2000.

1960

John "Jake" Kelly

I was in the first graduating class that had the benefit of four full years under Payton Jordan's guidance and friendship. My experiences on the track team were not only fun and rewarding but also have influenced the rest of my life profoundly. Simply put, Payton was always there when needed and said the right things at the right times. He was always enthusiastic and steady.

Stanford Years
In 1959 we had not beaten UCLA for years. I was barely leading in the long jump with one jump left and hurting. Payton came over and told me to go to the trainer to get ready for the low hurdles. This was at UCLA. A cheer went up from the crowd near the long jump pit. Payton ambled over and said we had a problem. He got me off the table and we headed for the pit. Another cheer went up and now I was in third place. Coach put a damp towel on my head and squeezed my shoulders. Someone in the crowd yelled, "Give it up Jordan, he'll never do it." My friend, Paul Gillespie, without my knowing, put a paper marker in the pit, 8 inches farther out than I had requested. My next jump proved to be the best jump of my life up to that time. I also went on to beat Jimmy Johnson in the low hurdles for a third place. We won the meet on the relay.

During my senior year (1960) I was honored to be co-captain along with Ernie Cunliffe. I graduated with a degree in physics then competed in the Olympic Trials in Stanford stadium, although in an injured condition (both ankles). I had been an All-American for two years (2nd and 3rd in the NCAA Triple Jump). I continued competing some with Payton's help while in graduate school at UC Boulder. I held the Kansas Relay record in the triple jump for about two years.

Post-Stanford

In 1964, I earned my Ph.D. at UC Boulder in nuclear physics and went to work at Sandia National Laboratories in Albuquerque, NM. In the 31 years there I developed methods and instrumentation to make radiation measurements (neutron and gamma rays) on nuclear weapons, reactors, and particle accelerators. These were designed primarily to support radiation effect tests on electronic parts used in missile guidance systems. I also worked in reactor safety studies and nuclear fusion projects. I retired in 1996 as a "Distinguished Member of the Technical Staff."

My wife and I both love sports. She was once ranked fourth in the US in women's 35's singles tennis. She served as president on the Western States Tennis Association and has been chairperson of the National Players' Development Committee for the USTA. She owned and managed a major tennis and swim club in Albuquerque. We are avid skiers and have a cabin in Colorado near Durango.

I competed in track, off and on, and won two masters championships in triple jump in 1988 and 89. We went to Melbourne, Australia in 1989 for the World Veterans Championships, where I earned a third place in the triple jump. Payton won everything in his age group.

I have been an artist in oil painting for about 15 years and am doing well at it, selling well, and winning a few awards.

Harlan "Jolly" Limmer

Pre-Stanford

Attended Culver City High School, Culver City, California: Varsity Football (All-CIF center, 1955; California High School 1956 North-South Shrine Game), basketball, baseball, and about three weeks of track and field — shot put (just for fun) at the end of the Senior year. Selected Stanford over California-Berkeley, USC, UCLA, and Ivy League primarily because of its prominent physics department with my intentions of being a scientist after an illustrious pro-football career.

Stanford Years ...

High jumping was pure joy! Signs of true athleticism were thought to be: jumping one's height, jumping up to touch a basketball rim, and being able to lift one's weight, and having equal measurements of calf, biceps and neck. See how seriously track and field was taken. But, finally, working to improve became part of my track ethic under Coach Jordan. He could be called Coach, Coach Jordan, or Mr. Jordan, but never Payton.

My performances for Stanford were ordinary at best. I did learn to throw the discus. But track and field became more than success at throwing a discus, just as it should be for a student who is also an athlete; it was all about life. In life there will be disappointments. Three of the greatest disappointments were: first, not being selected to travel to the Texas Relays one year; second, missing the Fresno Relays when the tip of a finger on the my throwing hand was cut off while breaking a dish at a Stanford dining hall an hour or so before the bus was to leave; and third, completely coming apart in Seattle at the Pac-Five Conference Finals and performing a personal worst.

Coach Jordan was disappointed. The team could have used my point or two. Personal and youthful disappointment was further covered up by singing, "Took a little trip down the Mississip" with an unnamed super shot putter on the airplane trip home, which probably didn't thrill Coach Jordan. But Coach never said a word. He understood my hurt and regret.

After Stanford
Right from Stanford ... Concordia Teachers College at Seward, Nebraska, was the destination ... to take religion courses and coach its track team. It is a blessing to be married to Donna Bremer and boast of five fine sons. Taught, coached, and served as principal at Lutheran parochial schools in Orange, California; Yorkville, Illinois; and San Diego, California. Served as Executive Director of a Lutheran retreat center in central Wisconsin for a time. Earned a Masters degree in Education Administration at Concordia University, River Forest, Illinois.

After twenty years as teacher, coach, and administrator, I attended the Lutheran Concordia Theological Seminary at Fort Wayne, Indiana, for four years, earning a Masters of Divinity degree. While at the Seminary, opportunities to coach high school track and collegiate basketball and soccer became available. Spent a year as a vicar at Waverly, Iowa, and then served as a Lutheran pastor in Chicago, Illinois, and coached basketball at its school for five years. Through all those eventful years, Coach Jordan often corresponded and offered a great deal of encouragement.

Then, for thirteen years, while serving a congregation in Burlingame, California, near Stanford, it was delightful to be near The Farm again! What a joy to participate in a recent track team reunion with Coach Jordan and teammates when the renovation and rejuvenation of Angell Field was announced! Watching the actual reconstruction of Angell Field was stimulating. The completion and its use for national competition have been inspiring!

And now
Gone are the days when a discus thrower during workouts at Angell Field would chase and retrieve a thrown disc, while at the same time, being on the lookout for gopher holes and excrement left by a canine after its afternoon romp. And, gone are the days when a certain discus thrower would sometimes attempt to hide down in the discus area away from Coach Jordan's watchful and mindful eye and enthusiastic exhortations. However, after decades, the thrower remains mindful of the Coach's deep, passionate yearning for that athlete to perform at his *personal best* in mind, body, and spirit.

Norm Lloyd

Prepared by Norm's widow: Dorothy

Norman was recovering from a stress fracture in his foot and unable to show his speed when he went to Stanford in the spring of 1957 on a full academic scholarship. But after a fall's worth of cross-country races in his legs, he won most of the collegiate open half-mile and mile events in California. Coach Payton Jordan described Norman's 1958 explosion onto the track and field scene thus:

> "Lloyd, a junior, was the greatest half miler and miler, as a soph last season, in [Stanford] history. Broke Ben Eastman's all time 880 mark with a 1.49.2 and smashed Paul Moore's 18-year old mark in the mile by more than 6 seconds when he ran 4.06. He was a key man in the 1958 relay team with a 47.1 440 yds. Jordan considers Lloyd one of the most devastating acceleration runners he has seen." (Stanford University Track and Field Prospectus, 1959.)

Norman twice broke the Stanford mile record, once with a 4:06, and a few weeks later breaking his own record with a 4:05. One of the greatest thrills in his life was when former World champ and Olympic silver medallist "Blazin" Ben Eastman congratulated him in person after he broke the tape to beat Ben's twenty-six-year-old record. As the two men stood together for a photograph, the reporters remarked how alike the two tall and lanky runners looked.

In June 1958, Norman was invited to the Mile of the Century in Vancouver, BC, to run against some of the world's fastest milers: Englishman Derek Ibbotson, Poland's Stefan Lewandowski, Aussies Merv Lincoln and Alex Henderson, and Americans Jim Grelle and Don Larson. In 1959, Great Britain invited him to train for the Olympic team; much to Coach Jordan's consternation, he decided to concentrate on his strongest event, the half-mile, and asked to compete only in the quarter-mile at Stanford. The excessive speed work probably caused the serious hamstring injury that curtailed his training that season.

In 1960, Norman thundered back with a smashing mile victory in the Big Meet over Olympian Jerry Sibert, and along with Ernie Cunliffe, Rich Klier and Bob Besse set a new national collegiate record in the Medley Relay. His time of 2:56.6 for the 1320 leg (three laps) was the fastest in track history, according to the May 19, 1960 edition of the Palo Alto Times. Although he ran some of the fastest times in the world that year, an NCAA title eluded him because Irish Olympic champion Ron Delaney of Villanova and Cal's Don Bowden-Norman's collegiate rival and good friend-ran even faster.

Victories off the track, however, meant the most to Norman: that spring he graduated Phi Beta Kappa and won a Woodrow Wilson Fellowship to Stanford for graduate study in economics. Already a CPA, he taught courses in the Business School while working towards his Ph.D. He was thrilled to remain in Palo Alto and soon became a member of the newly formed running club, the Angell Field Ancients, made up of Stanford faculty, staff and alumni.

Former elite athletes energized Angell Field in the 1960s and 1970s, as they helped popularize Masters track and field competition. Coach Jordan returned to serious training during this time and was soon a world threat on the Masters scene. Norman and the Coach were often out training at the same time, spurring each other on, and developing a great fondness and respect for each other. Norman also enjoyed a long and happy association with Chuck Cobb, a mighty hurdler and fellow teammate. While Chuck donated most of the funds needed to make Angell Field one of the best track and field facilities in the nation, Norman enthusiastically contributed his time and energy. Later, Coach Jordan and Norman would spend hours discussing the possibility of staging the Summer Olympics around San Francisco, with Stanford facilities at center stage.

Stanford Track Memories

Our earliest memory of Stanford was struggling up Palm Drive from the train depot to Coach Jordan's office with two suitcases apiece. Later, when he introduced us to all these well-mannered, crew-cut young men at the first team practice, the Coach looked at Norman's collar-length curls and remarked that a haircut would make him even faster. Norman came out of England's post-war generation of Angry Young Men, however, and Coach Jordan soon learned that a crew cut could never sheer him of his rebelliousness.

Only two women were brave enough to invade those training sessions in the late 1950s. One was Margaret Storey, a certified Official Timer who earned a Masters degree from Stanford in 1934. Clad always in her official's uniform of black Blazer and gray skirt, she never missed a practice. The other woman was Norman's wife, Dorothy, an Olympic sprinter who still enjoyed running even though there was no track and field for women at Stanford yet.

Norman and I [wife: Dorothy] also enjoyed our long talks with the noble and eloquent Sam McDonald as he sat outside his track house home and read chapters from his book. Sam was the son of a slave and the head groundskeeper at Stanford for whom Sam McDonald Park in La Honda and Sam McDonald Street at Stanford are named.

Beyond Stanford

In college, Norman considered himself a scholar-athlete in that order. In graduate school he kept training simply because he loved to run, but also to keep physically and mentally fit for study and work. After passing his PhD orals, he decided he could better use his CPA skills and Stanford education in the Bay Area's newly emerging hi-tech economy. He soon opened his own practice as a CPA and earned his MBA in Taxation in 1978. Besides Silicon Valley entrepreneurs, his clients included many fellow alumni such as professional football players, Olympic athletes and physicians.

Nonetheless, by the early 1970s Norman was chomping at the bit to race again. Inspired by Coach Jordan's career in Masters sprinting, he returned to the track and won or placed in various Masters half-mile and mile races. He even set the world half-mile record for 39-year-olds in 1973, a statistic that much amused him. Norman continued to train with the Angell Field Ancients and win track and road races in his age category for the rest of his life. Tragically, Norman passes away in 1977.

Bertil Lundh

In my hometown of Fredrikstad, Norway we had sports clubs in lieu of organized sports within the schools. I joined a track club at age 12 and participated in all kinds of events. Eventually, I settled on the 800 and 1500 meters. My best times were 1:47.8 (800m) and 3:41.1 (1500m), the latter a Norwegian record.

Journey to Stanford

It was a boyhood dream of mine to come to the USA. I had obtained an associates degree and wanted to get a BS and MS in engineering. I knew of Stanford's reputation. I discussed my interest with some Americans on a USA touring team, and Frank Hermann (Stanford long jumper) encouraged me to write to Coach Jordan, which I did. After several pleasant interchanges, I was accepted and received a scholarship.

Our journey to Stanford was quite a saga. My wife, Lollo, and I set sail for America on the SS Stavangerfjord. Lollo was booked as a passenger and I worked my way across as a seventh dishwasher in tourist class. Only the keel was lower than I on the totem pole! Crossing the north Atlantic in the winter wasn't exactly a joy ride. It was a miserable couple that arrived in New York. I developed pneumonia and initially was denied entrance to the US by immigration officials. After two day of quarantine I was released. Lollo's terrible "sea sickness" turned out to be "morning sickness" and we later would become parents to twins. As a result our plans to take a bus from New York to the West Coast had to change. The airlines were on strike but we were able to get on a charter flight to Oakland, then find our way to Palo Alto on a sunny day in December.

Stanford

I started the winter semester 1959 as a sophomore and got "upgraded" to a junior. Coach Terrill jokingly told me to stop running around among various engineering departments collecting credits for coursework in Scandinavia, " If you keep it up you will graduate before the first track meet!" That didn't happen, of course, but I did receive my BS in 1960 and MS in 1961, both with emphasis on computer science and operational research.

I competed in the 880, mile, and cross country plus several relays. In 1959 we hit the grand slam by winning the Drake Relays, West Coast Relays, and the Coliseum Relays. Unfortunately, my times at Stanford did not live up to what I had achieved in Europe earlier, but I was able to pick up points in various dual meets. My track career ended in 1960 when I sustained a foot injury, requiring surgery.

Post-Stanford

My first job, and only employer, was a large mainframe computer company specializing in scientific and engineering applications. Over a 30-year career we lived in Scandinavia for three years and spent the rest in the Bay Area. I have been retired since 1991. We have three children, the two twin girls (Anne and Bente) and a son (Espen). Anne received a MS in Social Work, is married, and lives and works in Norway. Bente received a BS and MD from Stanford, was a member of the track team, is married and lives and has a pediatric practice in Bermuda. Espen received a BS in Computer Science and works for Kaiser Hospital in Santa Clara.

Norm Pease

Stanford Years

I was part of Stanford Track from the fall of 1956 to the spring of 1960. Best time in college was a 9.6 in the 100-yd. dash and a 21.0 in the 220.

One day Coach Jordan decided he would teach us sprinters a thing or two about fast starts from the blocks. So he lined us all up (Dean Smith, Ben Anixter, Kurt Hauser and maybe Chuck Cobb was there too) and then Payton handed the starting gun to freshman coach, Floyd Strain, and Payton lined up to race with us. (This was just for 50 yards he told us). Well, all of us were determined to beat the coach so we were like high-strung coiled springs. So, right before the gun when off, Payton would flick his arm and at least one of us would false start. After about 4 false starts away went the coach with about a 3-yard lead and we could not catch him.

Coach Jordan was always very keen on staying healthy - many vitamin pills, and eating an orange a day. Sit-ups and pushups morning and evening (15-20 of them) was a routine he instilled in me.

Coach Jordan's Influence

I credit Coach Jordan with keeping me at Stanford. I do not recall the exact wording of some of Payton's "pep" talks but they made enough of a "mark" on me that my wife and I named our firstborn son: Jordan Pease.

Post-Stanford

What about running today - hard for me to admit to but this former sprinter has become a long distance runner. I have completed a dozen marathons, one on each continent. I recall during more than one Stanford track meet a few of us would watch Bob Monzingo run the two-mile, and we agreed that race was not for us. Never thought I'd run anything longer that a 220.

1961

Craig Barrett

I participated on the Stanford track team for 4 years. Events were sprints (100 and 220 yards), 4x110 relay, hurdles (110 highs and 220 lows), and long and triple jumps. Scored points in most meets but was just one of the guys on the team.

My memorable experiences on the Stanford track team revolve mostly around learning to compete and what it takes to be successful. Coach Jordan was a constant reminder of the need for dedication to the task at hand to be successful. I suppose I was something of a 'part-timer' for my first two years on the team, but I became committed during my junior and senior years. I really learned the lesson that you have to work if you want results. Subsequently, I have found this to be true in the business world as well as athletic competition. Coach was always patient with me and pushed just hard enough to get results. In return our dedication to his leadership was strong and consistent. We grew to understand that track and field, while very much an individual sport, still required teamwork and helping each other. We had a few great athletes on our team and several of us who could fill in where necessary, score the occasional first, second or third, and feel successful in the process. Perhaps my biggest disappointment was our inability to beat Cal in any of our meets. My biggest reward was the ability to move around between events and recognize the fact that Coach had some degree of confidence in my ability to perform. I always remember Coach saying that you have to want to win to win. It was true then and is still true today.

Since track and field at Stanford, I was fortunate enough to teach on the Stanford Engineering faculty for 10 years and then join a relatively new semiconductor company called Intel in 1974. I would rank my highest professional accomplishments as rising to become CEO of Intel in 1998 and also my election to the National Academy of Engineering. When book-ended with my time as an undergraduate at Stanford, I couldn't be happier with my overall career.

Don Bell

Pre-Stanford
Alameda High School: state champion and record holder in the discus in 1957 (173' 2-3/4"). Choice of college was between Cal and Stanford. Chose Stanford because I felt Coach Jordan was the best.

Stanford
Broke Bob Mathias' frosh discus record with a throw of 164"2" in 1959. Elected Co-Captain of the 1961 track team with Rich Klier. Finished Stanford career with the third best all time discus mark of 171'11". Also competed in the shot put, high jump, 220 low hurdles and anchored the weightmen's 440-yd.relay. Earned three varsity letters and finished no worse than eighth in three NCAA finals.

Served as cadet colonel and battle group commander of the Army ROTC unit.

Post-Stanford
Served two years in the Army, mostly "jock strapping" my way through the service. I coached and competed for the Fort Campbell, KY track team, Third Army team, and was assistant coach of the all Army team in 1963-64. I also competed on the inter-service team at Quantico, VA and the All-Army indoor team at West Point, NY.

After the military, I returned to Stanford to finish my Masters Degree and teaching credentials, then started my career in education in San Jose, CA. With Coach Jordan's influence a huge factor in my career choice, I coached track and field for 16 years at the high school level at Pioneer and Leland high schools. I spent the last nine years as Principal of Leland High School and served as President of the Central Coast Section and represented the Section on the California Interscholastic Federation Board for four years. I also chaired the C.I.F. track and field and cross country committee for two years.

Beside my dad, Coach Jordan was the greatest role model I ever had. His impact on my life made me want to follow the same path by working with young people in education in general and coaching in particular. What a great man he is, and what a great idea to chronicle his history.

Paul Schlicke

Pre-Stanford (Gonzaga Prep, Spokane, WA) 1957-61
A weedy adolescent, frustrated at my inability to excel in ball games, I took to running during my freshman year of high school and by training during the off-season (more or less unheard of in those days) developed into a successful athlete.

- Track 1958 - competed at 660 yards; fourth at Spokane city freshman championships in 1.34.
- Cross country 1958 - generally second on the school team.
- Track 1959 - competed in the mile, and won one race, in 5:03!
- Cross country 1959 - first at Spokane city championships over a 2-mile course; third at WA State championships behind Bill Pratt, then at Wenatchee H.S. and later a Stanford teammate.
- Track 1960 - first at Spokane city championships in 4:30.2 and first at WA state championships in 4:31.1; Phil Shinnick (later an Olympic long-jumper) & I scored all the school's points for third-place team standing.
- Cross country — undefeated season; first at city and state championships, led team to an undefeated dual-meet season; first in Spokane city championships and second in WA state.
- Track 1961 - undefeated season; city record 4.21.1; state record 4.19.3 - the latter a "miracle mile" according to the local paper! (That was before Gerry Lindgren came along two years later.)
- Awarded the Curtis Sharp Award for scholarship, leadership, and athletics at Gonzaga Prep.

Stanford 1961-65
Payton Jordan wooed me to Stanford along with other talented distance runners-Weym Kirkland, Harlan Andrews, Dave Steinbeck, Harry McCalla, Bob Miltz, Bill Pratt. On any given day somebody or other was sure to feel good, which ensured that workouts were invariably hard work - and a great deal of fun.

- Cross country 1961-generally second or third Stanford runner; tied with Harlan Andrews in an end-of-season 2-mile track race in a school freshman record of 9:20.4.
- Track 1962 - 4.10.6 mile for freshman record; 9:06.8 freshman record in 2-mile (I skipped out of a Russian exam halfway through the allotted time, in order to compete); 880 in 1:53.0 for second place, on a busy day competing against Cal, when I won the mile and 2-mile and lost the half-mile by a whisker.
- Cross country 1962 - set school record for 3-mile (on track) at 14:10.9, broken later the same season by Dave Deubner.
- Track 1963 - started season in best shape of my career, but broke a metatarsal early season; kept running and broke another - eventually managed only 4:09.7 & 9:01.0; seventh in NCAA 3-mile in 14:56.6 - on shoulder of eventual winner, Julio Marin of USC, with half-mile to go, but between altitude and lack of training ran out of steam to finish seventh; Wym Kirkland was fourth in the same race.
- Cross country 1963 - generally second or third Stanford runner; won intra-squad 2-mile on track in 8:58.2.

159

- Track 1964 - my best season: 4:02.3 & 8:58.8; first in Pacific Coast championships in meet record 4:02.5; dnf NCAA 5,000 meters (Olympic year) - I still don't know why I simply couldn't ever get going in that race at the end of a successful season.
- Cross country 1964 - won my only cross country race in four years at Stanford, at Strawberry Canyon, Berkeley, in a 4-mile course record 18:54.
- Track 1965 - elected Stanford team co-captain along with Bob McIntyre. Set school 2-mile record 8:51.4 (having run a 4:05 mile an hour earlier) - and damaged Achilles a week later; won LA Coliseum relays "miracle mile" in 4:04.4 and was awarded the Al Masters trophy for Stanford athlete of the year the same night; did not make the final of NCAA mile - 4:06.5 in semis; led coming out of final bend in AAU semi-finals-and finished last, unable to sprint on account of damaged Achilles, a sad way to end.

Post-Stanford

Took up road running, eventually running an average of 10 miles a day for over a year until another broken metatarsal put pain to that, in 1994. Before that I ran two marathons, the first in 1981 in 3:15.02 (having hit the wall spectacularly at 20 miles), the second in 1982 in 2:49.44. I also did a 75-mile run in 5-10 mile stages over two days for charity in 1984 - which cured me of mega-distances for life!

I started medical school at the University of Washington after graduating, but quickly realized that route was not for me, and switched to post-graduate studies in English (I was an English major at Stanford), getting a PhD from the University of California San Diego in 1971. While writing my thesis on Dickens I spent a year in London during the Dickens centenary celebrations (1970), and was offered a job at the University of Aberdeen (founded 1495) in Scotland. I thought that would be fun for a year, and have stayed ever since.

I have edited editions of four of Dickens novels, compiled a couple of major Dickens bibliographies and written a number of scholarly articles and reviews. My monograph *Dickens and Popular Entertainment* was published in 1985, and I was general editor of the *Oxford Reader's Companion to Dickens* (1999). I was president of the Dickens Society of America in 1994 and am currently (2003-05) president of the International Dickens Fellowship.

I have two grown-up sons by my first marriage, and a young daughter by my second. I live with my wife and daughter in a stone cottage near the northeast coast of Scotland, surrounded by fields, which are generally filled with sheep but occasionally by deer, badgers, and rabbits, and only last week by a fox.

1962

Art Batchelder

Originally, I was recruited to Stanford as a football player. In the process I developed a friendship with Don Bell, a.k.a. "the Camel." Camel was a great athlete. He had the size, strength, and incredible speed for a big man to become an all-pro tight end, except for his shoulders, which would dislocate in a moderate breeze. (How a guy with that problem could throw a discus 170 feet has always been a great mystery.)

Anyway, Camel was on the track team, and I played frosh football for Homer Smith, (strong coach) under Cactus Jack Curtis, (weak coach). Coaching aside, my future in college football was going to be limited to practice fodder, at best. Being either the smallest fastest lineman or the biggest slowest back was leading nowhere. (Later on all that turned around when rugby found me.)

After the frosh football season, Camel and I were pheasant hunting when he noticed that I had a pretty strong throwing arm. That led to the suggestion I take a look at the track team, as they had no real strength in the javelin at the time. So, in the spring of my freshman year Camel introduced me to Coach Jordan. Our first meeting was a routine hello in a "size-up" meeting in his office. Our second meeting after spring break was worrisome. I had gotten into an altercation, (minding my own business, mind you), that resulted in a black eye, a real shiner. With this painted on my face, I had to report back to Coach Jordan, and all I could think about was "What is a gentleman like Coach Jordan going to think of a roughneck like me?" Well, it was amazing! Instead of the disapproval I had expected, I got a pat on the back and a hand shake that made me feel we'd been old friends for a long time. "Art, I like a fighter, and clearly you are one. It's one of my prerequisites for a champion."

I was on the team and gave my heart and soul, to say nothing of my body, to the team and the Coach. Learning daily lessons on how to throw, how to train, how to compete at the highest levels, and most importantly, how to live life as a man. Payton became the second most important figure in my life, after my dad. Under his guidance, we set a freshman record in the javelin and later the university record. Being at the top of the "Top-10" board in the javelin at Stanford was a big deal to me, particularly considering those who had been there before.

Business and life took me away from Palo Alto, but whenever I could get back to the campus, usually for a football game, it was always one of the real pleasures of the day to go up and sit with Payton and Marge for part of the third quarter and get all caught up.

For me my life, particularly my business life, has been very competitive. The values and commitment learned from Coach Jordan have guided me well all these years. Whether it is in your personal life, growing your family, or participating in your community, no one could do better than to walk in the giant shadow of Payton Jordan.

Len Breschini
High School
I attended Salinas High School during Bill Kearney's tenure as track and field coach. His teams went undefeated in the 50s and 60s in dual and triangular meets, and had at least one athlete qualify for the CIF State Meet every year. Eddie King, who held every SHS record from the 75-yard dash to the 880-yd. run, broke the national interscholastic 440 record in 1955. I had a record setting year as a sophomore that generated some interest from local USC alumni. I missed my junior year due to a hamstring injury, but my senior year I qualified for the CIF Meet in the 440, even though I did not use blocks. Coach Kearney, a Cal alum, tried to steer me toward Berkeley, but Coach Brutus Hamilton was retiring, and I began looking more and more at Stanford. Coach Jordan

was the difference, as he made it a point to visit with me at the CCS and NCS meets. His enthusiasm for the Stanford program, and his genuine interest in me were deciding factors.

Stanford

I had a difficult freshman year academically and on the track, as nagging injuries and bronchial asthma hampered me. I recall Coach's letters wherein he challenged me to deal with my problems and not allow them to keep me from reaching my potential in school and in track. He did not give up on me. All Coach asked of any of us, whether we were a world-class athlete or not, was to perform to the best of our abilities.

I recall he had the team enroll in boxing classes so we could learn to persevere in a close race, to "fight" and not give up at the finish. As for aches and pains, the joke was to tape an aspirin to the sore spot and keep running! It was a good philosophy, especially for someone like me with hamstring problems. I remember being diagnosed with pleurisy and missing two days of practice. Coach called and strongly suggested that I get to practice the next day. Two days later, I ran life-time bests in the 100 and the 220. I don't know who was happier, Coach or me! My junior year, Coach had the entire team run cross-country during fall quarter to build up our strength and stamina. We proved to ourselves how valuable that training was by running 10 330's under 40 seconds and walk the turn. An added bonus for me was that I never had any more hamstring problems.

Coach was the premier promoter of track and field as a team sport. One of his innovations was the addition of the weight-men's 440 relay to our meets. What a sight seeing those big guys sprint around the track! He encouraged the team to ring the track in support of Ernie Cunliffe's assault on the school 880 record and the 4 minute mile. He was an inspiration to all of us. I remember the great dual meets with "speed city", San Jose State; and the double dual meets with Cal, UCLA and USC with crowds of 10,000 people. Led by Dan Moore, Larry Questad and Dave Weill, the '63 team was one of Coach's most successful, taking second place in the NCAA Championships. The biggest disappointment that year was the dual meet loss to USC. Rex Cawley anchored their mile relay team to victory and that was the meet. We almost ended their dual meet win streak. The season highlight for me was running in the Drake, Coliseum, California and West Coast Relays. What an experience and what great competition! My last day of competitive running was like three meets, with the Conference trials in the morning and finals in the afternoon at Berkeley, and then running in the California Relays in Modesto that night.

Coach was a real showman and promoter, as evidenced by the successful '60 Olympic Trials and 1962 US-USSR Meet held in Stanford Stadium. The Soviets were so appreciative that they invited Coach to bring some of his Stanford athletes to compete in Moscow.

Remember the red blazers and the conduct that was expected of us? Coach had no tolerance for deviant 60s behavior! I have many good memories of my Stanford track experiences; a lot of personal satisfaction and no regrets. I owe a lot to Coach Jordan for that. He was, and is, a class act.

Later

I have spent 38 years in the insurance industry. I sold my agency and now work with our local community hospital in the administration of their self-insured workers' compensation program. Dale and I spend most of our travel time in Colorado and Southern California visiting our three children and two grandsons (half a relay team)! Like Coach, we encouraged the kids to always perform up to their abilities in school, in sports and in their careers. Coach was gracious enough to accept an invitation to speak at my Rotary Club several years ago. His message, as expected, was well received, but it provided an opportunity for the three men who had the greatest impact on my life - my dad, Coach Kearney and Coach Jordan - to sit down and share a lot of great track and field memories. For me, that was a very special occasion. I am enjoying my work and the people, so retirement can just wait a while.

Chris Hungerland

At University High School in West Los Angeles I emerged as one of the faster quarter-milers in town. I was recruited by UCLA, Occidental, the Naval Academy, and Stanford. I chose Stanford because of its prestige and my high school coach, Jim Pursell, said Coach Jordan was great.

Stanford Memories

The competition at Stanford proved to be intense both in the classroom and on the track.

I particularly liked the few indoor meets. I recall our relay getting third at the Los Angeles Times Meet and a brief debate following as to whether accepting the "prize" (a wind-up travel alarm clock for each of us) would compromise our amateur standing with the NCAA. Valid question at the time; certainly different times, now!

Running indoors at Portland and seeing a quarter-miler get elbowed in a curve and go streaking up into a distant row of seats.

Watching Coach Jordan start with our sprinters (Larry Questad among them) and beat them out to the 40-yard mark.

Watching Ernie Cunliffe do the first lap of an 880 in 49.5 and... actually finish the race!

Feeling that the air would never, ever move again, but that lunch certainly might, while running - uphill - on the golf course.

Coach letting me keep my track scholarship (post-surgery) after I'd become about as useful to the team program as a traffic cone.

Coach: "Don't ask that you win. Ask that you do your best. If you've done the preparation and believe in yourself, you'll prevail."

Post-Stanford

I'd become quite active as a musician during my senior year and developed to the point where I was able to support myself singing (classical/opera mostly...some commercial) in Los Angeles. Got drafted in 1967, became a medic ("psychological research specialist") and was assigned to the Presidio of Monterey. I actually did go to Vietnam but only later as a Litton Industries employee. Then it was time to use my GI Bill and get a degree in architecture and construction engineering. Have been in the Puget Sound area ever since. My wife, Elizabeth, and I have raised two wonderful daughters.

Looking Back
Payton Jordan was the first person in my life to define "charisma" by personal example. His emphasis on preparation and self-belief have been touch stones ever since...I haven't always prevailed, but I've always known that I honestly gave it my best shot, and, thanks to Coach, I always felt good no matter what the result (given that "winning" is ... well... better).

Dan Moore
My life has been richly blessed in many ways... high on the list is the privilege of attending Stanford University, and coming under the influence of Payton Jordan. That experience provided not only treasured memories, but a host of lessons that have directed and shaped my life ever since.

Pre-Stanford
I participated in my first official track meet in the seventh grade. I quickly learned that I could jump higher and farther than the other kids, but my interests then were more inclined towards basketball and baseball. I "broad" jumped 15'3" in the seventh grade, grew 6 inches over the next year to just over 6', and jumped 18'1" in the eighth grade, and 19'6" in the ninth grade. I also tried my hand at pole vaulting on a bamboo pole my dad had gotten from a carpet store, and managed 11'3", which was a state junior high record at the time. I don't think I will ever forget the smell of fresh shavings delivered at the beginning of each season for the combination high jump and pole vault pit! I even fashioned a backyard practice vaulting/high jump pit, as well as a sand pit for the long jump, where I spent many happy hours when I'm sure my parents were wishing I was pulling weeds or doing other chores around the house!

My sophomore year at South Salem High School I was a starting guard on our basketball team that went to the state tournament and lost to the state champions by 2 points in overtime. In track I jumped 21'8" to place second in the state meet, and the following week won the Northwest Junior (under 16) long jump at 21'11 ¾". I earned enough money picking strawberries, after school let out, to buy a round trip ticket on a Greyhound bus to Los Angeles to see the 1956 Olympic Trials. I was there to see Charlie Dumas become the first high jumper ever to clear 7 feet; watched Greg Bell, who would go on to win gold in Melbourne, and whose long jump form I strived to emulate; and saw enough incredible performances to whet my appetite for that "Olympic Dream," that so many of us fantasized about at one time or other. The next 2 years I went out for cross country (to get in shape for basketball), and won our District meet my junior year. My best jump that year was 22'9", which won the National Jr. Olympics. I qualified for the State Meet my junior and senior years in the high hurdles and on our 880-yd. relay team. My senior year I was named to the all-state basketball team, won the state meet with a new state record of 23'10 ½", and the National Jr. Olympics with an identical mark the following week. No Oregon high schooler had ever broken 23' in the long jump in 1958, and I was able to do 23'8" or better in five consecutive meets, barely fouling jumps of 24'6" and 24'7" in the State meet. I knew I was going to Stanford, meeting Coach Jordan on a visit to the campus during our spring break. From that very first contact, his positive, charismatic influence fueled my determination to justify the faith he had placed in me by offering me a chance to attend one of the world's great universities.

Stanford

I experienced the first of several "academic shocks," when I sat down with my advisor (a Psychology professor) after fall registration, and told him I had to move the time of one of my classes as it would conflict with afternoon track practice. He looked at me like I was from another planet! A somewhat rocky start was made easier by the steadying influence and wisdom of Coach Jordan, whose open-door policy always made me feel welcome to come in and discuss any problem I might be having. My freshman season was great fun, participating in meets like the West Coast Relays at Fresno and the California Relays at Modesto, and actually being on the same field and figuratively "rubbing shoulders" with heroes like Rafer Johnson, Bobby Morrow, and Parry O'Brien. I was able to set a new freshman long jump record of 24'2" at Modesto, fouling 2 jumps of 25' or more. The most improvement, however came in the high hurdles, where thanks to the help of Chuck Cobb and Coach Jordan, I knocked a full second from my best high school time, running 14.6, and gaining real confidence that I might develop into an adequate collegiate hurdler. This was not to be however, as the next year I suffered a severe torn hamstring running the highs in an early season triangular meet with defending national champion Kansas, and San Jose State. This ended my season, in which I essentially "red-shirted," as I was granted an additional year of eligibility by the NCAA.

The next year I continued to be plagued by hamstring problems whenever I ran the hurdles. Concentrating on the long jump, I finally logged an official 25'1" in a dual meet at UCLA. I finished a disappointing seventh in the NCAAs in Philadelphia, then with a few teammates, took the train to New York, site of the National AAU, the following weekend. That night, on our non-existent expense accounts, four of us shared a cheap hotel room - Don Bell, and Art Batchelder took the 2 beds, and Harry Jerome (the Oregon sprinter, and the second man ever to run 10.0 in the 100 meters) and I got the 2 mattresses from those beds, and slept on the floor. Only one of many such experiences in the life of vagabond tracksters in those days!

The following year we spent much fall workout time on the Stanford golf course. Running barefoot on the grass felt exhilarating, but contributed to an Achilles tendonitis, which was to plague me throughout the year. To ease the strain on the tendon, I spent much of my workout time running in the old Encina pool. I was fortunate enough to win the conference championship in the LA Coliseum, and set a new Stanford long-jump record of 25'9 ½" in the NCAA meet in Eugene. The top 4 (I was fourth) were wedged within 3 inches of each other. The record held up for 15yrs., until broken by James Lofton. I have occasionally reminisced that if it weren't for 3 NFL Hall of Fame football players (James Lofton, Paul Warfield, and Mel Renfro), the record would have lasted 40 yrs., and I would have a silver medal instead of whatever color fourth place is!

Highlights of my Senior year including coming within 1 ½" of upsetting Olympic Champion and world record holder, Ralph Boston, in an indoor meet in Portland. I was honored to be named a Tri-Captain of the team along with Dave Weill, and Harry McCalla, and I won the conference long jump championship for a second time on a foggy day in Berkeley. Unfortunately, a week before the NCAAs, I learned I was ineligible to participate because of my fifth-year status... the team went on to take second place behind Oregon.

Post-Stanford
I stayed on another year for a Master's in Education, and worked out with the team and miscellaneous other athletes who had migrated to the campus to train for the Tokyo Olympics. I had the opportunity to compete in the big meets, Coliseum Relays, Modesto, Compton Invitational, and managed over 25' at the West Coast Relays.

Being greatly influenced by my mentor and role model, Coach Jordan, I aspired to go into coaching. I did my student teaching at nearby Los Altos High School, and before the end of the school year accepted a teaching position and job as head track and cross country coach. As soon as school let out, Elaine, my wife of one year, and I headed off in a borrowed, makeshift VW van to the East Coast for the National AAU meet and Olympic trials. I didn't jump far enough, and "camping out" for 2 months severely tested our marriage, but the adventure provided enough memories to last a lifetime.

I taught and coached at Los Altos High for the next 2 years, and sold insurance part-time on the side. The mid-60s was a period of turmoil and social change, which had its effect on authoritarian figures like coaches. I was very frustrated, for although we had some outstanding athletes, and 2 undefeated teams, it seemed to me that I often cared more about how my athletes performed both on and off the field, than they did. I know that Coach Jordan was going through a similar, but more intense experience, and we spoke often on the matter. To his great credit, he stayed on and worked through these issues.

I entered the insurance business full-time, and have my own company, specializing in estate planning and business uses of life insurance. We settled in our present location in Los Altos in 1970, and have 3 daughters, and one son, all of whom are living happy, successful, and productive lives. They have blessed us with 5 grandchildren who are our constant joy.

Memories of Coach Jordan
In one way or another for 46 years, Payton Jordan has had a positive influence on my life. Since Stanford we have met on several occasions to have a milkshake together at the Peninsula Creamery, or a sandwich in my back yard gazebo. His letters are always warm and uplifting. He has been a role model, a coach, a teacher, a mentor, and a dear friend. He is an out-spoken proponent of old-fashioned values: a man of principle, of character, and of courage and determination. He had a talent for making you feel better about yourself, and more confident in your ability to take on any challenge. He could look you straight in the eye and make you feel like you would climb mountains and swim through shark infested waters to meet his expectations of you...and then, the miracle of it all, was that those expectations became *your* expectations!

1963

Phil Lamoreaux

The 50s were a pretty quiet time in America, particularly compared with what would follow. Mort Saul referred to it as the "quiet generation." Growing up in the Napa Valley certainly fit that description. Wine appreciation had not yet taken hold, so when we competed against schools from the "more sophisticated" Bay Area, we often heard jeers like, "here come the hicks with the purple feet." This only emboldened our resolve to "stomp'em." How times change. One of the local high schools now is named "Vintage" and they are known as the "Crushers."

My strongest calling was in track and I concentrated on the sprints. I had a dance band, was on the honor roll, and president of the student body. My older sister, who graduated from Cal, told me "cool guys went to Princeton." I applied and got accepted but heard there was a great track coach closer to home, a place called Stanford. Is this sounding a bit like the screenplay for "American Graffiti"?

Stanford

I showed up as a walk-on (I thought everyone was) in the fall because I heard the track team trained all year. Jim Terrill was the freshman coach and would not even let me try out because my times were not good enough. He had guys on the team then that I had never lost to! Perhaps the times they submitted were wind-aided or downhill, but no luck. So instead I tried out for the rowing team. This lasted a year.

The next year Payton Jordan gave me a chance and I was introduced to the Stanford Golf Course, as were all my teammates. Not for golf, but for distance work. I wondered what a sprinter was doing running long hills, as did the weight men and most of my other teammates. I still have fond memories of seeing my classmate and future Olympian, Dave Weill (6' 6" and 265 lbs), thundering up and down the hills. I figured if he could do it, so could I.

I began to thrive under Payton. I learned both technique and mental discipline. By mid-season I upset the former California state champion, now at UCLA. Coach taught us that we were better than we thought we were. After every personal best I fondly remember his big smile and hug and the complimentary whisper, "Congratulations, that was great! You will be even faster, soon." What an amazing thing to say! He believed in me, and I trusted him completely. He proved to be right, and made me better than I truly was.

Coach introduced the idea of visualization in 1962 and brought a consultant in, just as sports psychology was beginning. We would write down on a piece of paper a result better than we had ever achieved and would look at it at the beginning and end of each day. We would use the first person affirmative, e.g., "I am an athlete!" I would close my eyes and visualize running my race and achieving that goal. I had visualized breaking the Pac 8 220-yd record of 21.5. At the Championship Meet in the LA Coliseum I achieved it by running a 21.3. However, I came in third, as many of the nation's best were in the Pac 8. Nevertheless, I qualified for the NCAA Championships and remember the dozen of us going to Oregon to give our best, which earned us a second place team result!

Coach's Influence
I believe the character-building experience with Coach and the team has served me well.
I have run a small investment management firm for the past 30 years. Not surprisingly,
our small team of five thrives on teamwork. We set high goals and help each other to
achieve them. I truly enjoy the work and have no intention of retiring. In 1996 I had the
pleasure of accompanying Coach Jordan on his 1996 return to Greece, subject of a
chapter in this book. What a thrill that was!!

Dave Weill

Athletic Biographical Information
My athletic career began at Los Lomas High School in Walnut Creek, California, where
I competed in football, basketball and track. I placed second in the discus throw at the
State meet as a junior when Northern California schools used the college weight discus.
I met Payton Jordan at one of the state meets and mentioned that Stanford was one of the
universities I was considering to get a degree in Electrical Engineering. My high school
coach could not say enough about Payton Jordan's talents as a coach. As things turned
out, I attended Stanford on academic scholarships but decided to compete in sports as
well. One half of one game terminated my career in Stanford football ending with the
characteristic Dr. Fred Behling knee surgery. I was then able to concentrate on track and
field at Stanford.

Under Coach Jordan's direction I was able to improve my throwing technique and was
able to place first in the conference championships, which was the "Big Five
Conference" in 1961, 1962, and 1963. As a sophomore in 1961, I placed third in the
NCAA meet. I placed first in the NCAAs in 1962 and 1963. I also placed in the National
AAU meets with a third place in 1962, a fifth place in 1963, and a third place in 1964.

After I graduated from Stanford in 1963, I went on to get a Master's Degree in Electrical
Engineering at Stanford. This allowed me to be able to train at Stanford in preparation
for the Tokyo Olympics in 1964, where I won the Bronze Medal in the Discus Throw
with a throw of 195' 2" behind Al Oerter (200' 1") and Ludvik Danek (198' 6").

My best mark was 206' 8" (62.99m), which was set in Sacramento, 6/10/67.

Memorable Experiences
As I think back on my undergraduate days at Stanford I remember some of the routines
that Coach Jordan had instituted for the entire team. In the fall, we were all encouraged
to run the cross-country course on the Stanford Golf Course. While the field athletes did
not compete in any cross-country events, we did spend time putting in 2 mile or 4 mile
runs on the golf course.

Daily workouts at Angell Field in the spring always began with a few warm-up wind
sprints on the infield grass prior to doing any throwing from the discus ring. Coach
Jordan would often join in and sprint alongside. His college background as a sprinter,
and indeed his later skills in Master's track ensured that he was quite capable of holding
his own with the athletes.

Coaching a team of track and field athletes can be quite a challenge because of the many varied skills and techniques involved. Somehow Coach Jordan was always able to find time to come down to the discus ring and give specific coaching instruction on technique.

Preparation always had an important focus with Coach Jordan. From the physical training to a focus on being mentally prepared on down to the details of the pre-meet meal of roast beef, peas, toast and honey.

While Coach Jordan was very serious in coordinating the track meets at Stanford, he also had a sense of humor. Why else would he include a special "weight men's relay event" near the end of the meet? I remember getting nervous in those 4x100 relays hoping that we could complete the handoff within the specified zone.

After the very successful US-USSR track meet held at Stanford in 1962, Coach Korobkov invited Payton Jordan to bring several athletes to the Znamensky Memorial Meet in Moscow in 1963. I was fortunate to be one of the athletes along with Steve Cortright and Larry Questad. Once in Europe we went on to the World Games in Helsinki, Finland and had additional meets in England, Ireland, Czechoslovakia, and Germany. I was very lucky in Prague to edge out Ludvik Danek by a mere one centimeter. This foreign tour allowed me to gain valuable experience in international competition prior to the 1964 Olympics.

I look back on the 1960s as the "heyday" of track and field. Coach Jordan showed his expertise in bringing in 150,000 people to the US-USSR meet in 1962. It was not uncommon to have a crowd of 60,000 at the Coliseum Relays in Los Angeles to witness the likes of Peter Snell breaking a four-minute mile along with a host of other great performances.

Payton Jordan had a number of colleagues who were also respected - Brutus Hamilton at Cal, Ducky Drake at UCLA, Bill Bowerman at Oregon and the list goes on.

Most Memorable Thing Coach Jordan Said to Me — or the Team
I can't say I remember any exact quotes that I could attribute to Coach Jordan but certainly his philosophy on preparation and training were important both for competition in track and field, and later as important attitudes for success in business and in one's personal life.

I am, however, reminded of a story that Coach Jordan once told about a man that went duck hunting. When he arrived at the lodge he was asked if he had brought a dog with him. When he said no, they said they would provide one for him. The man went hunting with "Champion" and was quite pleased with the dog's skill at retrieving ducks. The next year he returned and asked for "Champion" but was told that the dog had been renamed "All American" because of his improved skills. He went hunting with "All American" and was very happy with the results. The third year he requested "All American" but was told that the dog was now named "Coach". When he asked why, they said that all the dog would do now was sit around and bark. Needless to say, Coach Jordan's "barking" was very helpful to many of us at Stanford!

Post-athletic Biographical Information
After Stanford I went to work for IBM as a Systems Engineer providing technical marketing support. I retired from IBM in 1993 with almost 28 years of service. I then went to work at Visa as a Systems Architect, and retired in 2004 after working at Visa for 10 years. I am currently living in San Francisco with my wife Regula.

After putting down the discus, I began running with local fun running clubs. I competed in a number of marathons over the years setting my best time of 3:08:40 in 1979. Now retired from any road racing activities I still enjoy jogging for exercise but at a much more modest pace.

Reflection on Coach Jordan's Influence on Me
Coach Jordan emphasized not only physical preparation and training but also emphasized the need for mental preparation. His ability to inspire confidence in one's ability was a message that transferred onto my years in the business world. When you are prepared, you can be confident that you can get a job done.

1964

Steve Arch

Pre-Stanford
I was a three-sport athlete at Reno High School. I got a lot of attention for my football playing but also held the school high-jump record and the state shot put record (lasted for 20+ years!). I competed in the first Golden West Invitational the summer after I graduated and threw a PR, although I think I finished second. During my senior year I received a lot of recruiting pressure. Only one of my campus visits, Stanford, involved meetings with both the football and the track coaches. Even more important for me was the attention that Payton Jordan paid to academics as well as athletics in our dialogue. I was sold.

Stanford
During the first couple years I split my time between football and track, but eventually decided to spend my time in the track program. Little did I know what awaited me that first non-football fall. Apparently Payton had become confused about the different needs of weight men and distance runners. Sure, he encouraged us to lift weights but, and this is where he got confused, he also had us out on the damn golf course running inconceivable distances. And he told us it was fun! When I'd look around at Don Bell, Art Batchelder, and Dave Weill I just didn't see much gleeful frolicking. Though we persisted, Payton couldn't be convinced that we were in danger of hurting ourselves out there. It was straining our loyalties until Don began finding perfect spots where we could walk unseen by the coaches and, even better, he found a shortcut that got us back with impressive, but not suspiciously impressive, times.

Post-Stanford
After scoring points reliably, loving those wacky weight men's relays (hey, they only involved a hundred yards of running), and a couple trips to the NCAAs my interests were again diverted. This time it was Elizabeth and graduate school at the University of Chicago. Later during my postdoctoral fellowship at Caltech I started playing rugby.

When I went looking for a rugby team to play with after our move to Portland, my loving wife assured me that if I tried to play any more rugby she would give me a "preemptory injury." That very believable threat led me to a desperation that I couldn't have imagined in the Payton years, I started running!

We raised two terrific daughters, Alexandra and Victoria. Both are Stanford graduates and both are runners. We are both college professors and, while eyeing retirement speculatively, remain active; in addition to our regular workouts, we ski, kayak, and hike. As a result of our foray into javelin throwing, we saw Payton at the World Master's Games in Eugene. We chatted with him not long after he had set a new record in the 100-meters. It was a treat to see him, an inspiration.

1965
Eric Frische
The idea to attend Stanford came late in the game for me. I attended an eastern prep school (Choate) and I actually applied to Stanford after the deadline for applications. In retrospect I was incredibly lucky to get accepted. Although I had run track all through high school and had done well for an East Coast prep school boy, I had never heard of Payton Jordan and I am sure that he had never heard of me. I pretty much went out for freshmen track as an afterthought, which wasn't hard for Coach to figure out. My grades started to slip during the spring quarter of my freshmen year so I didn't go out for track sophomore year (I thought I'd use the extra time to study). As it turned out, all that extra time had the reverse effect and my grades went from bad to worse.

By the beginning of my junior year I was faced with a choice of doing better academically or leaving school. In an effort to put my failing college career back together, part of my plan was to try track again and what a surprise, Coach wasn't overjoyed to see me. I recall a brief but to the point discussion about commitment. After a short verbal thrashing however he did give me the chance for which I will always be grateful. That was the '62-'63 season. We trained with more intensity than I was used to as a sprinter with a lot of weight and over-distance work. Someone got pushed off the track without pushing back so we runners all had to take boxing during the off-season. As a slightly heavy sprinter with short arms, I found the boxing ring was not a healthy place for me. I wasn't the only one to suffer as Larry Questad got a bruised spleen. I recall the sessions we had with the sports psychologist and the megavitamin packs that I now must confess I didn't take because they made me feel sick. Most of all I recall Coach Jordan's admonition to "let out the animal in you" or to "let out the artist in you." We all learned that we were capable of accomplishments on the track we hadn't thought possible. We had a great season and went to the NCAA Championship Meet in Albuquerque and placed second. For the next two seasons, along with the usual dual meets, we went to all sorts of indoor and outdoor relay meets, from Los Angeles to Des Moines. It was the thrill of a lifetime and I couldn't believe I was lucky enough to be part of it. For me it all culminated at Fresno in May 1965 with our 440-yard relay world record - 39.7, still a Stanford record.

But Coach Jordan wasn't only helpful to me on the track. My academically disastrous sophomore year followed me when it came time to apply for medical school, and most schools wouldn't even interview me. The coach came through with a letter to someone at Tulane Medical School and I not only got interviewed, I got accepted. Although I didn't end up going to Tulane I was able to use that acceptance to get into Columbia's College of Physicians and Surgeons in New York City.

After finishing medical school I took an orthopedic residency and after finding my way to Oklahoma, compliments of the US Army and Fort Sill, I settled in neighboring Lawton and have been fortunate in having a very busy and enjoyable practice career. Like most everyone else I have gotten a little fat with age but after being totally sedentary for years I have started working out some. I recently completed a walk-run half marathon, something my fellow sprinters who shared the off-season Stanford golf course short cuts will have trouble believing. The thirty years have passed quickly here in Oklahoma but I have been blessed to be able to do something that I truly love to do, even on the "bad days". Along the way I have been given many second chances but Coach Jordan's "second chance" gift to me is the one I treasure most.

Harry McCalla

Pre-Stanford

My love for running and jumping started early. As a kid, I organized neighborhood track meets in front of my house including the 50-yard dash and the high jump in the back yard using my mom's couch pillows, mattresses, and anything else to form a high jump pit. Later during my years at Berkeley High, I got down to the low 4:30s in the mile during my junior year. At that time Track & Field News guys and Payton Jordan would come out to see who was running. The Stanford All Comer meets became a regular weekend event for me. I won many a race on that sandy, dirt track at Angell Field. During my senior year and with the support of Coach Rick Hacker and my teammates I won many cross-country meets and was a serious top-5 runner in the North Coast Section cross country. During my senior track season I established Berkeley school records of 1:55.4 in the 880, 4:15.7 in the mile, and 9:22.4 in the 2-mile. Since my grades were not good enough to get into the college of my choice as a freshman, Coach Jim Bush recruited me to Fullerton JC.

I had a fabulous year at Fullerton. Coach Bush had a very gentle coaching technique and great personal charisma. I was one of his early black distance running stars and he and I got along famously. I ran 4:09.3 at the JC Championships in Modesto and our team won the meet championship. Then I received the word: I had been accepted as a transfer student to Stanford!

Stanford

Initially, I was overwhelmed by the academic excellence, traditions, and caliber of student athletes. Coach Jordan was so terrifically organized and he too had a very special charisma about him. The Farm's T&F traditions were inspirational to me. Many of these were Jordan's ideas... the locker room had a record board in it showing the top-ten runners/field event men in each event. While at Stanford, I managed to win or place high in many dual and invitational XC meets. My high water mark was twelfth in the NCAA XC Championships in Michigan in 1964 and tenth in 1965, both good enough to earn me All-American status. One workout I will never forget is when Coach had me do a two-mile warm up, run some 100 yard strides, and then four 880s with a one lap jog rest between each 880 at the times of 2:00, 1:59, 1:58, and 1:58...and then a half-mile warm down. I know I should have broken 4:00.00 in the mile but the best I did while at Stanford was 4:01.5. I ended my Stanford career with PAC-8 victories in the steeplechase, and one and three-mile.

Under Coach Jordan I learned the importance of discipline, work ethic, fair play, being organized, and treating everyone the same. There were very few black athletes on Stanford teams at the time, but I always was treated as a key player. Jordan is the model of the Coach's Coach. As I think back I think about the team meeting before the big meets, I think about the bus rides to the meets, I think about the feeling of enormous pride that comes over me even today for having attended Stanford and had the privilege of being coached by some of the best at each stage of my development: Hacker, Bush, Jordan. I think about Coach Jordan preparing us mentally and physically. His media guides and his printed write-ups all inspired me to be a better runner.

Post-Stanford
I had been in Air Force ROTC while at Stanford so after graduation I entered active duty as an officer. Later I tried out for the 1968 USA Olympic team and ran my first and only marathon in L.A. on a flat course in a perfect day in 1968. To my surprise I ran 2:34.30 and came in eighth. I often wonder what I could have done with that distance had I continued.

I left the Air Force in 1969 with my Captain's Bars and a Masters Degree in International Relations from USC. I joined IBM and stayed with them for 25 years. I ran in many Corporate Relays but in the mid 70s moved into tennis, biking and jogging.

Bob McIntyre
Pre-Stanford
I started running in my senior year of high school and was the state 440-yd. champion and record holder. Stanford contacted me after the victory with an offer of a track scholarship.

Stanford
While at Stanford I was co-captain of the freshman team, ran the 100, 220, 440, relays, and long jump, received the Iron Man award during my junior year, and as a senior was an AAU All-American and part of the Stanford world record 440-yard relay team. Sadly, that was the only meet my father didn't attend.

Post-Stanford
After Sanford I attended the University of Oregon Medical School, anesthesia training, the Air Force, then an anesthesia practice in Medford, OR for 28 years, then retired in 2002. In 1968, I married a wonderful woman named Heather MacDonald from Canada. We have spent most of our 36 years together in Southern Oregon and have been blessed with two sons and three grandchildren.

I tried to use some of Coach Jordan's techniques during the early years of my medical practice, when I could make the time. I was an assistant coach for a local girl's high school team and a Catholic youth team in Dayton, OH. These years gave me a sense of accomplishment in a small way and made me realize how wonderful Coach Jordan must have felt to see his "guys" do well.

In 1978 I began running distance races for fun. The local half-marathon attracted my attention when Olympic Champion Frank Shorter ran...so I ran in the race. I ended up competing in ten of the 13 milers and two full marathons before deciding to leave the distance races to those who were better suited.

At age 40 I began to work out on the track with some friends with an idea to participate in Masters events. As a group we decided to try the decathlon. I won the Southern Oregon Decathlon 5 years, and then took second in the National Decathlon with 5680 pts. Along the way, I won the National long jump championship when it was held in Eugene, Oregon.

Reflections on Jordan

What can I say about Coach Jordan that hasn't been said? He had an ability to get the most out of everyone on his teams. Coach Jordan was for me an inspiration as a coach, athlete and as a person. I occasionally met him during Masters track meets. He was always upbeat and graciously wanting to know all about my family and me. Mind you, he usually set age group world records at those meets...it was most impressive!
I remember some Coach Jordan quotes such as: "...very rarely do you have a chance to be the best in the world at anything...this is one of those times". Another one, "to run faster you must run easier and more relaxed."

Some other great memories of Coach Jordan were times we spent as a team at his house in Los Altos. He would show us some of his awards, medals and watches and later his fighting cocks. I think he thought his chickens fought harder than we ever did!

Larry Questad

See Chapter "Stanford Years — 1962 through 1967", section "An Olympic sprinter in development: Larry Questad." Following graduation from Stanford, Larry attended graduate school at the University of Southern California, where he received his MBA in 1968. Here he made the decision to give his Olympic dream one more try. Larry worked out a training schedule with the USC track team and began training for the 1968 Olympics. The rest is history. Larry made the team and competed in the 200-meter dash in Mexico City. He made it to the finals, where he placed sixth. USA teammates Tommie Smith took the gold medal in a world record time and John Carlos the bronze.

After the Olympic Games Larry went to work for IBM and retired 26 years later. In 1972 he married Elizabeth and they have two sons: Christian and P.L. Christian is a professional engineer in Denver and P.L. works with Larry at Superior Steel Products, an Idaho company that Larry bought after retiring from IBM. Since retiring from running Larry has been honored in many ways including induction into the Montana High

School Athletic Hall of Fame, Stanford Athletic Hall of Fame, and *Sports Illustrated* "Top 100" Athletes of the Century. All of this with the only "stimulants" being desire and good coaching!

Weymouth Kirkland

High School

New Trier Township High School in Winnetka, IL has about 4000 students and was loaded with great athletes (national and world record holding swimmers, all-state football players, and wrestlers). Having gone out for football my freshman year and being relegated to the third string, I decided to try cross-country the fall of my sophomore year. I had run a decent 2:09 on the freshman track team the previous spring, so I had high hopes that I'd do well in cross-country. It was an amazing season. I went undefeated on the sophomore team and was given a chance to join the varsity squad for the state-qualifying meet. I totally surprised myself by winning the race and qualifying for the state meet. Unfortunately I was the only qualifier on my team and felt rather nervous heading to the State meet. After tripping in the first hundred yards I leapt back into action and somehow caught up with and passed all of the other runners by the 3/4 mark of the 1.95-mile course. A couple of runners passed me on an uphill stretch but I recovered and held on for second place. That was one of the most exciting races of my life, even more so than my winning efforts the following two seasons. In track I placed second in the state in the mile my junior and senior years. Both years someone managed to out-kick me, a phenomenon that would occur on a regular basis when I joined the Stanford track team. It was becoming apparent to me that I did better at longer distances.

Stanford

Although I had applied to three colleges (Princeton, Brown, and Duke), none particularly appealed to me as a place to test my metal as a runner, which is where my heart was at that time. As a devotee of *Track & Field News* I knew that California was the track Mecca of our nation. So, it was off to the "farm" for me. This was an exciting time for Stanford cross country. Coach Jordan had recruited three state champion distance runners and several high placers to complement upperclassmen Rich Klier, John Northway, Robin Ruble and Bill Pratt.

I was stoked on November 7, 1961, when I went down to breakfast at the Wilbur Hall cafeteria, opened the *Stanford Daily* and saw the headline "Kirkland Paces Harriers." Fellow Illinois transplant Dave Stineback, Paul Schlicke, and Harlan Andrews were right behind me that season of 1961. Nobody told us at the time that due to NCAA rules by running on the varsity as freshman we made ourselves ineligible to run in the NCAA Championships as seniors, when we were probably the strongest team in the country.

Some of the more fun training runs (is that an oxymoron?) while at the Farm were up in the hills around Woodside dodging along mountain paths. We sometimes paid a price for those runs. I recall a bunch of us gathering in somebody's room at Stern Hall with needles, gauze and alcohol where we broke open our itching poison oak blisters thinking this would cause them to dry up and stop itching more quickly. Sounds a little kinky perhaps, but it felt SO GOOD and it might actually have worked.

Some key additions to our cross country team in 1962 were JC transfers Harry McCalla and Bob Miltz and Oregon state high school mile (4:12) and half-mile champ Dave Deubner. Both the team and I individually won the West Coast Championships that season. My biggest disappointment while running cross-country for Stanford was that our team never got to compete in the NCAA championships held every year at East Lansing, Michigan. I am personally convinced we'd have dueled with our archrival San Jose State for the top spot in any of the four years I was there. Hey, but back then the Stanford cross-country team didn't even merit a photo in the yearbook. In 1963 Harry McCalla and I were scheduled to go to the NCAA meet, but President Kennedy was assassinated the day before our trip and our plans were cancelled. My junior and senior years I received the "Bert Nelson Award" for Most Valuable Runner. I think I shared it with Harry McCalla my junior year.

In Track & Field I managed to stay healthy my sophomore season (1963) and placed fourth in the NCAA 3-mile championships held at the U of New Mexico that year. Paul Schlicke placed seventh in that race.

My relationship with Coach Jordan was always great. I enjoyed those bus trips to various meets when Coach would relax with us and just shoot the breeze. He was always supportive of me not only when I was winning but also during difficult times when I would seek his private counsel and when I graduated and needed to find a job. To this day on my webpage there is a quote from Coach Jordan under a photo of me breaking the tape in the 1965 Big Meet 2-mile. I haven't been in touch with him for many years, but he is still a living presence in my life.

Post-Stanford
I joined the Navy and served on a coastal minesweeper in Vietnam. Following my discharge in 1969 I married Mary Lu Downing and soon became the father of daughter Amanda. I took a job as a salesman in San Francisco and moved to Marin County to raise a family. We moved to Sonoma County in 1977 and built a house on six acres in Occidental. This was the peak of the distance running craze that took over the nation. I began training again to see if I could still do my thing. I'm pretty sure I was the fastest 36-year-old pack-a-day smoker in the nation with a 32:03 10,000 meters (3rd place sub-masters finish at the 1979 National Diet-Pepsi 10K Championships in Purchase, New York) and a 49:14 15K (National Postal 15K Champion of 1979). Old injuries put an end to my second running career at about the time second daughter Laurel was born in 1980. Since then I walk the dog and play some golf for exercise. Oh, and I eventually did kick the smoking habit I picked up in the Navy.

A divorce took the wind out of my sails for a while in the mid-80s. I took a course in videography at the local junior college and got the opportunity to work in the department as the video editing lab supervisor. I eventually went back to insurance sales for another five years. During that time I flew back to my 25th high school reunion, where I met fellow Class of 1961 alum Margot Grimmer. Margot and I are 17 years into our marriage, now, and thoroughly enjoying raising our 16-year-old daughter.

Harlan Andrews

The Early Years

I grew up on a farm in Eugene, Oregon. There were not enough neighbors for team sports, so my sports activities tended to be individual activities like swimming and track. In those days track and field was big in Eugene because of Bill Bowerman and the University of Oregon runners. I lived right across the Mackenzie River from Mr. Bowerman, and his son, Jay, was one of my best friends. We spent many happy hours swimming and running on the mountain where they lived.

My first aspirations in track were as a pole vaulter. My father got me a bamboo pole and helped me build a pole vault pit. In junior high school I tried out for the team and had some minor success. I cleared 10 feet, but never improved much after that. In my ninth grade year, Eugene added a new event to the track program - the mile run. The coach had tryouts for the mile spot and I won the job. Since my pole vaulting was not getting off the ground, I became a miler. That year I won the city competition with a time of 5:03.

High School

My coach at North Eugene High, Bob Newland, mapped out a three-year plan for me to win the State Meet in the mile. Cross country was part of the plan. I won the State Championship in Cross Country as a junior, but I developed a stress fracture in the process. The walking cast slowed me down for a while. By track season my foot was OK again and I continued to run the mile and 880. I won most of the meets, but was unable to defeat the Springfield runner, Fred Dellinger. The State Meet was held in Portland that year and my school sent two representatives: Bob Graham in the shot put and me in the mile and 880. We won all three events to take the State Title. Strangely, the next year my high school won the same 3 events. Dave Deubner won the mile and 880 and Neil Steinhour won the shot put. Dave then joined us at Stanford.

After winning the state mile (with a time of 4:16), I was invited to the "Golden West Meet" in the Mile Run. This event included the best runners from all over the country. Unfortunately, while training for this meet, I broke my other foot and was unable to participate.

Stanford

As an A student, there was a chance I could get into Stanford. Bill Bowerman (Oregon track coach) wrote one of my recommendation letters and sent a personal letter to Payton on my behalf. Even though Bill and Payton were rival coaches, it was a friendly rivalry and I am grateful that Bill had my best interests at heart.

When I arrived at Stanford, I found a lot of really good runners in our freshman class. Paul Schlicke (the Washington State mile champion), Weym Kirkland (the Illinois State mile champion), Dave Steinbeck (second to Weym in the Illinois mile), and Dave Beck (a finalist in the California State meet). Harry McCalla was a year ahead of us, but he let us run with him anyway. We were to spend hundreds of hours training together.

I ran the ¾-mile in our distance medley relay team, which set a national freshman record. My best time in the mile was 4:06 and my best 880 time was 1:49.2 . All in all, my track career was very enjoyable but not spectacular.

After Stanford
During my senior year at Stanford I was working 20 hours per week at Hewlett-Packard. After graduation I continued there full-time. Work was interesting and demanding. It left little time for running. Before I knew it, I had gained 30 pounds and my running career was over.

About that time I met Carol, my wife to be. We were married in 1968 and are still very happy together. I have a daughter named Monique and a son named Brad. Both are great kids. I feel very lucky to have such a nice family.

I stayed at Hewlett Packard for 7 years, including 2 years in Geneva, Switzerland. Then I worked at BTI Computer Systems for another 7 years. (I must have had the 7-year itch). I have been at Apple Computer since then and I'm still enjoying work here.

About Payton Jordan
Payton was always an inspiration to us - as a person and as a coach. I remember he used to work out along with the sprinters. He was in great shape. He gave inspiring pep talks and worked with us individually to create and achieve our goals. He always encouraged us to work hard in our studies as well as on the field. When we traveled, he reminded us that we were representing Stanford. We should dress well and walk tall.

George Porter
I went out for track at C.E. Byrd High School in Shreveport, Louisiana in 1961 to get in shape for baseball. I was a pretty good pitcher and catcher in American Legion ball. Woody Turner, Byrd's perennial State Championship Track Coach back then, told me to try all the events and he'd let me know my sport in a week or two. Afterwards, he told me that I was too slow to run, too weak to throw and to just stay out of his way and I'd be OK. Oh, but if I quit track to go out for baseball, he would give me an F in his class!

He did say I could toss the javelin after school if I didn't hurt anybody. The first week I threw the wooden spear 168 feet and broke the school record! Woody gave me an old tracksuit and said I was his new javelin thrower. I started going to meets with our track team, then the reigning Louisiana State Champions.

The next year I threw 203 feet and set the Byrd High School record again, becoming the first junior in Louisiana history to throw over 200 feet. That year, Ed Red, who later went on to become a US Olympic javelin thrower in 1964, set the Louisiana state high school record at 214 feet, a mark I bettered in the Louisiana State Championships in 1962. In 1962 I set and held the Louisiana State High School record for the javelin... for 15 minutes until Delmon McNabb threw a foot or so farther and took the gold. My character was under construction!

To my delight and I think to Coach Woody Turner's amazement, in the summer of 1962 I got 11 college scholarship offers and 3 US Military Academy appointments. I accepted a grant-in-aide offer from Stanford, which proved to have been a great decision!

At Stanford I set a freshman record at about 220. In the next three years I threw 244' 10", leaving Art Batchelder with the school record by less than a foot or two. Humbling it was, but also a character building experience, or so I was told.

Over the next two years I attended USC's MBA program, graduated in 1968, and worked for TRW. I remained friends with Ed Red by then an Olympian. In a practice session at UCLA one day, Ed showed me a technique improvement that added twenty feet to my distances. From the 240s in a week, I was throwing in the 250s and 260s in practice, effortlessly! I started visualizing the Mexico City Games!

In 1968 at an all comers meet in Pasadena I threw in open competition against Ed Red, Larry Stewart and several other aspiring Olympic hopefuls, there tuning for the Olympic trails....and I won.

The LA times wrote me up as the "Southern California Track and Field Athlete of the Week" (in very small type) the next day! The 1968 Olympic trials in the USC Coliseum were just 30 days away. What I didn't realize then was that I had already pulled a groin muscle in Pasadena which would place me in the stands at the Olympic trials watching someone else place third on the US Olympic Team in the Javelin with a throw that day of 230 feet! My character exploded with disappointment! I hung up my spikes for 20 years.

Memorable Experiences
The next time I picked up a spear was in 1988 in Los Angeles, when Hal Connelly, an Olympic hammer thrower I worked out with at the Santa Monica Body Builders' Gym, talked me into competing in an 'All Comers' meet against the local Junior College talent. Then, at 44 years of age, I was in the best shape of my post-Stanford life physically and thought, why not? The answer follows quickly.

My first throw that day in the All Comers meet was a flat footed 168 feet (high school frosh mark), to get on the field and qualify for the finals. Seems I didn't have the 'new kind' of javelin boots with short spikes to use on the 'composition rubber runway' so I had to throw in warm ups. (In our day, real javelin men threw on dirt with 4-inch spikes...but not that day!) On my second throw I hyper-extended my left knee when my flats skidded, and stuck on the surface, ripping the back of my left cruciate ligament to shreds. Still, I came in second, was awarded a silver medal, and another dose of character.

Ironically, a TV reporter wanted to interview me, and the kid that beat me that day. She asked me on camera, when was the last time I had thrown the javelin? I asked the young man that had narrowly beaten me that day, when he was born then I told them that coincidentally, the last time I had thrown a javelin was the same year he was born, 1968!

Thus ended an inauspicious but character building javelin career that produced many great memories of Coach Jordan, many good friends, an abundance of character...and an occasional limp!

Most memorable thing Coach Jordan ever said to me - or the Team.
"George, never forget you are a champion...and don't cock your wrist!"

Post Stanford
After Stanford I worked for TRW for almost 10 years and became the Director of Management Information Services for the Industrial Operations Group. In 1978 I founded Custom Application Systems, Inc. in Los Angeles and became the largest HP Value-Added Reseller in Southern California. I was President of that company for 13 years. In 1986 I founded the Brentwood Consulting Group, Specialists in Strategic Marketing, which led me to Portland, Oregon, where I worked as a Consultant and later senior Manager for Intel until 1998. I worked for Sequent Computers for three years until they were acquired by IBM. Then I became a senior Project Manager for Wells Fargo Bank.

My wife Anna Louise is a Canadian citizen with a Psychology degree from the University of Toronto. Presently Anna is pursuing a second BA in fine art. We have an amazing talented and gifted daughter, Christina Lynn, (Chrissy), who is a straight A+ student in Middle School, an accomplished pianist, classical guitarist, level 5+ gymnast, jazz and hip hop dancer and emerging equestrian eventer, who owns her own 4 year old thoroughbred racehorse and jumper, a grandson of Seattle Slew. The Olympic dream lives on with Chrissy, whom I remind from time to time, "Never forget you are a champion!"

Coach Jordan's influence
"You can achieve anything for which you are willing to pay the price!"

Chuck Smith
Athletic Accomplishments
At South Torrance high school in Los Angeles, I was basically a high jumper, hurdler, and a sometime relay person during my first two years. I started to vault in my junior year because it looked like fun (somehow, falling into an old style, hard pack saw dust pit doesn't sound very appealing these days). After clearing 10'3" my first year, on a steel pole, I graduated to the new fiberglass pole (an old, green Skypole), and managed to do 12'10" my senior year. Not a particularly good height relative to my peers, I didn't expect much interest in my athletic prowess from colleges. However, as I was sweating out where I would go to college (Cal, UCLA, or Stanford), I got a call from Coach Jordan to explore whether I would be interested in vaulting at Stanford. He apparently had talked with my high school coach, Dick Scully, who had touted me as a late bloomer. I was thrilled to have Coach Jordan interested in me, and stammered something that passed for yes. I never knew if Coach pulled some strings with admissions, but it didn't matter-I was going to go to Stanford and vault!

My freshman year looked like a big challenge, since Coach Jordan had also recruited George and Dave Bardsley, from Palo Alto High School, where they each had vaulted 14'0". However, over the summer, I got faster and stronger and at the Big Meet with Cal managed to vault 14'8", a freshman record (which Jim Eshelman broke a year later). My sophomore year I managed to do 15'4" during the season, and 15'6" in the Pac-8 (as it was back then). I qualified for the NCAA meet, but finished back in the pack-behind the winner, John Uelses, who was first to vault 16 feet. I won the "Dink Templeton Award," for the most improved field athlete-an award I am still proud of.

My junior year started out well, reaching 15'8 ½" early in the season against UCLA in Stanford Stadium, and just missing 16'0". The next week I was entered in the Coliseum Relays in LA, and on a practice vault I felt (and heard) something pop in my left leg-I had torn my hamstring really badly which proved to be a season-ending injury. Although I was disappointed - heck, totally depressed after the hamstring pull - Coach Jordan was always very supportive. He was always so damn positive that I could get back to where I was before the injury, that I had to keep trying. A couple of times I almost quit the team, but Coach wouldn't have any part of that.

After a summer of rehabilitation, I came back to Stanford for my senior year, but never could regain the speed and leg strength to vault more than 15'6" again. But I had a great seat from which to watch my teammate, Jim Eshelman, push well over 16'0". I was glad I persevered, and have great memories of that year.

After graduation in 1966, I entered graduate school at Stanford, eventually getting a PhD in mechanical engineering. After letting athletic endeavors lapse for a couple of years, I got interested in the decathlon, and spent 1968-70 learning a few new events, and getting in shape to compete. I had a few pretty successful competitions, my best being a 6700-point outing, which won an AAU southern section championship in 1971 in LA. While working out for the decathlon, my leg had gotten stronger, and I managed to clear 16'4" in an LA All Comers meet.

After taking an appointment as an assistant professor at Purdue University in Indiana in 1971, I continued to compete sporadically in the decathlon and pole vault at All Comers meets in Indiana-never achieving any PRs, but having fun until about 1975.

In 1978 I moved to Lehigh University in Bethlehem, Pennsylvania. Later, one day in 1984, I got the urge to vault again (I happened to have two old poles I carried with me through the years). So at the age of 40, I started vaulting again, with the intent of competing in Masters Meets. I managed to make 14'6", and felt I was on my way to aging glory, when the other end of my body-my right tricep-popped, and I was permanently rendered an ex-pole vaulter.

Memorable Experiences

- The "affirmations" that Coach Jordan urged us to recite, I remember one: "I love to run long distances through open fields".
- The astronaut drink (a mixture of essential nutrients, which tasted just awful) that Coach Jordan gave the vaulters to drink, with the idea that we would weigh less

since all the food bulk would be gone from our body-we lasted about two days on that concoction. [Contestants on "Fear Factor" would be challenged by that stuff today]

- The inane commentary of Jess Bova (the assistant coach)-and the mimicking spoof of Jess by Bob Stoecker [those who were on the team during the Bova tenure know to this day why one must take care with drinking fountains].
- Standing out in the discus area and shagging 230' discus throws when Dave Weil and the Czech world record holder (Ludvik Danek) had an informal "practice."
- Watching Steve Cortright psyche out and beat Mel Renfro of Oregon in the high hurdles at Stanford Stadium in 1963-Renfro had previously run 0.5 seconds faster than Steve!
- Watching the sun set at the end of practice at Angell Field.

Most Memorable Thing Coach Jordan Said to Me — or the Team
"You need three things to be a great pole vaulter: The speed of a sprinter, the strength of a weight lifter, and the agility of a gymnast. You got 'em, Smitty, and you can be that vaulter."

Post-athletic Biographical Information
In 1969, I met a young woman from St. Louis, Christine Donohue, attending summer school at Stanford, and we were married in 1970. She works in university development (those folks who pester you for money), and after a successful career at Lehigh, she is now an assistant vice president for development at Georgetown University. Yes, the Georgetown in Washington, D.C.-we have had (for the last six years) a commuter marriage (she is there during the week), which seems to work.

We have two sons, Brian (31) and Christopher (27), who both live and work in Tampa, Florida. Both were great athletes, but had no interest in pole vaulting (darn).
A surfer, as well as a pole vaulter, in my younger years, I gave surfing up when I was stranded in Indiana. However, my brother [Steve Smith-a world record holder in the indoor vault in the 70s] got me interested in surfing again, and I have been back surfing in exotic places for the past 13 years.

Coach helped me learn to believe in myself, and to know that I could compete and win against anyone-and that quitting is not an option. I have applied that philosophy throughout my life, and it always works.

And maybe I can't pole vault anymore, but I never doubt that there is anything I can't do or overcome if I set my mind to it. Thanks, Coach.

1967

Jim Eshelman

Pre-Stanford
I started vaulting in sixth grade in my back yard in Palo Alto, using a thick stick for a vaulting pole and neighborhood kids holding up a slimmer stick as a crossbar. In eighth grade I began competition using a steel pole. My heights progressed and I acquired my first fiberglass pole as a junior. By my senior year I had done 14'1", which made me

attractive to college track programs. I originally accepted at MIT but a constructive talk with Coach Jordan led to a change to Stanford. Also, the realization that outdoor workouts were going to be limited in Boston and the fact that I had already bested MIT's school record by a large margin, were contributing factors.

Stanford

Freshman year went well, reaching 15'0" for a new Stanford freshman record. We were still using sawdust vaulting pits at the start of the year, though Dick Barkley soon came across a supply of foam scraps which, with some netting, we fashioned into a "modern" foam pit. Sophomore year I reaped the benefit of Coach Jordan's 1964 Olympic Team experience working with Fred Hanson, the vault gold medal winner. Coach Jordan was able to pass on to me a number of Fred's techniques. I won the AAWU Conference championship that year at 16'0 ¼", primarily because of that technique coaching. Junior year I progressed to about 16'6". During senior year I was trying to get onto a heavier pole - one rated at 175 pounds and I weighed 145. If I could get the energy into the pole with increased speed and strength, getting it back out with the right gymnastics timing would do the trick. It all came together at the Golden Gate Invitational indoor meet at the Cow Palace in San Francisco. I won the meet with 16'10 ½". At that time, it was the second-best world indoor height ever.

One of the first outdoor meets my senior year was the Santa Barbara Easter Relays. As it turned out, when the bar was set at 17'0", I cleared on my first jump!! That was the first collegiate vaulter over 17 feet outdoors (Seagren already had done it indoors) and only the seventh vaulter over 17 feet. Seagren and Wilson of USC also cleared the height so it became the first meet that three vaulters had cleared 17'0". Seagren was the only one to clear the next height of 17'4", then the controversy began. It turned out that the take-off point on the runway was ¾" higher than the vault box because the runway had been resurfaced. So the meet officials deducted that ¾" from all of the heights - leaving me with a vault of 16'11 ¼", which stood as the Stanford record for 20 years.

Post-Stanford

During my Army tour I was able to become a member of the Army Track Team, representing them in many meets, two foreign trips, and the 1968 Olympic Trials. I achieved a "real" 17'0" jump in the summer of 1971 in what I thought would be preparation for the 1972 Olympic Trials. Realization that my heights were not up to snuff for the competition level required for the Games led to the effective end of an enjoyable vault career.

I traveled around the world twice then finally settled into what would become my career - Computer Software Development. Lisa and I married in 1976, and when the Bay Area got too "busy" for us in 1982, we moved to the back woods of New Hampshire. I spent some time building our own house, and then returned to computers. I have been with The Echo Group for the last 12 years. We write software for non-profit behavioral health organizations.

Lisa has worked as a Registered Nurse and as Office Manager for some doctor's offices. She currently works at a children's toy store. We have a son, Evan, and a daughter,

Anna. Evan, a high school senior, is now looking at colleges - and Anna, a junior, is benefiting from his search experiences. Both kids are strong and accomplished in academics, athletics, music, theater, and arts.

Coach Jordan's Influence
Have goals - work hard to achieve them - overcome any obstacles that may get in the way. I have applied these lessons from Coach Jordan to most aspects of my life.

Glenn Havskjold

Pre-Stanford
At high school in Havre, Montana, I was the Montana state champion in the 100, 220, and 440, and the Montana record holder in the 440. Havre won the state championship in football two of the years that I was there, and I was an all-state halfback on that team. My high school principal encouraged me to apply and to attend Stanford - his son had been a fullback on the Stanford football team.

Stanford
My first impression of Stanford track was during some fall workouts. The weather was gorgeous (on my Montana scale of weather), but I had mononucleosis and had been in the hospital for the two weeks before coming to Stanford. Somehow I survived the workouts. I ran the 440 during my freshman, sophomore, and junior years, but I devoted my senior year to academics as I hoped to pursue a Ph.D. at Stanford. I have fond memories of my track experience, my teammates, and Coach Jordan. I recall Coach Jordan showing us a starting technique one day, and as he sprinted away from the blocks we were all impressed that the coach still had plenty of quickness and speed left in his legs.

After getting the B.S. degree, I continued at Stanford through the M.S. and Ph.D. degrees in Aeronautics and Astronautics.

Post Stanford
After finally graduating with the Ph.D., I went to the General Motors Research Laboratories in Michigan where I worked on automobile safety problems. After four winters, I left Michigan and joined the Rocketdyne Division of North American Rockwell, which later became Rockwell International, and which later was acquired by Boeing. Rocketdyne is by far the largest rocket engine company in the U.S. - all the engines that put men on the moon were made by Rocketdyne, as are the liquid propellant main engines on the Space Shuttle. Currently at Rocketdyne I write proposals to government agencies to win technology contracts, and then I manage the programs funded by the contracts. Over the years I have successfully managed over 100 programs.

While my son was in grade school from the fourth to the eighth grade, I coached a youth basketball "traveling team" in Thousand Oaks, was a member of the board that ran the youth basketball program for 1200 boys and girls in the community, and was also a member of the board that ran a youth basketball league of traveling teams encompassing eight cities across Ventura County. In those five years, the youth team that I coached won the county championship four times. The team also traveled to tournaments across Southern California and even to Las Vegas.

My daughter Marisa attended U.C. Davis, and my son David will be enrolling at Stanford this fall.

Jack Scott

Pre-Stanford
Growing up near the Villanova campus I got to know and train during the summer with some of their great track athletes (e.g., Rolando Cruz). I attended and competed for Penn State for two years, then transferred to Stanford.

Stanford
So this is California! Shortly after arriving I went to see Coach Jordan, who couldn't have made me feel more welcomed. He introduced me to Stanford's great pole vaulter, Jim Eshelman, and I felt at ease in what otherwise was a pretty intimidating environment. My recollection of the two years under Coach Jordan's influence was how encouraging he was towards not just the great athletes but equally so towards us not-so-great athletes. He taught us all to push ourselves to the limit and reach for possibilities, not just on the track but also in the classroom and life in general.

Post-Stanford
After Stanford I spent three years in the Navy, most of the time at Guantanamo Bay, Cuba. I competed in the 1969 Armed Forces Track & Field Championships, where I ran into my ole Stanford friend, Jim Eshelman, who represented the Army. After grad school at the University of Pennsylvania I began a career with DuPont (now retired). During the 1984 Olympics I had a great volunteer position working right in the Coliseum. Over the decades as everyone became a "runner" I ran some marathons. This gave me greater empathy for distance runners and the realization I should have taken up tennis and golf much earlier. Maggie and I have been married 35 years with two sons and live in Kennett Square, PA. Our older son, David, was a Navy SEAL officer (9 years), who tragically died in an accident while deployed overseas in October 2002. Our younger son, Michael, lives and works in Greenville, SC.

Bob Stoecker

I had the pleasure of competing for Payton Jordan at Stanford University from 1962 through 1966. Payton was then, and still is an incredibly inspirational man who brought out the best in his athletes. My high school coach, Leo Long, is a close friend of Payton and was a NCAA champion javelin thrower at Stanford. So, my coaching experience couldn't have been better.

While Payton coached me to All-American status two years in a row, and first place at the Berkeley NCAAs, what I remember about him the most was his dedication to the life style of an athlete. Payton lived it himself as the consummate example of not just "talking the talk," but he "walked the walk" 24 hours a day - and still does.

During my freshman year at Stanford Payton had me write a research paper on the effects of using steroids to enhance performance. He wanted me to learn how steroids could hurt my body. But most importantly, how it gave what he considered and unfair advantage. In those days many weight throwers used steroids, and of course this year's

2004 Olympics has been clouded by drug controversy. Payton was, as always, way ahead of the game with his clear image of the student athlete and the life style that dedication to sports should embody.

Bud Walsh

Introduction to Stanford

My first introduction to Stanford came with a visit from Stanford football coaches recruiting for new coach John Ralston in 1962. I grew up in Coos Bay, Oregon, a place not then known for track. But Marshfield High School had one of the best records in the State of Oregon in football and basketball. Marv Harris, an All-American linebacker then at Stanford, was one of the more successful alumni of Marshfield; Mel Counts, an All-American basketball player who attended Oregon State, also attended Marshfield. Later, however, one of my brother's friends, Steve Prefontaine, would bring track world focus to Coos Bay when he set the American high school two-mile record. We all know about Steve, one of the greatest track athletes in American history. His loss was a great tragedy. Walt McClure was our high school coach.

My football coach, Pete Susick, recommended that Stanford consider me for the football team. I was a halfback and defensive back. However, I had been injured and only played three games my senior year, one in which I gained 279 yards and scored on a 92 yard run but two in which I was injured. I also played guard on the basketball team, which had finished second in the State tournament in 1962. But I was certainly not what is called today a "Super-Prep" athlete in any sport.

During my recruiting visit to Stanford Spring Break 1963, I was, to say the least, overwhelmed, particularly by the facilities, the people I met, and the weather (I had never been to California before). I met Payton Jordan during the visit after expressing an interest in running track to the football coaches. I had finished fifth in the State in the 180 low hurdles in 1962. Payton, ironically, was meeting with the coach of the Oregon State track team when I entered his office for an introduction. As of that moment, my mind was made up and I wanted to be on the track team at Stanford, not play football.

Neither of my parents had been to college, and I had five brothers and a sister. My father told me that he could not afford college for any of us (at that time) and that I had to find some way to pay for the education myself. It was a life-changing day when I received my admission to Stanford, along with a David Starr Jordan Scholarship in April 1963. Payton Jordan had put in a good word for me. With this incredible motivation, I won both the high and low hurdle Oregon championships, the first to do so since Mel Renfro, the Oregon track and football star. Congratulating me afterwards was the Oregon State coach I had met at Stanford. We both enjoyed the coincidence of our second meeting.

It rained in Oregon almost all the time, not my cup of tea. Plus Bill Bowerman at Oregon was not interested. Thus, a life-time opportunity now opened up for me at Stanford, because of Payton Jordan. I later counted myself lucky that Bowerman was not interested. When I was a sophomore, we competed against Oregon and one of my acquaintances on the Duck Track Team expressed his doubts about the Oregon "system." To stay on scholarship, he needed to run a certain time, fairly regularly, or lose his scholarship. Bowerman picked the time. You lost the scholarship and, if you had no other source of income, you had to drop out of school. Education was not primary in that system. With my scholarship, so long as I made a bona fide effort at making the team and kept my grades at a passing level, I had a full four years at Stanford (I also had to "hash" at a women's dorm to pay some costs). The Stanford system freed one to focus on doing well.

Those Enjoyable Stanford Years
It is difficult (and perhaps impolitic) to explain to others what a tremendous place Stanford is and how terrific the athletic program can be. I know my Stanford colleagues who read this will generally agree, but then we all shared similar experiences. What Payton taught, even made routine, were those qualities of success that work well anywhere - in sports, business, public service, wherever. He started with a high level of careful organization, taught hard work and preparation, offered very skilled technical guidance, and, most of all, gave constant positive (but honest) reinforcement. Surrounded by motivated and successful students-athletes, coaches, and teachers, participating at a high level in Stanford athletics did seem routine - especially with the high level of competition we experienced.

I remember a freshman year track meet in particular. I was changing shoes for some event and I looked over to the back stretch of the 440 (yards in those days, remember). I noticed this tall, powerful black runner for San Jose State leading everyone by a considerable distance. I leaned over to someone and said "Who the hell is that?" Tommie Smith was the answer. He ran 46.5 that day. I watched or competed against him for four years. The most memorable experience was the day Larry Questad beat Tommie to the finish line in the 440 relay in the world-record beating time of 39.7 in 1965. Awesome. A few weeks later, when I filled in on the third leg, we lost to Tommie and San Jose but ran 40.1 to their 40.0.

Payton made us feel we could keep up with any competition and our teams were very competitive, although for two years in a row we lost dual meets to USC after losing the mile relay: 75-70. Too bad those great dual meets are no longer the staple of college track & field. And, of course, I will always remember that I ran a relay leg against the now infamous O.J. Simpson. Making friends with other athletes, even the great ones-Ralph Boston, Earl McCullough, Dave Williams, Phil Shinnick and many others-was easy in those days.

I certainly performed at a higher level than I ever expected coming out of high school. I participated in 3 NCAA championships, finishing fifth in the 440 relay in 1965 and fifth in the long jump in 1966. I was ranked second in the NCAA in the long jump in 1967 (25'2") but did not get a distance in the finals at the championship because of an injury suffered when winning the Pac-8 long jump title. I was in second place after the qualifying round. In 1965, even though I ran in the NCAA 440 relay final at Berkeley, I was filling in for an injured Questad on the last leg. Given a relatively large lead by Bob McIntyre, Eric Frische and Dale Rubin, I was nonetheless easily overtaken by Tommie Smith, Charlie Green, and some others down the stretch. I learned my limits that day, but Coach (charitably) said I did just fine.

I am proud of what I did at Stanford, accomplishments that I owe to Payton Jordan: I tied the school record in the 440 hurdles (52.3) as a sophomore, set the school pentathlon record, and won the Iron Man award for most points scored three years in a row. I also high jumped 6'6." My fastest high hurdle time for 120 yards was 14.1. At the University of Washington meet my senior year, Coach wanted me to enter the pole vault because all our vaulters were injured that meet. He wanted to put pressure on the two U of W. vaulters, and one of them failed to make the opening height! We had a good laugh about that one.

In 1967, Track & Field News ranked me fourth in the country in the decathlon for the Mexico City Olympics. That year, however, would mark the peak of my athletic career. I take note of the fact that if one finishes in top places (at least 1 through 6) in the NCAA finals, one is made an All-American. In the 60s, only the first three top finishers were named for that recognition. Oh well.

The 60s were also difficult years of social unrest and protest on campus, largely because of the Vietnam War but also because of rapid social change and civil rights issues. I never got the sense that Payton Jordan had any major difficulty in dealing with all the change going on around us all, although I am sure he had some. He tried to interact with all athletes as athletes first. No one gave him more challenge that a young sprinter from England named Pat Morrison, with his brilliant sprinting style, long curly hair, and openly socialist philosophy. I remember that UCLA coach Jim Bush used a picture of Pat as the reason one shouldn't go to Stanford. In the end, Pat did himself in with his behavior, and left the team and school. Payton suffered through the publicity and criticism as well as could be expected, which was undeserved. He always urged us to keep our eyes on our goals, which is very good advice indeed for all of life.

Post-Stanford

I entered the University of Washington Law School in 1967. Faced with the draft, I also joined ROTC but later only served 90 days for training as the Vietnam War wound down. After my first year of law school, spurred by the Mexico City Olympics where Payton was the head track coach, I started to train with the U of W track team, which I did for two years. Ken Shannon was the coach. I got to compete with Jim Seymour, who finished fourth in the intermediate hurdles at the Munich Games. But it was clear that a full-time commitment would be needed to be anywhere close to competitive for Munich. So I stopped training with the track team. I got my J.D. from the U of W in 1970, then an LL.M. in 1971. I became a lawyer instead.

I did not stay in touch with Payton after moving to Washington, D.C. in 1972, where I lived with my wife and three children until 1996. However, in my job as staff counsel of the U.S. Senate Committee on Commerce, Science and Transportation, I was assigned to handle legislation in the mid-1970s that addressed the long-festering fight between the AAU and the NCAA. I worked for the Chairman, Senator Warren Magnuson from Washington State, but he was not taking the lead. He had previously tried to broker a solution in the past, which also involved the International Olympic Committee, then led by Avery Brundage. The arbitration that resulted from his effort came to naught, but Senator Pearson of Kansas, the home of the NCAA bureaucracy, wanted to try again.

Our effort to settle the dispute, to include an athlete's bill of rights, failed when Walter Byers of the NCAA changed his mind and decided to oppose the legislation just before Senate Floor consideration. It wasn't until 1978 that Congress passed the Amateur Sports Act that began the transition to the modern system for amateur athletics, including the Olympic development program. The lead sponsor of that legislation was Senator Ted Stevens, a Republican from Alaska who was one of the Senators I worked closest with in my days on the Senate Staff and then afterwards, as the Deputy Administrator of the National Oceanic and Atmospheric Administration under President Jimmy Carter.

During the fight over the NCAA/AAU legislation, I experienced some of the "dirtiest" lobbying of my young career. One of the NCAA lobbyists tried to smear my relationship with Payton, because I was tasked with helping push Senator Pearson's bill after Walter Byers "dictated" that all NCAA colleges oppose the bill. I even had one of my former law professors (Harry Cross) call me, as the NCAA representative for the U of W, to argue against the bill. Professor Cross, not two weeks before, had been working with me to get an acceptable bill. It was embarrassing for him to have to switch his views, to say the least. In court, such a switch would likely lose a case, or be unethical. But such was (and is) life in Washington, D.C. To his credit, Payton stayed out of it.

I caught up with Coach Jordan again when I returned in 1996. I offered to help with legal assistance if the World Championships came to Stanford. Sadly, Stanford did not get the event and Payton eventually moved to Santa Barbara-the end of an era.

Reflections
My track and field career at Stanford provided me the base for a terrific college athletic experience, a wonderful education, and the platform to an enjoyable and exciting career. I do owe Payton a deep and abiding "thank you" for the opportunities his support has given me. He certainly got me to "play over my head." The methods he taught I have used routinely and I always have believed that I could compete with the very best. It requires preparation to be ready to play in all arenas. Payton and Stanford taught me how to prepare and be confident, while keeping one's personal life in balance. Thanks so much, Coach!

1968

Roger Cox

High School
I had the good fortune to attend Redlands High School, where Coach Jordan had taught and coached many years earlier. I had some good times, winning the sprints in the Citrus Belt League and placing in CIF and State several times, so Coach Jordan's old friends in Redlands brought me to his attention. I still have the many warm and wise letters he wrote me then. He emphasized academic preparation as well as techniques for strength and conditioning. He took the time to meet me and encourage me even when I was still a high schooler. It was obvious to me that Payton Jordan was a man who would always do more to win than the next guy. A fellow named Jim Hines beat me in the State Meet, but I scored my only win over him in the 100 at the Golden West Invitational at the end of the year. That was also where I first met the illustrious Jim Ward.

Stanford

Choosing Stanford was easy in a way, because it was the best in so many ways. It was hard for the same reason. Stanford was not a place for people who were willing to be second best. You had to try in every way to live up to your own goals. There were no jock dorms, very few gut courses, and the University did not revolve around track stars. Your fellow students were stars in their own way. It was also expensive, although not in the same galaxy as today. I could not have attended without the assistance of the university, and I have to thank for that, more than any other, Payton Jordan.

On the track there were many highs and lows. I remember winning the 60 at the Seattle Indoor, the 100 at the Big Meet, beating Busby of UCLA, running at the NCAAs at Indiana and scoring points in many dual meets. There was the exhilaration of watching our 440-relay team set a world record at Fresno in 1965 with the simultaneous frustration of being a freshman and so being excluded from competing with the varsity. I would like to forget the week in the convalescent home, the broken metatarsal, and the pulled hamstrings. West Coast track was the best in the country and it was a privilege to be there competing. In 1968 the great Larry Questad went to the Olympics as did, of course, Coach Jordan. I went off to Air Force pilot training. I got together with Jim Ward and Craig Vaughan a few times the next year in Southern California and had some thoughts of running for the Striders, but I was always on a plane headed for Viet Nam when it was practice or meet time.

I wonder if anyone else remembers flying down to LA on PSA and having them snap Stony Eshelman's vault poles, and having Bruce Wilhelm's shot roll all the way back through the plane when it rotated for takeoff. Who else was in the car going to Fresno when Larry Questad said of the car ahead, "Jordan must be talking. He always slows down when he talks." Does anyone else remember Pat Morrsion's haircut? How about the riots on the Sunset strip the night after the UCLA meet, or flying across Texas in Ward's new Corvette? Did anyone ever try to get you to carry their bags when you were wearing the red coats? We got out of it once by saying we were a singing group.

Coach Jordan presided over this collection of egotists and characters with grace and determination. He hated excuses and he hated to lose. He did not care to compromise with the long hair and social changes that washed over us all in the 60s, but he was a genuine friend to every trackman who ever made an honest effort. To borrow a phrase, he was a man of clarity in a time of uncertainty. My wife Connie and I were able to attend Coach Jordan's induction into the Stanford Sports Hall of Fame. It was well deserved.

Since Then

Although I got my MBA, I've spent most of my life flying airplanes and satisfying the wanderlust. Starting with Air Force Starlifters, I started collecting islands and continents. I landed at McMurdo, flew the evacuation of Saigon, flew 707s for the Saudis and a Falcon for AT&T. Like most professional pilots my age, I've worked for a number of airlines that are no longer here. For the last 17 years I've been a Captain at America West. I also served a tour as Chairman of the Air Line Pilot's Association there. I've got a flat rear and a big hat. Surprisingly, some people who make five times what I do think I have a great job.

Mike Jacobs

Pre-Stanford

I attended Burlingame High School on the Peninsula and became interested in Cross-Country and Track my sophomore year. I visited a Stanford Cross-Country (vs. California) Meet my junior year where I saw Coach Jordan (driving his white T-Bird) boisterously cheering on Harry McCalla and the other Indian harriers. Stanford won. After that, I had my heart set on attending Stanford. I won the King City Invitational 880 my senior year in a meet record time of 1:56.8. I was then accepted into Stanford and was thrilled to receive a telegram from Coach wishing me "winning results" at the State Meet in Los Angeles. (I finished seventh but it was a great experience. One of my Seattle neighbors, Larry Arnett, finished fourth in that race. It's truly a small world.)

Stanford

It was truly an honor and privilege to attend Stanford and to run track and cross-country. I remember seeing Howie Dalmar, John Ralston, and other great coaches such as Dick Gould. I recall running 20 milers with Jack O'Brien in Los Altos Hills in the heat, returning at 6:00 P.M., and raiding the Popsicle machine due to dehydration. I remember the time that Terry Fredrickson, I, and the team manager, Steve Shalken, missed the team bus to the Fresno State meet. We took Steve's Oldsmobile 442 and he was slightly speeding at 135mph+ (Steve would you please slow down!!) until arrested by the CHP. I barely made it in time for the 880 yd. race and placed third without warming up. When the 440-yard relay team of Questad, McIntyre, Rubin, and Frische set the world record my freshman year, I was especially proud to be associated with Stanford track. I was elated when Don Kardong placed fourth in the 1976 Olympic marathon. I remember how determined we all were to succeed including Jim Ward, Jack Scott, Dave Harrington, Jim Letterer, George Porter, Bob Stoecker, Jim Eshelman, Bud Walsh, Dave Duebner, and many other teammates. My best time in the 880 was 1:52.0 when I took second in the Big Meet my junior year. Coach was always positive. Everything he did was honorable. He always played by the rules. Everyone respected Coach Jordan even those who may have disagreed with him in some fashion. He worked hard to assist all his athletes to maximize their talent. He was simply a superb mentor, the best.

Post-Stanford

After graduation I moved to Seattle and attended the University of Washington School of Law. Since that time, I have enjoyed my 33-year career as a trial lawyer. I married in 1976 to Phyllis who grew up in Cupertino. We have two children, Amy, 25, and Jeff, 22. Amy just received a patent on a storage rack and is in business. Jeff is finishing up at the University of Washington and hopes to attend law school next year. I have coached youth basketball, soccer, baseball, and softball, and served as Little League President for many years. I run every day and play a lot of tennis. I follow Stanford sports closely and support the Cardinal/Buck Club because I look back at my experience in athletics at Stanford with fondness.

Jim Letterer

Stanford Years

Coach Jordan was the key reason why I chose to attend Stanford on a track scholarship. Although he did not coach the distance runners, Coach Jordan was an inspiration to the entire track team and to me. He helped me to run 20:23 for 4.2 miles on the Stanford home cross-country course and 30:32 for 6 miles. My personal best mile was 4:06 and 9:01 for 2 miles.

I had run 4:07 for 2 straight weeks in the mile and was up against a 4:04 miler from UCLA with a great kick. Before my warm-up for the race, Coach Jordan suggested that I start my kick early to take away the finish of the UCLA runner. I felt good with 500 yards to go, so I jumped into the lead and gained 20-25 yards on my opponent with 1 lap to go. I could hear Jordan yelling, "Keep my form and pump with my arms." I held onto first place by 5 yards, finishing in my personal best of 4:06.

I remember Coach Jordan's pep talks before every track meet. His encouragement to do our best, compete fairly, and represent Stanford to the best of our abilities was terrific. But most important of all to me was Coach Jordan's personal talks with me when I was injured my sophomore year in track season. He encouraged me to get therapy every day. As I healed, he emphasized not coming back too quickly or risk re-injuring my hamstring. I did come back stronger my junior year and finished as Stanford's number one runner in cross-country and ran personal bests in track.

Post-Stanford
I have continued to run for pleasure and competition. I still enjoy competing in 5K and 10K races almost every year. Seeing pictures of Coach Jordan and his continued efforts to stay in good shape has encouraged me to continue running, lifting weights, and other cross-training activities.

For the past 20 years, I have managed regional and national sales teams in the software and technology industry. I am currently the national sales director for the Manufacturing Business Solutions Division of Cincom Systems.

Coach Jordan was one of my most positive role models in my entire life. He was a great pillar of integrity, honesty with high moral and religious values. He will forever hold my admiration and respect.

Grady Means

Athletics
My best high school hurdles time at Notre Dame High School in Sherman Oaks, California, was 14.9. League Champion, Santa Barbara Relays third place, Mount San Antonio Relays third place, State CIF Championships fourth place.

At Stanford, I ran the 120-yd. high hurdles and the 440-yd. hurdles from 1964 to 1968. My best times were 14.7 in the high hurdles and 53.5 in the 440 intermediate hurdles.

Memorable Experiences
I was recruited by Coach Jordan during my senior year of high school. He met me during the USC meet at the L.A. Coliseum. Since I had recently moved from Kansas to Hollywood, I didn't know anything about Stanford - my kids find it hard to believe that anyone could be that out of it. I was very impressed with Coach Jordan (I had seen him at the Olympics), the team, and the school.

At Stanford, the lasting impressions of Coach Jordan are support and leadership. He took a very strong interest in each athlete, from the first day of freshman year. And through good times and bad, he was a great leader - the locker room signs, "lead, follow, or get out of the way." He researched every event and was extremely helpful on the fine details of technique and training.

And he coached attitude. Who could forget visiting his home and having him compare his athletes to the fighting cocks that he raised. He said he could tell from the attitude of the boys (and the birds) how they would do from how they walked, how they held their heads, how they approached competition. He loved brave, tough attitude.

He said I could beat (Olympic team and NFL star) Earl McCullough over the first hurdle. He was wrong, but I did get my best start ever and almost caught him at the tenth hurdle and ran my best time at the Coliseum.

Post-Stanford
➤ BS/MS Engineering
➤ Staff of Stanford Business School
➤ Assistant for Domestic Policy to Vice President Rockefeller in the White House
➤ Managing Partner of Corporate Strategy Consulting, PriceWaterhouseCoopers
➤ Chairman of Financial Market Solutions, a financial software company
➤ Wrote 3 business books
➤ Lived in Washington, D.C., New York, and San Francisco
➤ Wife and two children
➤ Sail, ride Harley across the country, write

Coach Jordan's Influence
He taught preparation and winning attitude. That has served me well.

Russ Taplin

While I am more anchored to the earth now, there was a time when my feet barely touched the ground and I seemed to fly. In my dreams and in my heart I am still a sprinter, I am still racing with Andy, Roger and Jim effortlessly flying around Payton's Angell Field. The passage of time and the times no longer matter but the cherished memories of running in my youth alongside my gifted companions matters. The total elapsed time of my entire competitive career couldn't have exceeded thirty minutes, but some of those seconds have been eternal. I began my Stanford career with sheer terror and dread. Stanford was highly charged. I deeply wanted to excel as a student and as an athlete.

In trying to distill my emotional, physical and intellectual experience of my Coach into a simple core description, I simply took the first three characteristics that came to mind. Payton was superbly positive, intensely enthusiastic, and deeply kind. Not all of us were or could be record holders or super stars but all of us could continually set personal bests. Coach is an infectiously positive true believer and his persona at its core is simply and completely upbeat. Negativity had no place at Angell Field. Coach's positive approach made me believe I could reach into the self I did not know and become something that I did not know existed.

Payton had a unique way of sharing the moment with you and being genuinely enthusiastic about your own personal success. When I nearly caught the Arizona State anchorman at the tape of a 440-yard relay at the Santa Barbara Relays, Payton ran up to me like I had just set a record. While I had not, I certainly felt that I had. Similarly, at my last conference championships and the conclusion of my leg of a mile relay, Payton, with stopwatch in hand, exuberantly gave me my split time. I had just run the best quarter mile of my life, Payton knew it, and with the race still in progress brought triumph to my own personal best.

Payton also believed in the concept of team and community. Coach wanted all of us to practice together in the same area. Which is quite a trick considering that some of us were essentially tossing ancient weapons around and some of these weapons could make you do an instant imitation of a shish kabob. I was never sure that having our modern Achilles tossing their spears around Angell Field was such a great idea; one mistake and we runners could become shish kabob.

I also saw calmness under attack or extreme pressure. In 1968 Coach Jordan and Harry Edwards, a social science professor at San Jose State, were to share a podium at Stanford to discuss contributions of black athletes in America. Edwards took the opportunity to attack Jordan, the then current head USA Olympic Coach, with a vicious, blind-sided, scripted, personal attack that I felt was outrageous, degrading, demeaning, and politically motivated. Coach handled the sustained attack with calmness and dignity.

After Stanford I did volunteer community service, tutoring younger less successful students and developing tutoring opportunities for more successful older students. Subsequently, I returned to Stanford and experienced the full thrill and joy of law school. Professionally, I carved out a niche in estate law. My legal work paid the bills and I have tried to use my problem solving skills in real estate.

I have a son who I will proudly tell you has graduated from the London School of Economics and a young daughter I recently adopted from an orphanage in India.

Craig Vaughan

I entered junior high school a "P.E. Nerd"...always the last person picked to be on a team. That all changed one morning in April when my teacher explained the "running broad jump" during a track and field unit. We all lined up to have a try and, amazingly, I had a talent for it and broke the 7th, 8th and 9th grade school records on my first jump. From then on I spent most afternoons for the next twenty years getting sand in my socks and shorts. I discovered that I loved the camaraderie and routine of practice, and always another meet or season ahead.

My high school, John Muir in Pasadena, California, had an exceptional track and field program, generating dozens of nationally ranked athletes and many state championships over the years. I recall it took a 9.7 or better 100 yd. time just to make the relay team. The intense and competitive practices, along with some much needed technique work with my coach, Mr. Walter Opp, helped me to jump over 24 ft. in my junior year. Kidney surgery and a hamstring injury made improvement difficult my senior year, but much to my good fortune, Coach Opp had known Coach Jordan in Redlands and put my name in his ear. I visited Stanford during spring break and Coach Jordan graciously showed me around and was very positive and encouraging. I don't know what magic he worked or what arms he twisted but I was accepted to Stanford with financial assistance from the Buck Club and I will be forever grateful to them for making such a quality college experience possible for me.

I told Coach Jordan a few years ago that my Stanford track and field experiences were some of the very best times of some of the best years of my life, and that comment still rings true. I had never been to the Pacific Northwest before and it was a wonder to me to wake-up in Pullman my sophomore season with snow falling. Or, slogging through the Oregon rain and landing with a splash in a liquid long jump pit. Does anyone remember a bunch of us watching "George of the Jungle" in the motel before the meet? I roomed with the great Larry Questad on another away meet and remember his running out of the room yelling, "Oh, no. He's a nudie!", when he found out I slept au natural. For the home meets there were the pre-meet lunches of roast beef, peas, and mashed potatoes at the student union. For sheer horror it was trying to run a competent mile around the golf course. The highlight of the year was the Coliseum Relays were I met and competed against my hero, Ralph Boston, the world and Olympic record holder. Representing Stanford at various indoor and outdoor invitational meets, I had the opportunity to compete against the great long jumpers of the day...still one of my proudest accomplishments. I might never have done so without Coach Jordan's help. In other years I remember the ultimate agony of 150% maximum heart rate and world class oxygen deprivation sprinting up Ward's Hill; or, the simple pleasure of an after-practice orange juice bar from the vending machine in the locker rooms. All good times I wouldn't trade for anything.

I very happily have found my niche in life as a middle school teacher for the last 34 years (Los Angeles County "Educator of the Year" in 1999), a career choice cemented on Angell field. Coach Jordan would have us work the freshman meets and I loved helping, encouraging, and coaching our freshmen and their junior college competition, like Hancock. Best of all was working with the new long jumpers entering the program, like Chris Gibson, and helping them to improve and be successful. Not everything was always wonderful with Stanford track and field, however, especially when campus politics reared their ugly head. Several faculty tried to pressure me into signing some petition against Coach Jordan because of an issue with Pat Morrison. Overall, though, Angell Field was my island of calm in the turbulent 60s. Does anyone remember the great Astroturf experiment...an interesting surface to run on until you fell. Or any event Bud Walsh didn't excel in. Or, what an incredible sauna the team locker room was; I'd sweat so much in there I couldn't get my clothing on and off. And Coach Jordan's team motto, "Lead, follow, or get out of the way." Still good advice; although, I would never tell my classes, "Teach, learn, or leave." I might wind up with an empty room.

After Stanford I continued to compete, finally jumping 25 ft. for the Southern California Striders, until the end of '72 when I had to have a knee rebuilt. To rehab I started jogging and discovered the joys of "slow and long," eventually running a fair number of marathons. In another kind of distance event I took up sailing and made three trips to

Hawaii in a 27' boat, the longest time at sea being 28 days. Now, meeting my monthly mortgage and taking my kids to soccer practice is about all the adventure I get. My red blazer has long ago been consumed by moths and I haven't put on a pair of spikes in almost 30 years, but I still feel like a Stanford track and field athlete and Payton Jordan will always be "my Coach."

Jim Ward

High School
My introduction to Stanford University came in the National AAU Track and Field Championships held in June 1963 at St. Louis. As a high school junior, I qualified for the Men's Outdoor Championships in the long jump (called the broad jump in those days) and the 220-yard dash. The preliminary rounds saw me eliminated in both events, but it was a tremendous experience; competing against the likes of Bob Hayes in the 220 and Ralph Boston and Paul Warfield in the long jump. What really caught my attention, however, were Stanford athletes, Dave Weill and Larry Questad, and their coach, Payton Jordan. They made a lasting impression on me that played a huge part in my eventually accepting a scholarship for academics/track and field at Stanford.

Experiences such as the 1963 AAU meet truly opened my eyes to so many opportunities. My hometown of Columbiana in northeastern Ohio is a small farming community of about 4500 people. Perhaps only 30-35 percent of high school students went on to college. The decision to attend Stanford was a big step for me. My father, Ralph, was my high school track coach, so this period was a special father-son time for us. Dad and Coach Jordan got along very well from day one. Their relationship was very helpful in my eventual decision to attend Stanford. I played football, basketball, track, and baseball (summer American Legion ball) all through high school. I was skilled enough in football to be offered some division one scholarships as a running back, including the University of Michigan. Looking back 40 years later, I am so grateful for the guidance that my father and Payton gave me on making my college selection.

I was able to qualify for the Ohio state track and field championship in each of my four high school years. I won the Ohio State Championship in the 440-yard dash in 1964. During my senior year I also was fortunate to defeat both Emmette Taylor and Martin McGrady in the state 440 finals. Emmette later won the NCAA 440 and Martin set several world records in the 600 indoors ... in some epic duels with Lee Evans. I also qualified for the National Golden West Track and Field Meet in three events after my senior year. Perhaps the most enjoyable part of my journey through high school athletics was winning a state championship with my father as my coach.

Stanford
I arrived as an 18-year old frosh in the fall of 1964. This trip to Stanford was only my second airplane ride and my first time actually seeing the beautiful Stanford campus. Needless to say college was a pretty big step for me, but I enjoyed the challenge from day one. Frosh year turned out well. I found out I was able to do the class room work at an acceptable level and that I was able to compete well in a division one track and field program. Frosh were not eligible to compete in those days, but I was the top 440 runners on both the frosh and varsity teams. That year I ran a season best of 47.5 for the

440-yard dash, breaking Olympic champion and world record holder Ben Eastman's frosh record which had stood since 1932.

By the start of my sophomore year, Stanford was truly an enjoyable place to live, study and compete in sports. I learned much about the world and myself during these first 12 months in Palo Alto - new friends, experiences, and challenges. This was a special time in my life and always will be. I had a solid season in 1966 with a fifth place finish in the 440-yard dash at the Pac-8 Championships. Probably the most exciting races of the year were dual meet 440 wins over Cal's Forest Beatty (national record holder in the high school 220) and USC's Geoff Vanderstock (world record holder in the 400-meter hurdles). I ran a season best of 47.0 for the 440 yards. Our 440-relay team, with a terrific anchor leg by Larry Questad, upset the great San Jose State team that included Wayne Herman and Tommie Smith. I still remember the big smile on Coach's face after we pulled that win out of the hat. I ran the 3rd leg for our team. I qualified for the NCAA outdoor national Championships in both the 440-yard dash and also the 440-yard relay. That year the NCAA track and field Championships were held in Bloomington, Indiana. Stanford finished fifth in the 440 relay. I advanced to the final round of the 440-yard dash and finished a competitive seventh. I surely would have liked a better result that day, but I ran my best. If I am correct, I share with the great Ben Eastman (1930) and Ray Mallott (1936) the distinction of being the only Stanford athletes to advance to the NCAA finals in either the 440-yard dash or 400-meter dash. I have some great memories from that second season and I cherish the things I shared with Coach and my teammates. We were all close as friends and teammates.

The highlights of my junior year at Stanford were selecting a major (Economics) and continuing to enjoy the Stanford experience. I won several individual 440s in key dual meets and placed third in the Pac-8 440-yard dash. This year turned out to be my best chance to win the event but I came up short by a few tenths in a strong final race. I also ran in the finals of the 220-yard dash and finished seventh. The field for that race included the infamous O.J. Simpson. I set the Stanford record for the Indoor 600 that season and qualified for the NCAA outdoor championships in the 440-yard dash. I advanced out of round one, but was eliminated in the second round of competition.

My senior year at Stanford went well culminating in my graduation with a degree in Economics. I continued to enjoy my last year of track and field at Stanford. I was elected captain of the track team. That honor will always be extremely special to me as it came from my teammates. I ran very well early in the year with a strong second to eventual 1968 Olympic Champion Lee Evans in the San Jose/Stanford duel meet. I won the 440 in our duel meet competition against UCLA's Len Vanhofwegan in my personal best time of 46.9. Mid-season I developed some foot injuries, which hampered me for the remaining part of the year. I did qualify and run in the NCAA Outdoor Championships, in the 440-yard dash, but I was eliminated in round one. This was not the way I wanted to end my career, but it was how it was to be. Looking back over my experiences, 40 years later, I am so fortunate to have experienced Stanford, been able to run track at this great university, and been part of Payton's teams and of his life. Coach Jordan has remained a close friend all these years. He has taught me so much about life and I will be forever grateful. I have 4 young sons and the influence of Coach will affect their lives in such a positive way. I try to pass on many of Coach's wonderful lessons and teachings. Coach and I have exchanged monthly letters for many years now. These terrific letters constantly remind me of how one should live a quality life.

Post-Stanford
I am a married to a beautiful and talented woman, Julie. We have three sons Nicholas (8), Zachary (6), and Grayson (2). I also have a son from a previous marriage. Travis is 13 years old and lives in the Netherlands with his mom.

My career involves real estate lending and development, and publishing. I enjoy and remain active in my businesses. Being involved in the preparation of this book has been one of the great joys of my working life.

I have raced open-wheel Formula Cars throughout the USA and Europe for the past 20 seasons. This has been a dream come true for me and I have had success in my professional race-driving career. Most notable season was a seventh place finish in the 1988 Detroit Grand Prix and an eighth place finish in that year's final season points standings. I still race a little when I can. At age 58 my best racing days are behind me, but the memories and excitement remain.

Conclusion
There is no question that the decision to attend Stanford changed my life forever. I am grateful for the whole experience. Hopefully, some day, one or more of my sons will attend "The Farm." There is rarely a day that goes by during which I do not think of and do feel most grateful for my friend and my Coach, Payton Jordan. What a terrific and wonderful man. Payt has truly touched so many of our lives and in such positive ways. Thank you, Coach, for so many things.

Dick Warwick

Pre-Stanford
Oakesdale (WA) High School 1963-1964
Oakesdale is a small farm town in the Palouse Country of eastern Washington state. When I attended, the local four-year high school totaled about 70 students. I was ten percent of my graduating class. It had been a track and field power during the first decade of the 1900s, but had not had a track program for decades. As I was not good at baseball, I was happy when a new coach, Don Trueblood, started a track program when I was a junior.

As a kid on the farm I was always running and jumping, lifting and throwing things. That helped develop an all-around athleticism that served me well in football and basketball, but especially in track and field. Under Coach Trueblood, I took to the jumps right away, and went to the state meet in the long and high jump that first year. He also had me throw the javelin in one meet and, without any practice or training of any kind, I threw it 146' 1 1/2" on my first try. Oddly, I never threw the spear again during my high school career. My senior year I again went to State in the high jump.

Stanford Years 1964-1968

Matriculating at Stanford, I tried out (as a walk-on) for the Frosh football team. I was injured the first day of practice by a blind-side block during a "half-speed" drill. This put me in the Intensive Care ward of Stanford Hospital for a few days, and a slow and painful period of subsequent healing from a lacerated kidney.

When spring came, I tried out for the track team. We already had freshmen who had been superior long jumpers in high school, among them Jim Ward, Craig Vaughn and Steve Coy; and the great Ed Hanks in the high jump, who had 6"10" to his credit. A couple other high jumpers had also exceeded my personal best of 6'1". This was in the days of the old western roll style of leaping.

There were several of us strapping lads who were athletic and strong, but with no outstanding marks in any particular event. This group included Cam Benjamin, Carter Newton, Patt McDermid, and me. Since most states did not allow the javelin in high school track & field, we had on the frosh team no javelin recruit, so we were put to work on that event. Chuck Smart, a great all-around high school weightman, also trained with us. We were a convivial cadre and helped each other a lot.

This is when the javelin became my main event. Upperclassman George Porter, a 230-plus performer, and the soon-to-be NCAA champion discus thrower Bob Stoecker (who could toss the spear 220' whenever he wanted to) worked with us, showing us the technique and, with Coach Jordan, helping to refine it. When I unleashed a toss of over 190 feet during practice, the die was cast. I became a committed javelin thrower. My best throw that year was 199' 4 ½" at Angell Field during a dual meet with West Valley Junior College.

For the rest of my Stanford career I was a pretty good journeyman javelin thrower. After George Porter graduated, I was for a time the best thrower on the team. Then came Tom Colby, a transfer from Tulane, whose personal record was less than 220 feet. He was a somewhat lackadaisical trainer but was strong and highly motivated and suddenly, at an all-comers meet in the early spring, had a throw of 249'1". Not long after that he became the school record holder at 265 feet. Witty and high-spirited, he was always a lot of fun in practice.

My senior year we had an early season dual meet at Washington State University in Pullman, not far from my home in eastern Washington. It was cold and there were intermittent snow showers, which disheartened our sprinters and jumpers, who did not want to risk pulled muscles. My lifetime best throw of 229'1" earned me fourth place in that dual meet, behind Colby and the two great WSU throwers, Carl O'Donnell and Foss Miller. All three of those guys finished in the top six of the NCAA meet that year.

The Monday after that meet I was throwing the best I ever had in practice when I heard a pop in my right elbow. That injury basically derailed my career. Although I continued to throw over 200 feet the rest of the year, I had to eliminate throwing in practice and I was in pain after every meet. I never let the coaches know the extent of the injury - I wanted to compete. My mark at WSU qualified me for the NCAA meet, which was in

Berkeley that year, and it was a thrill to be included in that event, even though I did not do well. It also placed me on the then "Ten Best Ever" board.

It was exciting, that year of 1968, that our own Coach Jordan was selected to be the head coach of the US Olympic Team. I felt that was really a feather in our cap, and I was proud of him and of us.

Post-Stanford
I was never a star, but I thoroughly enjoyed track and field and continued to compete in mostly all-comers meets fairly frequently during the five years after college, and sporadically after that. The last time I threw the javelin over 200 feet was in 1980. I have managed to place third in my age group in the National Masters Meet in the javelin the three times I entered - 1992, 1996, and 2003. I believe it was in 1996, when the national meet was in Spokane, that I watched Coach Jordan show his astounding sprinting ability - still a magnificent runner nearly 60 years after setting his world record. My lifetime best marks were 229'1" in the javelin, 22'6" in the long jump, and 6'2 1/2" in the high jump. I might have been an OK hurdler - I ran a 42.4 in the 330-yard intermediate hurdles when I was a sophomore, but since we already had a good performer in Grady Means, I never ran it in an official meet.

All in all, track and field has been one of the joys of my life. I have been competing now for over 40 years, with no plans to quit. Coach Jordan has been a great influence because of his consistently positive attitude and his example as a person of rectitude, discipline and integrity. And he always takes time to write letters, even to those such as me, who certainly did not enhance his career but who benefited greatly from being one of his "coachees." Thank you, Coach Jordan.

1969

Peter Boyce

Growing up in Australia
Like most of us, my track and field career began simply enough. At Deepdene Primary School in Melbourne, Australia, it was announced that the "school sports" were to be held in a few weeks. This was an annual event with a limited number of running and jumping events.

Many of us fancied ourselves as the next Chilla Porter, the Australian silver medalist in the high jump the previous year at the 1956 Olympic Games, held in our fair city.

As in most grade school playgrounds, the high jump pit was not a scene of democracy in action: the bigger kids of course could jump higher than (a) most of the smaller and younger ones, and (b) tall but gangly and uncoordinated sixth graders like yours truly. Naturally, the bar tended to remain at the higher end of the ability range. Then that aforementioned vacation arrived, much of which was spent in the Boyce back yard working on my best scissors jump over a bamboo bar supported on homemade stands. The wonder of being 11 is that a year's worth of improvement can occur in a week. I returned to school able to keep up with the hot shots.

By the time I was 14, I was training most days, now under the eye of Franz Stampfl, coach at Melbourne University. The improvements continued through high school: 6'-6 1/4" at 16 (A National Sub-junior (U17) record); an invitation to the National trials for the 1962 British Commonwealth Games, and later that season fourth place at the Australian championships in Adelaide; 6'-9 3/4" at 17, winning the Australian Junior title, a record, and passing the qualifying height for the 1964 Tokyo Olympic games. I was the number three qualifier - they took two.

On to Stanford
A mutual friend introduced me to Coach Jordan. After exchanging letters and school records I was off to Stanford.

I remember my first Stanford competition, a squad meet a little before the end of fall quarter at Angell Field, followed by invitations to a number of West Coast indoor meets, my first. My performances were consistently good on the whole, but did not show the substantial yearly improvement, which I had come to expect. The spring freshman team season followed, with similar results, highlighted with a frosh record 6'-10 3/4".

Sophomore year started with some early successes during the indoor season, and highlighting with my first seven-foot jump, in Stanford Stadium at the Big Meet. As luck would have it, though, Cal freshman Clarence Johnson cleared an NCAA freshman record 7'-3 1/4" earlier in the frosh event. I actually was happy for both of us. It certainly put things in perspective. Favored to win the AAWU meet, I placed a relatively disappointing second to some unknown from Oregon State with a strange style, named Fosbury I believe. A poor performance on a chilly night at Provo, Utah, at the NCAA meet was also disappointing; the consolation prize was a return
trip to California with Jim Ward and his parents, delivering his brand spanking new 1967 Corvette.

Junior year brought anticipation of the 1968 Olympic Games. A tender jumping knee curtailed much of the indoor season, but a personal best 7'- ½" in early March vs. San Jose State and Occidental put things back on track. During that time 1941 World record holder Les Steers arrived to volunteer his additional coaching help. The stars were all in perfect alignment on March 30, 1968, for the Stanford - Fresno State meet, held at the end of an actually pleasant bus ride on a glorious early spring California morning. By meet's end, I had equaled the fifth best all-time outdoor jump at 7'-3", and, I hoped, earned a place on the soon to be announced Australia Olympic Team, it being the end of their track season. In April the team was announced: I was included! Exciting stuff to write home about.

Unfortunately, the rest of the story has few moments close to the foregoing. I was not able to match that early season success again: I placed third at the AAWU (6'-10"), and the same at the NCAA (7'-0)", both held at Berkeley, although becoming an All-American on the basis of the NCAA placing was indeed thrill for this Aussie.

Dick Fosbury continued to improve all the way to the Olympics, winning the gold medal decisively. I did not pass the qualifying round, clearing 6'-10".

Given the above, and a continuing knee problem, senior year saw performances at a markedly lower level, although reasonably solid and consistent. I had my share of dual meet victories, but little above that. My last competition was that summer at the Los Angeles Times International Games where, according to the trophy, I placed fourth. The height jumped, kindly, is not recorded.

Post-Stanford
My career has been in the field of structural engineering. After my first job with Bechtel Corp. in San Francisco, I took a Master's degree at San Jose State, worked in the San Jose area until 1979, then began my private consulting practice, which consumes much of me to this day. It has been a one-man affair, with the exception of part-time administrative help, which is probably appropriate for one who took to one of the most individual of sports.

I have two wonderful children, David, 24 and Marisa, 21, he is working on a degree in computer science at San Jose State, she a Berkeley senior Development Studies major. They are both doing well for themselves, and they are good to their parents. Their mother and I divorced many years ago; my partner Juanita and I have been together 17 years now, I am very happy to say.

Memories of Jordan
I do not recall so much memorable quotes from Coach Jordan, as an overall conveying of support, genuine interest and a positive attitude. I rarely saw him without his engaging smile, twinkling eyes and a ready pat on the back. Even when things were not going well, he always managed some much-needed words of encouragement, and when things went well, he was usually the first to offer his congratulations.

When he moved from Los Altos to Santa Barbara a few years ago, he very kindly tracked me down and sent a plaque that had been on his wall for many years taken from the cover of 1968 Coach and Athlete magazine showing a much younger Peter Boyce and a slightly younger Payton Jordan looking up at a high jump bar.

It is safe to say that Coach Jordan and I are of quite different personality types. I am not always able to muster the everyday enthusiasm that Coach Jordan always conveyed to us. As it is for all of us, he has certainly had his disappointments, some of them major I know, but he has managed to embrace all that has been good in his life and to allow that to determine his attitude and his demeanor with those around him. It is a quality that I have tried to call upon in difficult moments and times, particularly since I have received more than my share of blessings. A major inspiration at such times is Payton Jordan.

Tom Colby

Stanford
I was an All-American javelin thrower in 1968 and set the Stanford record for javelin in 1969.

Memorable Experiences
Once Coach and I agreed to disagree on our politics, we were friendly and had mutual respect

Post-Stanford
Went to Med School at U. Michigan from 70-74
Was resident and faculty at Stanford Med School from 74-83
83-86 U of Utah
86-93 Mayo Clinic Rochester
93-present Mayo Clinic Scottsdale
Have been a Professor of Pathology since 1989

Brook Thomas

I graduated in 1965 from Catonsville High School in the suburbs of Baltimore, Maryland. During my high school years Catonsville was known in the area primarily for its big fireworks display every 4th of July. But the town would gain national recognition a few years later because the Berrigan brothers chose it as the site to pour blood on draft files (including mine) to protest the Vietnam War. (Copies of the files were in Washington D.C., so the protest did not affect my draft status.)

Until 1961 high school track in Maryland was pretty backward. For instance, my brother, who graduated that year was the first in the state to break 50 seconds for the 440 and almost the first to break 2:00 for the 880. The pace had quickened by the time I graduated, however, in large part due to the efforts of Charlie Messinger and Dave Patrick from rival Kenwood High. A year ahead of me, Messinger won the High School National Indoor and Golden West Outdoor two miles in 1964 and Patrick lowered the state mile record to 4:12.4. Both went on to star at Villanova. My junior year I ran 1:58.4 in the 880, behind Patrick, but at least breaking my brother's school record. My senior year we were state champions in cross country. I came in second. Indoors, we won state again, and I won the 1,000 (yards), breaking my brother's record. Outdoors, at state I tried to double in the 440 and 880 and lost both with a 50.6 and a time I have successfully forgotten. I did record 1:56.4 in the 880 and 4:19.4 in the mile that season.

Wanting to avoid the cold, I decided not to go to an Ivy League school and opted instead for Stanford, in large part because of television images in my mind of the 1960 Olympic Trials and the 1962 US-USSR meet. Never having flown on an airplane or been west of West Virginia, I flew to Palo Alto in September 1965 and did not return home for nine months.

Those nine months were fascinating, but disappointing as far as running was concerned. I arrived in great shape, but my best time in cross country was in the beginning time trial. In track I did not even match my high school times. One problem was over training, a problem that continued my sophomore cross country season, although I did come in second in one race. Winter and spring I attended Stanford-in-Britain, where I trained on my own. Spring break included an overnight train ride to Florence and, the next morning, the Tuscany cross country championships with Allen Sanford, who was finishing up his stay at Stanford-in-Italy. After traveling in Europe during the summer, I returned for cross country my junior year, and finally had some - if mixed - success. By track season I was back to my pattern of leaving my races on the practice track, although I did win the steeplechase against UCLA and scored a couple of points one meet when I hopped into the 440 hurdles after a lane opened up just before the gun went off. I also significantly lowered my 2-mile time in the Cal meet.

The summer before my senior year I had a job teaching tennis in Catonsville, and I spent the start of vacation trying to regain some lost speed in short, 50-minute sessions before work. Fall of 1968 was magical. We had a new distance coach, Marshall Clark, who guided us to an undefeated season and second at NCAA. Greg Brock and I were All Americans, and most of us made the list of top performers on the Stanford 4.2 mile course. In preparation for nationals, we also inaugurated a six mile race, which allowed me - for one short year - to hold a golf course record. Track season was marred by a bad hamstring pull in a time trial. I recovered to place in the Pac-8 steeplechase and to qualify for NCAA.

I had enough credits to graduate a quarter early, but with a year of eligibility in track left because of my time in Britain, I decided, with the threat of the draft looming, to return for another year. It was a great year for Stanford distance running. Brock and Don Kardong broke school records for 2, 3, and 6 miles. At conference Duncan Macdonald became the first Stanford runner to break 4 minutes in the mile. I was not quite as impressive, but I did run 8:59.6 in the steeplechase, tying Harry McCalla's school record. I made the finals but did not place at NCAA.

After Stanford I continued to run competitively, while in graduate school at UCSB. I qualified for the 1972 Olympic Trials in the marathon, and enjoyed rooting for ex-teammates Brock, Kardong, and Macdonald in Eugene. I also had a couple of decent races in the national cross country championships and set PRs in the steeple, 3-mile, and 10,000, the latter two by barely beating Tony Sandoval, who was a Stanford freshman at the time. (That was the last year I would ever be able to beat Tony at any distance.)

I got my Ph.D. In English literature in December 1975, and by Spring 1976 I was back in Germany as a visiting professor, helping the track club in Constance win the state of Baden team championship. After watching Kardong and Macdonald at the 1976 Olympics from a TV set in a Paris hotel lobby, I flew back to Maryland and then onto Hawaii, where I had a job at the university. In Hawaii I won a number of road races, so long as Duncan was out of town. An operation on my knee slowed me, but during a fellowship year back in Germany I managed to be the first American in a 1979 marathon south of Paris. By fall 1980 I had to have another operation. This time the surgeon completely botched it, and although a second operation relieved the pain caused by the first, I have not been able to plant my foot properly ever since.

Too addicted to running to stop, I continued to try to train and could still run a 32 10K at the age of 40. But the years of favoring my foot have caught up with me. My body is so out of balance these days that I spend most of my exercise time trying to rehabilitate aching muscles all over my body. There are so many to rehabilitate that I keep relatively fit. The botched operation did have one positive effect. It forced me to concentrate more on my job. After Hawaii, I taught for awhile at UMass, Amherst, where Bob Miltz was also a professor, although our paths never crossed. In 1988 I moved to UC Irvine and have been here ever since, except for a few other stints teaching in Germany. In 1998 I married Jayne Lewis, a professor of English at UCLA. 1999 our son Peter Ramsay Thomas was born.

I first met Coach Jordan in 1965 the summer before I headed for Stanford. He was coaching for the International Games for the Deaf held in College Park, Maryland, so I drove down to introduce myself. I was immediately struck by his enthusiasm and informality. The years I was at Stanford were turbulent years, and the nation continues to experience some of the divides that opened up in those years. It is, I think, fair to say that Coach and I did not always share the same political beliefs. But we did share a mutual respect, one that would continue over the years as I occasionally visited Stanford and as my brother—a successful Master's runner-reported Coach's numerous victories and records on the Master's circuit. When I last saw Coach he delivered a moving and gracious tribute at the October 12, 2002, memorial service for Marshall Clark after his untimely death.

1970

Mike Flannery

I grew up on a middle class block in the center of Downey, Calif. It was a great place to be a kid. Within this one block, there were eight kids within a year of myself, all with dreams to go pro in several sports. For us, there was no wasting that idle time, especially during the summer. We were constantly in competition in the major four sports at the time. We had to organize into our favorite teams to compete. For baseball, it was the Dodgers, Giants, Yankees, Red Sox. For basketball, it was the Lakers, Warriors, Celtics. For football, it was the LA Rams, Forty Niners, and of course, the Raiders. However, when it came to track competition, we were united, all competing at the Central Downey Olympic trials for a spot on the Olympic Team.

The competition at the Downey Olympic trials was fierce among the eight of us. The sprints were run on the asphalt street out front, timed between the flow of cars. The distance was around the block several times, a feat I always swore I would not duplicate as I matured. The long jump and high jump was rugged for me, having short legs for the former and first coining the term "white man can't jump" for the latter. However, I found my competitive niche in the pole vault. With a thick mattress on the ground, a bamboo fishing pole in my hands, and standards made of 1"x2"s, I went to work on clearing six feet. Not much in retrospect until one remembers your bum penetrates the mattress, leaving a lasting impression on the ground underneath.

Having shown my particular agility with the fishing pole, the local junior high scouts signed me to pole vault for North Junior High in Downey. Trying to maneuver a much too heavy Swedish steel pole, the only pole they had, I managed to clear the top height on the only scrawny standards they had. Now what? Well, we quickly borrowed standards from the local high school, standards that had the potential to go higher. Not only was I given the chance to vault higher, but more importantly, I now had the eye of Warren High School's scouts.

Entering high school was a challenge. This is where I had the thrill of first meeting Paul Wilson and Bob Steinhoff. We quickly became the Warren High Vaulting trio. Paul was the first high school student in the nation to clear 16 feet. He then went on to USC, where he held the world record for a period of time. Steinhoff cleared 15' 6" before going off to Kansas State. Well, with this competition, what could I to do to leave a legacy. Well, I was so small compared to these guys, I vaulted my sophomore year in the "C" classification in the Southern California. Perfect!!! I was able to set the CIF C record of 13' 4" at the time, only because Paul and Bob weren't small enough to qualify for the C category, but I had the advantage of having their coaching and encouragement. As I grew big enough to actually get a fiberglass pole to bend, I cleared 14' 4" my junior year and 14' 8" my senior year, where I managed to take third in the State Meet.

As my 5' 7" frame and my speed became a factor, I was pleased to have Coach Jordan offer me a position on the Stanford track team. What a thrill. We had Coach Jordan, who always pushed us to be the best. We had Eshelman as a mentor, Ostrander as a colleague and friend, and a whole team of great people and athletes. My dreams formed on that neighborhood in Downey had come true. It may not be the Olympics, but Stanford was the place to be.

Freshman year, 1967, at Stanford was a wet year. Lots of running in the tunnels of the Stadium to try and stay dry. My performance that year was disappointing. In retrospect, it must have been the lack of any positive female response to my attributes, or lack thereof. I know this is what Ostrander would claim, having set new heights that year for himself, and definitely doing better in the female category than the Flan.

I can still remember watching Eshelman break 17 feet and Ostrander setting new highs. Trying to pole vault at Washington State as the snow continued to fall harder and harder on the runway. I can remember setting my best official vault of 15ft 6 inches at Oregon, with Jordan and my teammates cheering me on. I can remember my introduction to Moscow, Idaho with Ostrander and the boys. I can remember working out with Ostrander, landing on a hurdle (who put that there?), landing many times head first in the box, and getting a good view of long distance runners from overhead as I landed in the middle of the track amongst them. I can remember trying to vault against Cal, my back continuing to spasm, as the team pulled out a victory.

Stanford was a phenomenal time. Coach Jordan was a great teacher, leader and friend who gave us all a purpose on the track and an ability to compete in the world. His great influence allowed me to go on and build and lead a number of high tech companies to success. I now enjoy a great family of two college almost-graduates and a loving wife.

Clint Ostrander

Pre-Stanford

I grew up surfing in Southern California and started pole vaulting in my back yard around age 14 or 15. My poles were made from whatever I could find and my cross bars were the chain link fences that separated the neighborhood yards. The spikes at the top of the chain link fencing served as a real incentive to clear each height and probably helped me develop some consistency in the event. My coach at Taft High School, Dale Lythgo, was a great mentor who did so many good things to help kids develop as athletes and as individuals. Fiberglass poles and modern vaulting pits were very expensive but he somehow made these available on a limited budget. Some years ago, I had an opportunity to take Coach Lythgo to dinner and to thank him for his kindness and the difference he made in my life.

Tom and Dave, two of my best friends at Taft, were also vaulters and the friendly competition between us only served to make us better. During our senior year, I don't recall losing a single point in the event and our combined heights were supposedly the highest team total in the country. While I had the best height, Dave actually made the most amazing vault I have ever seen. He was a very large football player, one of the top rated centers in Los Angeles, and I still vividly remember him walking over to the vault area one day after football practice, picking up a pole, and clearing 12 feet in cleats and full pads. His takeoff was similar to that of the Space Shuttle and, to this day, Dave is still the largest thing I have seen on a runway with the possible exception of certain wide-body passenger aircraft.

I ended my high school career with the Los Angeles City Schools record as well as various other records and honors. However, the importance of these was insignificant compared to the invaluable lessons I had learned from my teammates, my coach, and from competition itself. I credit my teammates, particularly Tom and Dave, for teaching me how to set goals, stay focused, and be a competitor. As for coach Lythgo, I not only credit him with showing me what personal character is all about but I am also deeply in debt to him for contacting Coach Jordan on my behalf. The resulting scholarship offer from Stanford allowed me to attend a great university that was otherwise out of financial reach. While I did not understand the significance of this at the time, it proved to be a pivotal event in my life.

Stanford Years
To say the least, my first year at Stanford was an uncomfortable period of adjustment. While I set a freshman record in the vault I also established another record for switching majors in one year (I went 3 for 3 in math, physics, and engineering). The track team offered an identity to a somewhat lost kid and Payton Jordan was a pier of stability. Throughout my 4 years on the team, I always saw Coach Jordan as the most dedicated individual I had ever met and I think I gained some strength from his example. It wasn't that he was focused solely on winning, although he was most certainly a winner, it was rather his emphasis on putting out your best effort in everything you did. He made it very clear in both his actions and words that win, loose, or draw, you could walk away proud if you knew you had prepared well, fought hard, and accepted the outcome on your own terms. To him, it was as much about character as it was about being a winner and to be a true champion in life you had to have both.

I eventually adjusted to Stanford after clearing the hurdle of the first year and my overall experience was both enjoyable and rewarding in almost all respects. Unfortunately, my performance in track did not fall completely into this category. After entering college as a top-rated vaulter with lofty expectations, I ended my career as an athlete who consistently scored points but, in my own mind, was otherwise unexceptional despite a lot of hard work and commitment. It was extremely disappointing but as I have reminded my children over the years, you can learn more from one disappointment than you can from 10 successes. I think Coach Jordan would agree.

My memories of track include my teammates, many of whom became life-long friends. I also remember the incomparable rush of being thrown into the air by a fiberglass catapult, Angell Field in the spring, vaulting in the snow at Washington State, and competing against the best guys in the world, some of whom I occasionally beat (it was always a fluke but I'll take the win anyway). While the academics at Stanford taught me how to think, training and competition taught me much more about myself and how I wanted to approach life. I have always considered the combination to be unbeatable.

Post-Stanford
Following my undergraduate degree, I did some graduate work in engineering and then spent another 10 years at the university doing medical research. In total, 16 rewarding years in a place that was initially so formidable! Who would have thought it? I continued my workouts at Angell Field and frequently saw Coach Jordan going through his own preparations for Masters competitions. What an amazing guy! At age 30, I doubt that I could have come close to his times in the hundred despite the years he gave me. Another vision of dedication to put in the memory books.

I finally left Stanford to start my own company in a small back yard garage. Over the next 18 years Trace Analytical grew to become a major niche player in the semiconductor industry. The academic preparation I received at Stanford was an invaluable asset in this undertaking, but it was what I learned on the track that guided me through the most difficult times, those times when focus and determination were about all we had to fall back on. That, and the satisfaction of knowing we were giving it our absolute best shot. Thank you, Stanford and Coach Jordan.

Life Now
At this writing, I am a 56-year-old idle CEO who has tried retirement and is once again thinking about changing majors. Interestingly, the question of "what do I really want to do in life" is no less of an issue now than it was when I graduated. My wife and I continue to lead an active life and, over the last 25 years, Jackye and I have raised three great kids including two daughters, Nikki and Karin, who played soccer, have graduated from college, and are happily out in the real world. T.C., our youngest, entered Stanford this year as a member of the football team. As a quarterback, he follows in the footsteps of some great players at Stanford. As my son, he shares some of the same dreams and expectations held by his father almost 40 years ago and still alive today.

1971
Charlie Francis
I really enjoyed my time at Stanford, even if they did call me Chuck at the track. I first heard of Stanford from two members of my home track club, Ian and Dave Arnold, who went there ahead of me. It sounded good from their accounts and I figured the weather wouldn't be too bad in Connecticut. It sounded better when I found out it was in California, but, fortunately, I didn't hear much more about the place or I might have been too intimidated to apply.

My mother bought me a copy of Payton Jordan's book: "From Childhood to Champion Athlete" which impressed me greatly - and made me want to get down there to find out how to do the "eggshell drills"! But, back to why Payton gave me a shot in the first place: I grew up in Toronto, Canada (just head north, you can't miss it) and was fast as long as I could remember (of course, that's not very long these days). I was the provincial high school champion 4 years in a row and was Canadian Juvenile and Junior Champion and record holder in the 100 and 220 yards, at 9.6 and 21.3 respectively, and I'd won the 220 yards at a junior international match against England and France.

So, a lapse by the admissions department and it was off to Stanford in the fall of 1967... a big trip, a swollen left arm from hauling my suitcase up Palm Drive, and the start of a big adventure! These were tumultuous times... Jefferson Airplane, Vietnam, Riots, Frosh Track, and, oh yes, classes. One of my first stops was Coach Jordan's office. He cut a dramatic figure in person - handsome, ramrod straight, and terrifically fit for his age. Of course the image was enhanced by the fact that he'd been named Head Coach for the upcoming Mexico City Olympics.

He showed me the photographic history of Stanford and the people who'd run there, including the great Bob Hayes, and the breathtaking aerial view of the crowd for the first USA vs. Soviet Union dual meet held at Stanford Stadium, which he'd organized. He also showed me photos of Larry Questad winning the NCAA 100 yards in 1963 and the Stanford relay team that broke the 440-yard relay world record in 1965. Impressive stuff!

Dementia has mercifully dimmed my memory of many first year results, though I do recall a couple of wins, one against Simms of Merritt JC, the national JC champion and one at Cal against Masters, the Golden West Champion. I never got back the feel for dirt tracks and I missed the 'latest technology' on the track front - Grasstex (basically asphalt with 3% rubber thrown in), which I'd competed on at home.

The season closed out with an exciting trip to "Speed City"- San Jose State, where I'd gone to see their new, ultra-fast "Tartan" track and to watch the world's greatest sprinters in action. No sooner had I entered the stadium than I ran into John Carlos. I struck up a conversation, which he promptly redirected: "Why are you watching when you should be running?" When I explained that I hadn't brought my track gear, he reached into his bag, pulled out a pair of shorts, and said: "There you go! I can't help you with the spikes, cause I'm size 13, but I know who can!" John took me over to meet Tommie Smith and asked Tommie to loan me a pair of his spikes! Tommie agreed, saying: "Don't let Coach Winter see these (they had 12mm spikes instead of the 9mm specified for Tartan)- and don't run slow!" I equaled my Canadian Junior Record for the 220 yards but the real excitement was meeting those guys! That summer I ran a windy 10.4 100m to finish second at the Canadian Olympic Trials, behind our world record holder, Harry Jerome - a good result for me but not good enough to go, so I consoled myself by winning the National Junior 100 and 220, while Coach Jordan was off to Mexico City as the Head Coach of the greatest US Olympic Team ever assembled.

Sophomore year was spent recovering from a quad pull and learning to tread water at Angell Field, which became a lake after it rained for 43 days in a row (it was only 40 in the Bible!). In my first collegiate 440 at the San Jose State dual meet, I won, but what an experience! As dumb as I was, I thought I could save energy by warming up as little as possible, doing just enough to stave off injury - a mistake that allowed me to set the record for the most lactic acid ever accumulated in a living being. Payton came over afterwards and said: "You see! It's not so bad!" Of course, I couldn't see much as I was still bent over, thinking that he really shouldn't have his shoes right there in my present condition. Fortunately, I (and Coach's shoes) survived.

A highlight of sorts was our victory over the defending NCAA champions from UCLA in the 440-yard relay, despite three of us having injuries. I was there for the fallout when their anchorman told UCLA head coach Jim Bush: "I never want to run this relay again!" To which Coach Bush replied: "Don't worry! You won't!" That summer I made the Canadian team for the Pacific Conference Games in Tokyo.

Hallelujah! My junior year started with the introduction of Grasstex in the main stadium at long last. This faster surface was impervious to the weather, and, like the proverbial umbrella, guaranteed that it would never rain again during practice for the rest of my career at Stanford! Fair weather or not, I was bedeviled with injuries all season, sending me up to the dreaded 440 on occasion. The most memorable of these was at the USC dual meet, run in the LA Coliseum. In those days, pollution caused twilight to descend by mid-afternoon, as the sun, distorted into a giant red ball, could barely cut through the murk. A swirling wind and the presence, one lane in, of Edsel Garrison, USC's 44.5 man, completed the grim picture. The race would be for second place.

A slow learner, I used the same warm-up as the year before, with the same effect! Though I did get second place, the only record I set that day was a new one for lactic acid. My muscles were so rigid that I couldn't even blink when the sun caught me in the eye and I had to turn my whole head to avoid the glare. Coach came over and asked how I was doing, but I think he had a pretty good idea already, as he kept his shoes a little further away this time!

I came into my own that summer, running a windy 10.1 for the 100 meters and 20.8 for the 200 meters, winning the National Seniors for the first time, and beating Harry Jerome in the process. Senior year went fairly well, though I was stuck at 9.5, running it a number of times but unable to find a way under. I suppose my best result was at the USC dual meet at Stanford, winning over a great field, but in an appalling 10.0, a time I'd first broken at 15. The headwind was howling in my ears at the start line, so, with faint hope, I asked Coach if the race could be turned around, but, after I got the expected answer, Payton said: "Keep relaxed and stay down just as far into the race as you can!" Advice I put to good effect, as I was well clear by the time I got upright. The victory was bittersweet, for, despite the blast on the straight, the wind had swirled at the wind meter, registering only minus 4 miles per hour! This meant that if the race had been turned around, as was the custom at UCLA, I would have gotten a tremendous legal time. This was backed up by the fact that the USC guys ran 9.2 and 9.4 legal at the UCLA dual meet the very next weekend.

After wins at the Washington and Cal meets, it was time for the Pac 8 (as it was called then) Championships in Seattle. Coach felt I was ready for the 100 there, and it turned out he was right. I had a great start in my heat and built up a huge lead by 50 yards, but instead of just relaxing and letting the race take care of itself, I got excited and pressed for even more. Disaster struck a step later and a strained hamstring forced me to shut down completely. I was hardly moving when I crossed the line and had given back all the margin I'd built up, yet I still ran - you guessed it- 9.5 again! At least I knew I was capable of something big, but now I was injured and time was fast running out for the NCAA.

Three weeks later the NCAA was on, again in Seattle, but this time conditions would be tough, as the weather had turned bitterly cold and damp. I was relatively healthy by now, but not back to the level I'd reached before the Pac 8s. The 100 would be contested in heats, semis, and final, and now I saw how the lost opportunities at the USC dual and the Pac 8s had come back to haunt me. With only a 9.5 to my credit, I drew a nasty heat, as the ranks were swelled with sprinters with faster, and, as it turned out, bogus times who got better draws. There was a blanket finish in my heat and I ended up 5th, eliminated in a photo finish for the last qualifying spot by JJ Jackson from UTEP in, of course, 9.5. And how did the final go? The four qualifiers from my heat went 1,2,3,4 in the final- with JJ Jackson the winner!

Well, my college career was over, and I wouldn't be returning to Stanford with the team, as I'd arranged to stay in Vancouver to await the Canadian Pan American Games Trials, which would be held in two weeks. Coach Jordan and I said our goodbyes and he presented me with my competition singlet, which we used only for meets and always handed back afterwards. He was very gracious, though he must have been disappointed, as I'd flirted with bigger things but never came through. I wouldn't get to see him again till 1978, when the insurance business took me to a conference in San Francisco, and I got a chance to stop by the "Farm."

The two weeks after the NCAA allowed me to return to the form I'd had at the Pac 8 for the Trials in Vancouver, where I recorded a 10.1 100 meters, a time which placed me fifth on the world performance list for 1971. That summer, I was fifth at the Pan Ams, behind Don Quarrie, Lennox Miller, Del Merriweather, the US champion, and Montez, the 68 Olympic finalist from Cuba, and I won a dual meet in Italy against their up-and-coming star, Pietro Mennea. I competed through 1972 and went to the Munich Olympics before packing it in (and, eventually, packing it on!)

I'm living in Toronto and have been married to my wife, Angela, for 15 years and we have a son, James, who just turned 5. Some of you probably know I did a little coaching myself and I've continued to work as a consultant to professional sports teams and individuals. In that vein, I was with the St. Louis Rams a few years ago and I went out to dinner with then Head Coach, Dick Vermeil, Offensive Coordinator, Mike White, and a retired coach who did scouting assignments for Dick named John Ralston (sound familiar?). Amazingly enough, we'd all been at Stanford at the same time, though, as coaches of the Rose Bowl winning Football team, they'd been a tad more successful! Turns out that Payton had been instrumental in getting the job for Dick at UCLA later. Shows you how small the world is and how many lives Payton has touched.

This Christmas holiday season, we were visiting friends in Santa Barbara and we got to visit Payton at his retirement villa. He's had a few health challenges lately, but he looks great; in fact, if you haven't seen him for a while, it's a bit of a shock to see how much he looks like he did 34 years ago! Of course, many of you who've followed his exploits on the masters' track circuit already knew he must have stayed in great shape! He's as upbeat and positive as ever, and though his hamstring has been bothering him, at least he waited till he was over 80 to injure it for the first time! If any of you get a chance to visit, I'm sure he'd love to see you, and I bet he remembers all about you too.

We also took a few days to visit the old homestead and Angell Field looks amazing these days! I got to show James my name on a plaque there and have a race down the old straightaway. James won the 100 meters in 30.2, but I'm pretty sure he could have gone faster if his old man hadn't been holding him back!

Don Kardong

I ran sprints in elementary and middle school track meets in the late Fifties and early Sixties, but my real athletic interest in those days was basketball. So when my basketball coach suggested I turn out for cross country in the fall of 1964 to get in shape, I acquiesced. Within a month I discovered a talent for distance running, and by the end of that sophomore season I was Seattle Prep's top runner. Unfortunately, that was in many ways the best season of my high school career. I had lots of solid races in the next two years and competed well enough my senior year to finish second in the Washington State XC Meet, but I had largely lost interest, and my times reflected it. I failed to qualify for the state track meet as a senior, and I received no college scholarship offers. I almost quit the sport. My decision to attend Stanford was purely academic and climatological. Good school, nice weather.

When I got to Stanford I decided to give running another chance. Through that first season of freshman cross country, Duncan Macdonald and I-both sadly lacking in preseason conditioning-steadily got into shape and worked our way up the freshman ladder. By season's end we were number one and two on the team. Things went well that spring, too, and my half-mile, mile and two-mile times all improved dramatically. Most important, my passion for distance running reignited.

I had come to Stanford with no aspirations of running varsity cross country or track, but in the fall of my sophomore year, 1968, I found myself training with a group of dedicated and high-achieving teammates under a new cross-country coach, Marshall Clark. Coach Clark's knowledge and style brought out the best in our group, and senior Brook Thomas was an outstanding captain. I scrambled to get my game up to speed. During that season our team went from being Bay Area afterthoughts to finishing second in the NCAA Cross-Country Championships at Van Cortlandt Park in the Bronx. Our group - Brook Thomas, Greg Brock, Large Al Sanford, Chuck Menz, Bob Anchondo and I - were mostly journeyman runners who rose to a unique height through hard work and a clear vision of what we wanted to achieve. My chest heaved and my legs buckled during the final mile of that NCAA meet as I struggled not to let the team or Coach Clark down. I finished 40th, and proudly helped carry the enormous second-place team trophy through the New York City subway system afterward, happily explaining to anyone who would listen what we had achieved.

As wonderful as that experience was, I had already signed on to spend winter and spring of my sophomore year overseas, so I missed the 1969 track season. The next fall I was woefully out of shape, and my cross-country season showed it. By the spring, though, I was back in good condition and running well. In one meet, Greg Brock and I traded laps and ran a two-mile in the 8:45 range, which was about a 15-second improvement for me. Our team performances in those days were disappointing, but at the NCAA Track Meet in Des Moines, Iowa, our distance runners performed well. I finished fourth in the three-mile (13:28) behind Steve Prefontaine, Gary Bjorklund and Dick Buerkle, all of whom would eventually become Olympians.

The next fall, my senior year, our cross-country team showed promise, but injuries cut into our success. By season's end only Arvid Kretz and I were given the go-ahead to run in the NCAA Cross-Country Championships at William and Mary. A persistent side stitch had ruined a couple of my races that fall, but in the nationals everything worked, and I finished third. I was ecstatic, and eager for my final track season.

My times improved in the spring, but to be honest, my memory isn't too good with number retention, and my record-keeping is worse, so I have trouble dredging up details. Sometime that year I ran 4:03.2, my fastest college mile time. I remember that Arvid Kretz, Duncan Macdonald and I earned a lot of points, but that our team struggled through most of the dual meet season. This was frustrating for Coach Jordan, as it was for all of us. 1971 was still the Sixties in terms of values, and pursuing athletic greatness wasn't part of the zeitgeist. It was hard to rev up for track competition when Vietnam politics were front and center. Given the era and a disappointing win-loss record for the season, our upset over Cal in the Big Meet was especially sweet. It felt like winning the Rose Bowl, which Stanford had done earlier that year. My most poignant memory from the year was from that meet, when Arvid and I sealed the team victory with a 1-2 performance in the two-mile, leaping into team captain Alan Meredith's celebratory embrace at the finish. That victory overshadows all other highs and lows I experienced that season, which includes the high of nearly beating Steve Prefontaine in the PAC-8 three-mile (13:19.8), and the low of being a total washout in the NCAA Championships in Seattle-a devastating, demoralizing conclusion to my collegiate career, made worse for having happened in my home town.

Since the final race of my senior year was a disaster, I came close to calling it quits. Timely encouragement from Coach Clark buoyed my spirits, and I decided to stay around for another year and take a shot at making the 1972 Olympic team. I lived in Menlo Park during the 1971-72 school year, doing nothing more than training. I upped my mileage a notch, ran my first marathon (2:18:06), and made my first US team indoors. Great expectations, though, ended in disappointment. I got mono that spring, and my Olympic Trials performances in Eugene were, to say the least, lackluster. In the 10,000 I was nearly lapped.

In the fall of 1972 I enrolled at the University of Washington. I had a B.A. in psychology from Stanford, but over the next two years I earned a second bachelor's (English) and a teaching certificate. My development as a runner continued, and in the spring of 1974 I ran a 3-mile in Eugene in 12:57.6, my personal best. In the fall of that year I moved to

Spokane and started teaching elementary school. My training continued, but without the support of teammates, and often in the cold and dark. It reminded me of how special those days at Stanford had been, training in an ideal climate with other runners who were pursuing high goals. Somehow I was able to tap into that spirit on many long, lonely runs, and during intense, solo sets of intervals, and I maintained a high level of training in spite of the isolation. I continued to run decent races at three and six miles, but in the spring of 1976 I decided my future might be in the marathon. I entered the Olympic Trials Marathon that spring, and surprised a few people by taking the third spot behind Frank Shorter and Bill Rodgers. My experience in the Montreal Olympics was even better, if bittersweet, as I finished fourth in 2:11:16. I ran faster than the Olympic record. Unfortunately, so did the three guys ahead of me. I missed the bronze medal by three seconds.

Looking back, that was clearly the apex of my running career. In the years following that I continued to compete, managing a few nice victories and thousands of great memories. I have been active in the sport over the years, helping bring prize money competition to road racing and open competition to the Olympics, founding a 12-kilometer road race in Spokane that attracts 50,000 entrants each year (the Lilac Bloomsday Run), and enjoying a wide variety of running adventures. After leaving the teaching profession, I opened a sporting goods store, then sold it nine years later and began making a living writing for national running magazines, most recently Runner's World. In 2002 I became executive director of the Children's Museum of Spokane, my current profession. I've been in Spokane since 1974, where I live with my wife Bridgid and, until their departure for college, daughters Kaitlin and Catherine.

I run about 30 miles a week now, most of it slow and ragged. But those memories of training and racing at Stanford remain fast and fluid. Being part of Stanford's athletic tradition and, most important, a teammate of so many great athletes and high-quality, oddball, and immensely entertaining characters, is something I'll always cherish. Man, those were the days!

Jim Kauffman

Stanford

All I ever wanted to do as a kid is go to Stanford and, of course, play sports, having grown up on the Peninsula and gone to countless football, basketball and track meets. I was smitten. At Capuchino High School in San Bruno I worked my tail off to get the grades I knew it would take to get in. Getting in was for me a dream come true.

I came in on a partial scholarship shared between football and track. But of course, my true love had always been basketball and so frosh year I also played basketball. I soon saw, however, that my BB days were limited and it was, in fact, my frosh defensive back coach, Dick Ragsdale, who urged me give rugby a go. From the moment I played my first game, I felt I'd really found my game. Though liking football, I hated to have to come out when the offence had the ball. Rugby, on the other hand, had a flow more like basketball, where one moment one is on attack and the next on defense.

I had a great frosh year running track, but after I switched from BB to rugby, I found that at the end of those two seasons (football and rugby) I had no more pop in my legs, where, for whatever reason, basketball had been a great lead up to track... rugby was not!!!

I still, however, loved track and wished to compete. I particularly recall the warm springs afternoons out with Bud Spencer (an x-440 great at Stanford) who came out to generously give us his time and encouragement.

Post-Stanford

I've been living and working in Florence, Italy since 1990..hard to believe... even for myself. To summarize, I came here with my wife and Stanford mate, Priscilla, to spend a year living in a different culture with our two kids age 9 and 12 - at the time. Part of this was driven by the fact that for the previous 10 years I'd been in the restaurant business in the Bay Area; having been the opening manager of MacArthur Park when it opened in Palo Alto in 1981; but later, with this outfit (Spectrum Foods), I worked as the director of operations working mostly with Italian restaurants such as Ciao and Prego in San Francisco. Probably even a bigger factor in making this move, however, was based on the fact that directly after Stanford, I went to Australia to teach and play rugby. After 2 years of "doing my time down under," Priscilla joined me and we traveled overland across Asia; for what was supposed to be a 6-month trip but in the end took a year and a half. This trip changed our view of the world forever...as, we realized how wonderfully diverse we all are in the world, but how much we also really do have in common. We returned home and did all the normal, conventional things...got married, got jobs, bought a house, had kids, etc. but somewhere, deep-down in there we always wanted to give our kids the idea that not everyone lives like (or has what we have) in the Bay Area. We weren't going to return to India, but Italy seemed the right place...not only due to the food bus. but Priscilla had gone to the Stanford campus here in Florence and even I, as a 12 year old, had been here briefly with my family (my Dad on sabbatical) and Florence had been our favorite city. So...Firenze for a year...perche non???

I immediately got a job teaching English at the Istituto Americano, which I later ran, but at the end of our first year, we felt we had just begun to settle in and understand our new culture, so we decided to stay, "just one more year"....well, here we are 13 years later so that about says it all. The reasons for our staying are subtle and diverse, but aside for the fact we enjoy the Italians, their life style and values, we also thought our kids were getting an excellent education in the Italian public school system and, in fact, they were as, both attended Stanford and felt they were very well prepared going in.

For the past 3 years I've been the Asst. Director of Student Services here at the Syracuse U. campus in Florence. It is one of the oldest and largest in Italy and Europe, for that matter... the best! I had started here teaching a course called, "Cultural Assimilation through Journal Writing" and when this other job came up they offered it to me. Priscilla works in a variety of ways with tourists coming to Florence helping them to arrange housing (villas to apartments), itineraries, essentially whatever they need.

My son, Casey graduated in 2001, came right back to Italy where he worked for nearly a year as an intern for Associated Press but now works for the news network here in Italy, SkyItalia, and believes he's found a great profession as a tele-journalist. My daughter, Clara, graduated last June and is currently getting her masters at Columbia University in Modern Art and curatorial studies.

In Summary

I suppose what will distinguish my time at Stanford was the fact that I played 3 sports all four years I was there. Fortunately for me and in particular, in those days, this was still possible. I loved them all and ever since I could remember this gave my life the discipline and rhythm I guess I craved. I loved the action, the camaraderie, the strive to do one's best, the praise of coaches, parents and others...it was my identity and life for many years and it gave me, personally, a tremendous amount...in terms that are not easily measurable!!!

Rick Tipton

High School

I grew up in the thriving metropolis of Silver City, New Mexico, attending the local high school. At that time, we still had Bermuda grass tracks; cinders would have blown away in the wind. I took up track in the ninth grade, only because the football coach made everyone do something in the spring to stay in shape. I was devastated to learn he wanted me to become a hurdler - the hurdlers I knew were geeks. On top of that it was really hard, and painful. Every day I trudged home with battered ankles and trail knee - I was a slow learner, I guess. At the first meet I won the race in a fairly good time. Then, a few weeks later, I won a race against some really great runners from a larger town. My attitude and motivation changed overnight. I had an event! Although I continued to like football and basketball more than track, I kept at it and continued to improve. I went on to run the 120-yd high hurdles in 13.8 on a grass track, and was ranked third in the nation. At the state track meet in 1967, I won 5 events, setting 3 state records. I was promptly dubbed the "Silver Bullet" in the newspapers around the state. Pretty heady stuff!!

Stanford

Coming from small-town America, my transition was quite a challenge. At times I longed to return to the southwest, where I could be a big fish in a little pond. Coach Jordan and Bud Spenser encouraged me to hang in there, so eventually, like everyone else, I began to realize I belonged. Track represented a familiar aspect of college life. I looked forward to practice and the fellowship every day. The bull sessions with Bud, while stalling for time between 330s, remain fond college images. Great teammates and the brief respite from academic pressure provided necessary balance.

I never knew about indoor track before coming to Stanford. I got to run at the Cow Palace freshman year, my first taste of big-time competition. Willie Davenport and Earl McCullough were at that race and I think O J Simpson ran the 60. I was fourth or fifth that night, but it didn't matter. It was magic. Over the years, several of us - Peter Boyce, Casey Carrigan, Charlie Francis, TC Jones, and Duncan Macdonald come to mind - traveled to meets around the country. I remember winning several times and beating some great runners.

Outdoors, I had a good season as a sophomore, winning the highs in the Pac-8 and again, as a senior, placing second in the highs and the 100. I liked racing more than worrying about my P.R. [personal record], so Coach always had me run a lot of races each week. You gotta love a guy who doesn't hide at mile relay time!

One of my favorite memories is from the 1971 Big Meet. As always, Coach had analyzed the meet forwards and backwards, and had announced that it was going to be very close. He was always saying that kind of thing, however, and we were not as sure of the outcome as Coach. So, on the way to the locker room Jim Kauffman and I decided we would help Coach out, and show up at the meet in war paint - we were still the Stanford Indians then. We figured the team could use a little loosening up or firing up, as the case may be. We carefully avoided running into Coach until it was too late for him to do anything. As you can imagine, the fans, our teammates, and the reporters really loved the stunt. The Cal runners couldn't believe we were such hotdogs. It was really a hoot. Fortunately, we both had a good day, so made no apologies. I couldn't quite tell whether Coach appreciated our spirited effort, or wanted to strangle us. We won the meet and I think the war paint helped.

Later
After graduating, I spent the next two seasons running in Europe. Duncan Macdonald and I went over each spring and barnstormed during the long European season, hustling a little money for each race, just enough for beer and gasoline to get us to the next meet. There were a lot of runners from all over the world doing the same thing, so it was an incredible experience. There is big money in it now but we probably had more fun. Every meet was a unique adventure. Of course, the stories and times have improved over the years.

I spent one more year in Europe, teaching at a small private school in Spain. I raced a couple of times, but it wasn't as much fun as when we were true track bums. After that, I spent six great years at the Robert Louis Stevenson School, in Pebble Beach, teaching and coaching track and cross-country. I quickly discovered how little I knew about track. I had some good athletes, however, and we all learned together.

For the last 18 years, or so, I have been in the hotel management business, with my own small company. My wife Marcia and I have lived in Palo Alto since leaving Pebble Beach, and have three children: Alison is starting her sophomore year at Oregon; Melissa is turning 16 and is a sophomore at Palo Alto High; and Jamie, our son, is an eighth grader. I stay in touch with Duncan Macdonald, Jim Kauffman, Dan Moore, and Jim Ward. Would love to hear from others.

1972

Duncan Macdonald
Running as a sport began for me in about second grade. We lived at the time a block away from the University of Hawaii's track. We watched the meets there and when no one was around did our own racing, including digging holes for starts, bicycle racing, and running from the maintenance workers. A year or two later President Kennedy's fitness test appeared in our schools and I discovered that I excelled in the 600y run-walk.

The first competitive efforts came in seventh grade when a handful of us went to our athletic director and asked if we could have a track team. That season consisted of two meets, but for me was the beginning of continuous competitive running through age 40.

I spent my 10th grade year in California at El Cerrito High (Berkeley) where I received my first real coaching from Hale Roach. He definitely opened up my horizons and gave me some goals. We ran our own "mini-Olympics" - that sounds a lot like what Harry McCalla was doing a couple of years earlier. My year in California ended by working the hurdle crew at the NCAA Championships at Cal. The release that summer of "The Tokyo Olympiad" was the last straw. I became a track junkie.

My final two years of high school back in Hawaii were spent at Kailua High School. I lucked out in coaches again with Vern Davies (CC 11th grade) and Chuck Richeson. Both were instrumental in my continued growth as a runner (best prep times: 440 - 50.2; 880 - 1:52.7; mile - 4:11.6).

I was recruited at Cal, Yale (too cold), Oregon State, and Stanford (my brother and uncles went there). All had legendary coaches. I was also recruited at the University of Hawaii, and I will always admire how Moses Ohmes recruited me. "I can offer you a full scholarship, but I think it would be better for you if you went to the mainland." I did not personally meet Payton Jordan during the recruiting process. Still, his letters and my familiarity with Stanford led me to Palo Alto.

My first two years at Stanford were traumatic. This was 1967-69. The Viet Nam war and protests at home were raging. The "summer of love" in San Francisco had just ended. Mostly, my Hawaii public school education hadn't prepared me for Stanford. I arrived on campus wearing a suit, which I wore to my first meeting with Payton and his distance assistant Jerry Barland. I never wore that suit again (or any other for that matter). My freshman cross country season was actually pretty good despite the usual freshman weight gains. Track was another matter. Payton didn't have much direct coaching contact with me and most of my problems were in the classroom, so I don't think I gave him too many headaches that year.

Jerry Barland took the head coaching position at Iowa the following year. Marshall Clark was hired as cross country and distance coach. He was so mellow that not even Pete Fairchild and I could shake him. To say that Marshall Clark was a positive influence is a gross understatement.

The remaining years at Stanford were mostly unremarkable from a performance standpoint. The only really memorable performance was my school record sub-4:00 mile at the 1970 Pac 8 Championships at UCLA. At the other end of the spectrum were last place NCAA performances. Off the track, however, there were a lot of memorable events. Pete Fairchild inadvertently locked me in the restrooms at Fresno St. minutes before the start of the mile during a triangular meet with FSU and Oregon. I escaped out a trellis window just in time to make it to the starting line, where I think I actually ran fairly well. That day I decided I was sick of seeing the back of Oregon jerseys at the end of the race and vowed to do everything I could to prevent it in the future. Another race with Oregon in Eugene led to my disqualification when I retaliated against the entire Oregon field after Alan (Large) Sanford was pushed off the track by an Oregon runner. They all retaliated against my retaliation and were DQ'd as well, leading to Alan and one Oregon runner being the only finishers in the race. This probably helped our scoring that day. I know, technically that happened on the track. It really wasn't part of the race plan. Most of the stuff that happened should be kept from public view to protect our reputations. One other memorable event has to be mentioned. We were in Seattle for an indoor meet. A rare snowfall hit the city and everything came to a halt downtown where we were staying. Somehow Rick Tipton, Pete Boyce and I found ourselves in a bar near the hotel. Never mind that Rick and I had fake ID's. The bar seemed strangely silent. Is it the snow? We finally realize that we were the only patrons in the bar who were not deaf-mutes. We finished the evening by stamping out a message in the snow 20 feet high for T.C. Jones to come down and join us at an all-night diner. Another great road trip. Speaking of road trips; how about rest stops in Los Banos?

Payton's patience with me must have worn thin at least once. After a winter in which I couldn't seem to stay healthy I felt a need to get warm. When spring break arrived I borrowed my older brother's Jeep and went to Baja California for a few days of sun before joining the team for the Santa Barbara relays. When I met Payton at the meet he couldn't decide whether to stare at my new mustache or the running shoes I had painted in da-glo colors. The mustache seems to have stuck, but the shoes mysteriously disappeared from the locker room a week or so later.

My running career really took off after I finished at Stanford. I seemed to run pretty well during medical school in Hawaii and residencies in Internal Medicine and Anesthesia in the Bay Area. I don't know why I was more successful after my college career. It was probably just physical and mental maturity happening after what seemed likely to be a career ending injury. The highlights were making the 1976 USA Olympic team and establishing an American record at 5000m. There were several European summers on the track circuit and lots of local and national racing at home. After starting in private practice home in Hawaii in early 1984 I mostly disappeared. At age 40 the Masters scene beckoned and I had a brief hold on the American Masters record in the mile run. Injuries, work and coaching, not necessarily in that order, have kept me away from training and racing since then. My own children have continued on to run in college. Eri (born 1981) has just finished at the University of Oregon, and Pippa (born 1985) is just starting at Cal. I spend most of my "spare" time coaching at a local high school, assisted by my wife Darby. Having the guidance of coaches like Payton and Marshall during my own developmental years made all the difference in the world to me. It only seems natural to try to carry on that tradition.

1973

John Anderson

Getting to Stanford

Growing up in Newberg, Oregon was almost a natural stimulus to get involved in Track & Field. There were runners there before it was a craze and the high school track programs were strong and well coached. By the time I was in High School, I was committed to track as a sprinter, hurdler and relay team member. In my senior year, I was running both the 120 yd. high hurdles and 180 yd low hurdles at Newberg High school and running in invitational meets, often with my colleague from the Oregon high school circuit, Steve Prefontaine. During my senior year, I was the Oregon State champion in both the high and low hurdles and was contacted by Coach Jordan. Who could turn down that invitation! When the acceptance letter was received from Stanford - there was no question that Stanford was the place, and the Coach was going to be the coach.

At Stanford

Going to Stanford to run the hurdles was a dream come true. Only problem was that an early knee injury in freshman year (caused by hitting a hurdle, not a more skilled reason), and the growing realization that maybe the speed requirements in world class hurdling were SLIGHTLY higher than those on the Oregon high school circuit, caused Coach Jordan and me to decide that maybe the 440 and relays were more my cup of tea. And that set the course for the next four years.

Being a Mechanical Engineering major, and having Bud Spencer driving the training with Coach Jordan made for full days and nights. But the Stanford experience was great. You learn humility (as when you race a 440 with the current world record holder - John Smith at UCLA - and the two fastest 440 runners of that year), you get that incredible feeling of being with a world class coach and teammates, and you develop that respect for the balances in life between athletics, academics, and inner character building that Stanford is so good at fostering.

In both my junior and senior years, Coach asked me to be the Captain of the team and I enjoyed working with him, as well as the Co-Captain in our senior year, Ralph Bakkensen. One of the true highlights was anchoring the 880-yd. indoor relay team that set a world record at the Pocatello Relays with Matt Hogsett, John Kessel, and Ken Curl. This honor and the thrill of earning a fourth letter in Track & Field at the awards banquet my senior year made an indelible impression on me. All in all, Coach Jordan and the track team formed a foundation stone of my Stanford experience.

After Stanford

Having met my wife, Wendy Sargent, at Stanford, and getting married the week after graduation, we set out for two years fulfilling my Army ROTC obligation in the Corps of Engineers. After that tour I got my MBA at Harvard (the "Stanford of the East"). I then worked at McKinsey & Co., the consulting firm, in Los Angeles, for 13 years. Following that, I moved on to spend ten years as the Executive Vice President of two railroads: Burlington Northern Santa Fe and CSX. We were married 14 years before we had our first child (we had our free time before the kids came) and now have 4 children in middle and high school. I'm now a partner with a New York private equity firm, but we've chosen to still live in Jacksonville, FL and Cape Cod rather than move to the big city. Wendy and I will always remember the towering influence that Coach Jordan had on us (even on Wendy as she got to know him during our time together at Stanford). The Stanford/Jordan partnership was a winner and the Coach's continuing legacy of shaping young men will live in Stanford minds for decades to come.

1974

1975

Jim Bordoni

Stanford

Ran cross country at Stanford all four years (thank God we had "JV" cross country back then!) but was primarily a track runner.

Did the 440 and the horizontal jumps in high school; tried to continue with the 440 my freshman year at Stanford but the quarter-milers at Stanford were way out of my league (guys like John Anderson, John Kessel). I needed tons of work to run well, but these guys ran well with workouts consisting of merely one or two 220s or 330s, interspersed with listening to Bud Spencer tell stories about how he used to "kick ass." While highly entertaining, it was not (for me) a productive training regimen. I decided then to try the 880.

Spent sophomore through senior year as an 880 runner. Was blessed to be at Stanford when there were no outstanding 880 runners, so a mediocre one like myself could have a role to play. Best time was 1:52.9 (Big Meet against Cal at Stanford, May 1975).

Other highlights (although that's kind of a generous term): Went overseas (Stanford in Italy) fall-winter of junior year but came back in good enough shape to run in a couple meets spring quarter, including leading off the winning 4x880 at the West Coast Relays in Fresno where we were awarded watches! That sure was a big deal to me then. Maybe a bigger deal is that the watch still works!

Another favorite memory is Mount Sac Relays senior year. Ran the 880 on the distance medley on Friday night (I think we were fourth) and was supposed to be done for the weekend. But by Saturday afternoon the sprinters were dropping like flies so I was recruited (coerced?) to run on the 4x220 relay. Lucky for me my teammates were Marvin Holmes, John Foster, and James Lofton. Also lucky for me: two teams dropped their batons on the first handoff (in lanes adjacent to me but I swear I had nothing to do with it; they must have been stunned and/or distracted by my lack of any kind of speed whatsoever). Anyway, I got the baton around safely and I believe Lofton ran an incredible anchor for us to salvage third, which I think was one of Stanford's best finishes of the weekend. We got a set of silk-screened glass tumblers for third (kind of an odd award now that I think of it); all but one has broken over the years, but it still sits in the back of our glass cupboard as one of my all-time favorite prizes for running.

Reflections on Coach Jordan

The most memorable thing I remember about Coach Jordan is the day I first met him. I definitely was not a recruited athlete, nor had I filled out any sort of questionnaire regarding my high school track career. I merely hoped to be accepted as a walk-on. I had heard the cross country team would be working out the week before freshman orientation so made arrangements to stay with some relatives in Mountain View until the dorms opened. When I first arrived on campus I made my way through the maze of hallways that eventually took you to the track office, and poked my head through the doorway and introduced myself to Marshall Clark, whose desk you could see from the door. Marshall greeted me and steered me toward the "inner sanctum" (Payton's office) and introduced me to Coach Jordan. Much to my shock and amazement, Payton proceeded to tell Marshall about all my high school accomplishments as if he had known me for some time. Talk about making a sheepish freshman feel right at home! Here was the legendary coach of the '68 U. S. Olympic Team rattling off the best times and jumps of a two-bit high school kid from Vallejo! From that day on Coach Jordan has always had a special place in my heart, and he is a large part of my motivation for coaching middle school kids as I do today.

One of my favorite memories of Payton is as his "vineyard consultant" about ten years ago. When he heard that I had gotten into grape growing and winemaking, he asked if I could come by the "Rancho" in Los Altos and guide him in his pruning. So for a few years, until he got the hang of it himself, I would go over to his place every spring and spend an afternoon with him in his incredible back yard pruning back the myriad varietals he had growing back there (amongst the chicken coops and the fruit orchards and whatnot).

About this time I also started coaching track at my sons' grammar school. My boys were in third and fifth grades at the time, and, not being real confident in my coaching abilities, I thought I might bring in a true expert as a "guest coach" one day. Of course, Payton never hesitated to say yes to my request, and he spent a memorable afternoon mesmerizing a dozen or so kids who could not really grasp the magnitude of their good fortune. One of my favorite pictures is the group shot I took of the kids with Payton. To me it just sums up how magnanimous the Coach is: a true gentleman and ambassador of the sport.

Post-Stanford

Got a masters in education from Stanford, but then got married (Diane Simpkins, Stanford '75) and headed off to dental school (University of Pennsylvania). Practiced for 8 years in San Jose, then "retired" from dentistry to grow grapes and make wine on the ranch were I grew up in Vallejo (Bordoni Vineyards). Have three boys (whom Payton regularly checks up on, bless his heart!): Mike, a sophomore at Stanford; Matt a senior in high school and going to Yale in the fall; and Jack, a fourth grader. All three boys are runners.

Personally, I've never stopped running. Thanks to the inspiration of Payton Jordan and Marshall Clark it has become an integral part of my life that I am not willing to give up as long as the Lord blesses me with knees that are willing to keep bending comfortably. Although I still do a lot of road races, my preference in still on the track. Last year I turned 50 and set a goal for myself to try to do a sub-5:00 mile which I had not been able to accomplish for several years. I treated myself to a trip to Eugene for the USATF National Masters Championships where I was lucky enough to take third in the age 50-54 men's 1500 meters in 4:35.8. A couple weeks later I ran a mile in 4:55.6.

Coach Jordan's Influence

I think the best lesson I took away from my time with Payton (and Marshall) was how important it was to believe in myself. They always had faith in my ability long before I did. My progress started when I started buying into the idea myself. Also the concept of the "PR" (i.e., personal record), measuring my achievements against myself. I've tried to instill these principles with the kids I coach, today. I only hope they someday look to me with the same reverence and appreciation that I have for Coach Jordan.

Kenny Kring

ACHIEVEMENTS	AWARDS
NCAA Decathlon, 1973 & 1974 Two-time finalist	1973 Iron Man Award
Stanford school record, 1974 Pentathlon, 3150 points	1973 110% Award
Stanford Decathlon list, Second to Bob Mathias, 7151 points	1974 Track & field, Co-Captain
Two-time World Maccabiah Games Gold medalist— Decathlon, 1973 & 1977 Gold medalist-Pole Vault, 1973	1974 Iron Man Award
World Record, 4X440 intermediate hurdles (Kring, Hogsett, Mason, Bagshaw) 3:37.8 Stanford Stadium, April 17, 1974	1974 John C. MacFarland Outstanding Achievement Award
Stanford school record, indoor distance medley Pocatello, Idaho, February, 1974	

MASTERS TRACK

1999 U.S. Indoor Pentathlon- Men's 45+
Champion and new American record

Memorable Stanford Experiences

Appearing along with Coach Jordan in the cover story of Coach & Athlete Magazine, August/September 1974.

On the humorous side: The look on Payton's face when he saw me boarding the team bus in my mandatory meet day necktie. The tie was standing firm and perpendicular, the victim of spilled pole vault "firm-grip" while in my travel bag.

Following my particularly hard fought, second place finish in the 400 intermediate hurdles in the USC dual meet at the LA Coliseum, the ole coach put his arm around me in apparent support and whispered, "Tuck in your shirt, Tiger, you're on national TV."

I remember many memorable speeches covering a variety of topics ranging from coaching technique to more personal matters like health and hygiene. Some of my favorites included - the importance of a firm handshake; Coach Jordan's theory of choosing a spouse the way you buy a horse - you need to look at the teeth; a nutritional speech on why eggs and hash browns create "the perfect carbohydrate enzyme action" for meet day performance. Coach Jordan was a uniquely effective communicator. You always knew exactly where you stood with him, but he combined that directness with a dramatic and colorful sense of surprise!

Post-Stanford

I have lived and worked in New York and Philadelphia, since coming east for my masters from the Yale School of Management. My wife, Pamela, and I are constantly humbled by the task of raising three children-Jake 16, Lydia 13 and Abby 8. The joys, rigors and vicarious pleasures of being a parent now occupy many of the places that athletics once held for me.

I have competed off and on, however, in Masters track & field over the years, enjoying the benefits-both competitively and in association with the sport. And, I've remained committed to staying in shape and workout religiously, just in case I am ever called upon to run another leg on a 4X400.

Professionally, I have spent nearly twenty years in the executive search field. Most of my work today is dedicated to top level recruiting engagements for leading not-for-profit and higher education institutions.

I remained on the farm for two years after my graduation to extend my competitive career and to support Payton and Marshall Clark, as an assistant coach. When I finally concluded that I had raised the bar about as high as I could, I turned from track to a business career. Now, nearly 30 years later, having thrived in the suit and tie world, not a day passes without a thought about or a lesson learned from the ole coach. Long forgotten are the rebel encounters with Payton, the authority figure-"Get your hair cut, Champ"; "Tuck in that shirt, Tiger" - those memories have been replaced by a timeless, enduring sense of integrity, self respect and personal accountability. As I parent my three children, coach their teams, listen to their dreams and attempt to imprint solid values, I am never far from Payton and his teachings.

Thanks, Coach.

Derek Toliver

Youth

I was born and raised in San Francisco to parents who had migrated from the South. The oldest of three children, I was raised in the United Methodist Church where I got my first taste of the Civil Rights Movement, leadership, college-educated African Americans, and my love for track and field. My father took me to all the big track meets in northern California. I started out as a junior high school high jumper. At age 13, I represented San Francisco in the US Youth Games, held in New York City. After placing second in high jump for my age group I returned to "the City" to be recognized before my church congregation, in the *San Francisco Chronicle*, and even had my picture taken with the mayor. That was quite a thrill for a thirteen-year-old.

High School

I was Senior Class President and Captain of the track team at Woodrow Wilson High School in San Francisco. I focused on the high jump and won the Pacific Association AAU Junior Olympics. But shortly thereafter I developed a hamstring injury, which would both haunt and plague me for the rest of my athletic career.

Stanford

During my first year at Stanford I worked out only briefly with the team. My hamstring problems persisted, so Coach Jordan placed me on the junior varsity and encouraged me to focus on adjusting to college, academically. I had just switched to the triple jump and already had a mark of 45'4". I desperately wanted to compete in the Big Meet [with rival Cal Berkeley], so I approached Jordan. He listened then told me if I felt truly ready, he would have me compete for the varsity against Cal. My Big Meet jump gave me third place and the distance, 47' 11-1/2", catapulted me to, then, third on the Stanford All-Time list.

Sophomore year I continued to battle hamstring injuries. I also became a constitutional activist with respect to the search procedures implemented throughout the Bay Area in an effort to capture the so-called Zebra Killer. The police announced a broad profile (i.e., black male, age 20-30, 5'6" to 6'0", and 150-180 lbs.). Word quickly spread of random stops and searches, which not only spread terror among those of us fitting that "profile" but also represented, in our view, a loss of our fourth Amendment protection against "unreasonable search and seizure." As a result, I wore a black armband during the 1974 Big Meet and encouraged other black competitors from Stanford and Cal to do the same. When asked by the press about the silent protest, Jordan told them that we had a right to be concerned and to demonstrate silently and respectfully. Coach Jordan was a father figure. He coached me, disciplined me, challenged me, taught me, and, most appreciated, treated me with respect.

I made fighting for injustice my passion and, as a result, lost my academic focus. My school work suffered and I became ineligible to compete in track. I told Coach Jordan how sorry I was for letting my teammates and him down. He never criticized me. In fact, he surprised me with his reply, which I will never forget. He told me never to regret committing myself to a cause that I truly believed in. He said that everything that I had done outside of track and field was important and that it didn't matter what he thought. It was more important that I hold my head up high and take pride in the fact that I was a man of my convictions.

Post-Stanford

Since Stanford I have been working in the medical products field, primarily in sales and sales management. I currently am employed by McKesson Corporation, the large healthcare information services company. Anitra and I have been married for 23 years and have three daughters: one an Occidental College graduate, one a student at UC, Riverside, and one in high school at the San Francisco School of Arts. I have remained active with track and field, but now as a coach and clinician. I am currently researching a book, which will examine the socio-economic impact of the 1968 Olympic Games.

1976

John Foster

Pre-Stanford

I played football and ran track at Los Altos High School in Los Altos, California. My specialty in track was the hurdles and the sprint events. In football I played halfback and defensive back. We had an excellent sports tradition at Los Altos High. My track & field coach at Los Altos High was Leo Long, who was the 1954 NCAA javelin champion while at Stanford. He had created one of the most successful high school track & field programs in California, and was known for his many outstanding discus throwers. We won the California State Meet in 1970 and many of our athletes went on to Cal, Berkeley. Dave Maggard (Cal Athletic Director, Olympic Organizer) had been a weight coach at Los Altos for a few years. Los Altos High had many ties to Stanford being just a "stone's throw" away. Famous Stanford and 49er QB, John Brodie, lived a few blocks from the high school and his kids all attended.

After high school I enrolled at Foothill Junior College, where I became the State JC runner-up for two years in a row with a best time of 14.1 in the 110 hurdles, and 53.2 in the 440-yard hurdles. I was the West Coast Relays Champ in the 440-yard hurdles. I ran many "all-comers" meets in those days at San Jose City College, and would run against and train with Olympian Bruce Jenner. I also got to run against Stanford's great hurdler, Rick Tipton, and made it a very close race.

Stanford

I came to Stanford in the fall of 1974, as a "J.C." transfer. Also recruited and accepted to UCLA, Cal, and Washington, I chose Stanford mostly because of my meetings with Coach Jordan. The three things that impressed me most about him were his positive energy, compassion, and good sense of humor. In those days Stanford only offered a few track & field scholarships yet we had to compete against the nation's best teams of UCLA, USC, and Cal that offered 20 plus full-scholarships a year. I always was proud of how well Stanford did despite our "handicaps." We regularly won meets against Fresno State, San Jose State, and Occidental College; plus placed among the top teams in most large West Coast Relay Meets. Coach Jordan would often run the Masters 100 meters to thunderous applause and standing ovations. This in itself provided huge motivation to do your very best.

My thoughts of those days are of the great group of men on the team, and in addition to Jordan there were coaches Marshall Clark and Bud Spencer. I remember Bud often standing with his little dog watching Coach Jordan practice his starts at the Stanford Stadium. I recall the words of Marshall Clark to me at the 1976 PAC-10 Championships, "John, I have never seen anyone walk the last 50 meters of the 400 and still run a 48.0 relay split."

My best race at Stanford was a 13.7 in the 110-meter hurdles at the Modesto Relays in May, 1976. I placed second in the Invitational Race. This allowed me to compete in the

1976 Olympic Trials in Eugene, Oregon - along with teammates Tony Sandoval (10k, Marathon) and James Lofton (long jump). I made it to the semi-finals with a 13.92 time. After that I ran in Canada in four "International" meets before the 1976 Olympic Games running a best time of 13.82. I had run in a few "big races" before that, including the 1975 (BYU) and 1976 (Univ. Penn) NCAA Championships. At Penn I made the finals and placed sixth.

I stayed on for my M.A. at Stanford in Social Psychology and "volunteer coached" for the track team. Coach Jordan allowed me to run with the team in Mexico City in a meet he organized in the spring of 1978. Coach seemed to know everyone, and was a fantastic organizer and planner. George Berry was a terrific team manager in those days.

Post-Stanford
My dad was the Athletic Director at the College of Notre Dame in Belmont, California, where I worked as his assistant for a year or so. He was a big Stanford Sports fan, and graduate of the School of Education.

After that, I tried "my hand" as an actor in San Francisco playing many roles at The American Conservatory Theater (A.C.T.). I moved to New York City to play "Romeo" in Romeo and Juliet - "Off-Broadway." I was the fastest man ever to get off stage in a New York production (13.2).

Currently, I live in the Pasadena/Los Angeles area and have worked as a College Administrator at Cal State-LA, USC, and also at NASA-JPL. I assisted in organizing the Judo competition at the 1984 Olympic Games and have been a volunteer in every Olympic Games from then through 2000 (Sydney). My interest in sports, theater, and film has continued since my days at Stanford.

I have traveled this "blue little world" of ours a bit in my life, and I have found few places nicer or more memorable than the Stanford track on a sunny spring day.

My best wishes to everyone.

Matt Hogsett

Pre-Stanford
How did that education come about? Track, quite frankly. I grew up in Newport Beach, wanted to play football in high school, surf and then join the Navy. It didn't exactly work out that way. I played all sports in junior high school, but found out I could run about as fast as anyone. Since I was not the largest kid around, however, my father suggested track instead of football. He said I wouldn't be big enough to play football in college, but there was a chance I could run. He was right. I ran track for four years at Newport Harbor High School under my first great coach, Bob Haley, and I was taught to hurdle by a former Stanford runner, Jeff Pierose. Bob retired from teaching a few years ago at a dinner well attended by his adoring former athletes. Without athletics I would have been a middling high school student. Didn't work out that way.

Advised by a high school counselor to apply to college, she suggested USC, UCLA, and Stanford. My dear neighbor, Kay Spurgeon, was a friend of Coach Jordan; they both vacationed in Avalon on Catalina Island. I learned I was going to Stanford one afternoon after school. Mrs. Spurgeon came to the house with a letter from Payton. She had written Payton to inform him of this kid who could hurdle and he had written her back saying that they already knew of my running and would be offering a scholarship. For a kid without the means to attend a first-rate school, her news was one of those life-changing events we all hope for but too few ever really experience.

Stanford Years
I loved the school. Being something of a traditionalist even then, it was not lost on me that I was living something of an anachronism - traditional school, jock, away from home, wonderful surroundings, and a first-rate mentor, Payton Jordan. Bud Spencer was then volunteering his time as a quarter mile coach and he took me under his wing.

The intermediate hurdles were a perfect fit, except that I led with the wrong foot, my right, not the best on the turns. It turned out to be a small impediment, however. In 1973, my freshman year, a Stanford indoor team (John Anderson, myself, Ken Curl and John Kessel) set a world record in the indoor half-mile relay. Each time we are at Stanford, my wife takes the kids out to the new track facility to show them the names at the west end, saying, "That was your daddy." I don't mind the past tense. My best year was my sophomore year, 1974, when I won the then Pac-8 Championships in the intermediates at the LA Coliseum, much to my surprise. Injuries my junior year were frustrating, and I tore a meniscus cartilage in my lead leg my senior year which ended the hurdling. I still ran the mile relay and vividly remember the last 50 yards of my leg on the mile relay at the Pac-8 Championships at Berkeley my senior year. I remember thinking, "this is it, take a look around" just before I handed off. And, then it was over, or so I thought.

Post-Stanford
I never ran competitively again after college, but I had learned so much while running about competition, self-control and confidence that I can honestly say I was a changed person. Stanford changed my entire horizon. Law school followed and, probably inevitably, I was drawn to the courtroom. I now tell my kids that 90 percent of the people never go head-to-head, you win or you lose, no excuses, making those who do a somewhat rare breed. At least in my opinion, not a bad characteristic to pass on. The whole road of my life now seems to have been something of an odyssey and no part of it was more magical than the four years in college. As time has passed the years running at Stanford have become more dreamlike, the walks past Angell Field, afternoon workouts in the stadium, and so on. The mementoes from those years now hang on the walls of my office, not to impress others, believe me, but to remind myself there was a time when I was truly celebrating youth. For those I have encountered during my life who consider athletics to be brutish, I have told them there is one time in your life when you are the strongest, the fleetest, the most alive, those young years in a person's life, when you choose what you are, whether you're in the game or not. For the great or, like myself, the not-so-great, the lesson is the same.

Coach Jordan Impressions
Regarding Coach Jordan, no one ever knew better what young men and women can do or how better to motivate them to do it. Coach Jordan has my greatest admiration, always did, and my gratitude that he would be the last person to acknowledge. Such is the man. I hope he knows what a legacy he has left.

Life Now
At present I am a near fifty-year old insurance defense lawyer in Denver, Colorado. We have two kids: a 14-year old girl, Murphy, and an 11-year old son, John. I married my college girlfriend, Mary Ann, and we are still married after 26 years. I live in a refurbished 1906 home in downtown Denver. For pleasure, I watch the kids' sports (volleyball for the girl, hockey for the boy), travel to Europe every other year or so, sail here in Colorado and in the Virgin Islands, still read lots of history, and love woodworking. In summary, it is your basic fairly traditional existence - an existence much molded by my experiences at Stanford.

David Schreiber

Pre-Stanford
Sprinters are born, but competitors are cultivated. As a child, I was gifted with reflexes and anatomy that created quickness. I first realized this at age 8, on the playground. Elementary and high school records seemed to follow along all too soon, as I look back so many decades now. Medals for league 100 yd., 220 yd. and 440 relay, Southern California CIF championship meets and medals were gleaned with natural talent. I thought I was working hard, but I hadn't yet met Coach Jordan.

Stanford
I walked on to the Stanford Track Team in the fall of 1974, and was immediately struck by the history and talent of the Head Coach. Imagine, running a 9.3 second 100-yard dash — barefoot! He regarded me with a skeptical eye at first, but was willing to give me a chance. He presented me with workouts previously un-fathomed by me, enabling me to gain incredible cardio-vascular and strength conditioning. This, along with many sprinting tips gleaned from instruction and from observation of Coach Jordan himself competing, increased my quickness as well. All of us, walk-ons and those few with scholarships, were treated equally by the Coach, all given a chance to prove ourselves. At Stanford, my 100 yd. dash time fell from 9.9 sec. to 9.7 sec. and my 200-meter (we switched that year) time fell to 21.3 sec. during my first season. I competed in some dual meets with some tremendous athletes on our team and on others in the Pac - 8. My career was cut short in the middle of the second season due to a knee injury (cartilage damage), most likely sustained on that old asphalt track, which of course was immediately replaced upon my graduation. There was no arthroscopic surgery in those days, so my choice was a major operation with no guarantees, or to quit sprinting. I chose the latter.

My most memorable experiences with Coach Jordan revolve around the one-on-one attention he was always willing to give me. He treated me like he was not only proud of who I was, but also proud of what I could become. Little pointers like not wearing socks (less slippage in the shoe), finishing a longer run with a sprint (putting in the extra effort when you think you have nothing left to give), and showing me proper running form and insisting that I maintain it. Finally, I will never forget two of the most important moments I shared with Coach Jordan, the day I met him in his office, before I was even accepted to Stanford, and the day I sat down with him in his office and resigned from the team. He understood my decision, and felt my loss and pain; however, he understood. He knew that I learned a lot more than about sprinting from him over the previous two years. He knew that I would not forget him, the team or the lessons he taught me about sprinting and life, the parallels. He was right.

I'm paraphrasing; it's been awhile. But I recall this quote from him, "The greater the adversity and effort required to achieve your goal, the more satisfying the attainment."

Post-Stanford
When my track career ended in my second year, I concentrated on academics, graduated at the end of my third year, and went on to medical school in North Carolina. I returned to Stanford for my residency and two fellowships in Radiation Oncology and two subspecialties. I moved to Denver and joined a hospital-based practice for twelve years, then went on to open my own facility, Littleton Radiation Oncology, create the Prostate Seed Center (35 urologists are part of this company, of which I am the CEO) and am now organizing the Breast Brachytherapy Center to treat breast cancer with a quicker form of radiation treating only a part of the breast at less cost than conventional radiation therapy. I am a commercial/instrument pilot and own a turboprop aircraft, which I use to attend conferences, give lectures and consult around various parts of the country, mainly the Southwest. I am married with children aged 23, 21, 11, and 9. The two boys have some speed, but I think the gift skips a generation, as my grandfather was also a talented sprinter in 1916.

Coach Jordan's Influence
Life is a challenge. Coach Jordan gave me a wonderful gift when he provided tools for me to meet that challenge. The Coach taught me how to maximize and capitalize on my strengths and minimize or overcome my weaknesses. He helped me utilize every ounce of mental and physical strength I could muster to take on any task, no matter how daunting. He taught me that it pays to be persistent both mentally and physically. My career has blossomed and I enjoy excellent health, strength, quickness to this day - all thanks to the lessons gleaned from a mentor, a coach, and a friend, Coach Payton Jordan.

1977
John Olenchalk
Athletics
Stanford Football (1973-1976)
- 3 varsity letters
- Only non-scholarship "walk-on" freshman to play in a varsity game in 1973 (first year the NCAA allowed freshman eligibility for varsity football, Division 1)
- Awarded Stanford Football scholarship commencing 1974.
Stanford Track (1973-1975)
- shot put and discus (injured 1976)
- shot put best 53'11"

Professional Football
- Montreal Alouettes CFL (1978-80)
- Kansas City Chiefs NFL (1981-83)

Path to Stanford
My choice of Stanford, as a seventeen-year-old freshman in 1973, was driven by my desire to play football at the Division 1 level in the (then) Pac-8 conference. Having been accepted at Cal, Stanford, and Oregon academically, I was disappointed at not having been recruited by any of them despite achieving all state honors (North-South Shrine Game, etc...) and felt Stanford offered the best opportunity for me both athletically and academically. My parents, both schoolteachers in Antioch, California, preferred Stanford over the others, and offered to come up with the money for at least the first year. Having grown up in the east bay, I had little desire to spend four years in Berkeley, Stanford had recent Rose Bowl appearances, and in that era, Oregon football was abysmal, so Stanford was the choice.

Stanford
Achieving recognition in the freshman football program, I was activated for the Big Game as a freshman, and after a strong showing in spring football, asked for and received a football scholarship for tuition for my sophomore year, with the promise of an upgrade to a full ride as a junior and senior. I knew who coach Jordan was, and had competed in the shot and discus in high school with some degree of success. Subsequent to the football season my freshman year, I spent a lot of time in the weight room with another football player, Andrew Kolesnikow who'd been a hurdler in high school, and we decided to talk to Coach Jordan, who easily convinced us to try to compete in both sports to the extent our football commitments would allow.

As a freshman, given my age and size, it was quite a struggle adapting to the heavier implements, and when spring football came around, coach understood I would have to focus on football, but graciously left the door open for me to continue to compete in his program to the extent I could. I returned as a sophomore, and with benefit of some added maturity and strength, in the early season managed a shot put of 53'10 ½ " but suffered a hand injury that never allowed me to improve or compete effectively in track and field from that point on, although I came back as a junior and senior to try.

Following the football season my junior year, I had lost my starting position at linebacker halfway through the season, head coach Jack Christiansen had reneged on his promise of converting my tuition scholarship to a full ride, and I was extremely discouraged, full of self-doubt. For some reason, I stopped by Coach's office. He engaged me in a long conversation and showed extraordinary concern and consideration for my situation; going further, he offered to provide me with the opportunity to take a psychological profile test developed by sports psychologists' Ogilvie & Tutko at San Jose State. I still have the results and analysis, which he shared with me several weeks later. The insights revealed by the simple diagnostic were quite stunning to me, and helped me characterize and cope with what I was experiencing.

Despite having his athletic scholarships and team budget drastically reduced, despite the lack of cooperation from the football coaching staff in sharing many of the much more talented dual-sport athletes at that time, Coach Jordan invested money, time, and effort to rebuild and reinforce the confidence, attitude, and sense of purpose in a football player who was never going to make a major contribution to his program, at a time when I was literally being thrown away by the football staff. I had a whole new appreciation of Payton Jordan as a person, beyond the storied athletic achievements, here was a guy that was a fierce competitor, was fighting for his program, but had such depth of character and compassion, and I believe he freely gave of those qualities to every athlete who ever came through his program. I truly believe he is one of the greatest people I have ever been privileged to be around.

Although I continued to be an important special teams player, I never started another football game at Stanford, but I never allowed a coach from that point, until I hung up my cleats years later, to destroy my sense of self worth. I became even more determined to prove them all wrong.

Post-Stanford
Ultimately, I "walked on" as a free agent and was involved in professional football for the better part of six years, in two different leagues, playing longer and more successfully than any of the linebackers the Stanford football staff had promoted ahead of me during those years. I came to measure the quality of every coach I encountered in my football career, by the standard set by Coach Jordan.

I was truly fortunate to have worked with and learned from some great football coaches (Marv Levy, Rod Rust, Ted Cottrell, Lamar Leachman, to name a few) after I left Stanford. All of the truly great ones manifested a humility and greatness of spirit, as well as a professionalism and commitment to their athletes and teams, that were embodied by Payton Jordan. Those transcendent qualities are at the heart of a true champion, no matter what his chosen field. He is an archetypal human being, and that about says it all...

Jeff Parietti
Jeff attended Seattle Prep High School, where he was a standout in both cross country and track. As a result, he earned a scholarship to Stanford.

At Stanford Jeff continued to perform well in both cross country and track, lettering in each for four years. In addition to his active sports schedule, Jeff also found time to be the sports editor for the Stanford Daily.

After Stanford Jeff has worked in public relations for the American Electronics Association and more recently has served as public relations manager for Kenworth Truck Company in the Seattle area. He also has authored several sports-related books.

Actual performances on the track include:
800 meters - 1:55.8
Mile - 4:10

1,500 meters - 3:50.2 (equivalent to 4:08 mile)
Two mile - 8:55.6
Three-mile - 13:49 (6th all-time at Stanford - back then!)
5,000 meters (3.1 miles) - 14:20

Highlights include:
Qualified for Pac-8 in 1500 and 5000 meters. Entered 5,000 meters and finished 10th in 14:22 at UCLA in Los Angeles.

Running against the great Steve Prefontaine of Oregon freshman year in Pac-8 cross country championships. He beat me by 4 minutes over 6 miles!

Finishing 7th (almost 6th) junior year in 5,000 meters in Pac-8 track championships. Also qualifying for conference meet in 1,500 meters.

Running 13:49 in three-mile at Stanford - 6th best all-time...

Finishing third in the Open 5,000 meters at the Mt. SAC Relays in Walnut, Calif. by beating one Olympian (Paul Geis) and a number of other top runners with my time of 14:20.

Earning the Most Improved Runner award from Stanford by junior track season.

1978
Stacy Geiken
Pre-Stanford
I had an early start as a distance runner in the Bay Area. As a 15 year old I was ranked second nationally in the 2- mile (9:56) and third in the 3-mile (16:11). In high school I was an AAU age group state champion in cross country and improved my mile time to 4:21 and 3-mile to 14:32.

Stanford
I was the first freshman to break 9 minutes in the 2-mile, with a time of 8:58.6. I went on to improve my times in the mile to 4:15, steeplechase (9:08), and the 5K (14:57). But only at Stanford could one recall crossing the finish line as the third runner for Stanford in the Pac-8 cross country championship on the Stanford golf course to the sound of the Stanford Band playing the William Tell Overture! Received the 1976 Frank Angell Award.

When I arrived at Stanford Coach Jordan's reputation was so legendary I was absolutely petrified to speak with him. I soon found that he always was there at the finish of a good race with a pat on the back and words of encouragement. One of the important learnings I took away from the Ole Coach is "the importance of saying what you mean and meaning what you say."

Post-Stanford
Continued to compete for the Converse Aggies (80-84) then the Reebok Aggies (85-90). Managed to post times of 8:27 in the 3000 meters, 14:58 in the 5K, 31:45 in the 10K, 1:08.42 in the half-marathon, and 2:26.56 in the marathon.

Mark Hadley

Pre-Stanford
I was a track and field enthusiast and participant at an early age. My father, Jack N. Hadley, was a high school track phenom in Southern California (100yds: 9.8; 220 yds.: 21.8) and was awarded a scholarship to the University of California at Berkeley. My dad knew Coach Jordan long before I did. I was successful in cross country and track in high school. I ran for Napa High School (1971) and subsequently, Vintage High School (1972-74) in Napa, California. I posted times of 1:52.6 in the 880 and 4:17.6 in the mile in my senior year, ranking among the nation's top-20 high school performers for both events that year.

I was offered a variety of potential collegiate opportunities and was delighted to be recruited by and ultimately accepted at Stanford. My father having been a Cal Bear, his familiarity with and respect for Coach Jordan, combined with my early impressions of both Coach Jordan and Coach Marshall Clark, made my selection of Stanford easy and exciting. I received a combination of academic/athletic grant-in-aid all four years on the Farm and was an active member of the cross country and varsity track teams all four years (1974-78).

Stanford
My tenure on campus centered around the Athletic Department, the golf course (cross country) and the track, and my teammates. I was a good student (Economics and Biology), but I wanted to be considered a "jock," not a "pre-med." While a "big fish in a small pond" in high school, I was a journeyman trackman in college. My best times in the 440 (47.3), the 880 (1:50.6), and the mile/1500m equivalent (4:10-ish) were few and far between, but won a few points at selected dual, relay, and invitational meets during my Sanford career. I made the varsity traveling squad each year and was an occasional alternate on the mile relay/4x400 relay teams. I was not a "star" in college but had a great experience and supported my team and my teammates. I worked out twice a day most every day at Stanford and loved being part of those Clark/Jordan teams all four years. I enjoyed Coach Jordan's doctrine and philosophy. I met with him regularly in his Athletic Department office and made it a point to greet him daily on the track. He provided me with insight, encouragement and inspiration in all aspects of my collegiate life.

Visiting Coach in his office was a highlight. I did it often. He was warm and upbeat and had that incredible, engaging smile. His office was like a museum filled with photos, awards, medals, and trophies. He was disciplined, conservative, caring, and compassionate. He was inspirational and a great motivator, always very positive. He was a great role model, leader, and coach. He seemingly treated all of us the same, from the All-Americans and Olympic hopefuls and team members to daily-grind low-level contributors like me. It was an awesome experience and I grew to love the "ole Coach" like a father.

We had some great guys on our teams from 74-78. Lofton, Foster, Shellworth, Holmes, Wingo, Banks, Crowley, Margerum, Sheats, Wells, Geiken, Nelson, and many, many others...and we all were friends and comrades. I recall a mile relay at the Stanford Invitational our junior year. Sheats opened with a 46.4, Banks ran 47.0, and handed off to me tied for second place with USC. I ran 47.4, lost ground, and passed the baton to James Lofton. I had slipped to third place, well behind the leading USC team. Lofton ran 44.06 and won running away! That was the most incredible relay race I was ever a part of.

In the spring of my senior year, I received a medical school acceptance, culminating my years of study at Stanford. I ran to the Coach's office to inform him. He was already down at the track with the sprinters and field event guys. When I informed him of my news he suddenly picked me up by the waist, hoisted me in the air and announced my good fortune to the team. He then told me to run to the golf course to inform my distance coach, Marshall Clark. "You're a champion, Hadley," he said, "on and off the field." I ran through campus to the golf course with tears in my eyes, pleased by my good fortune, but most pleased that Coach Jordan was so proud of me, one of "his guys." Finally, it was an honor to receive the Al Masters, Stanford Track and Field Scholastic Achievement Award at the conclusion of my senior season, and a Stanford blanket, signifying four consecutive years as a Stanford varsity athlete.

Post-Stanford

After graduating from Stanford I attended medical school in upstate New York at Albany. I completed my Residency in Neurosurgery at Barrow Neurological Institute in Phoenix, Arizona. I spent three years in the Air Force after residency to repay a three-year medical school scholarship. In July 1991, I took a position in the Department of Surgery, Division of Neurological Surgery at the University of Alabama at Birmingham. UAB is a very large, productive, successful, tertiary care Medical Center. In thirteen years I have developed a very busy practice focused on the treatment of spine and spinal cord disorders. I am the Director of the Residency Training Program in Neurosurgery at UAB and am on the Medical Student Teaching Faculty. I participate in scientific study and publishing. I have recently completed a ten-year-term on the Executive Committee of the Congress of Neurological Surgeons, our national specialty organization of 5400 members. In 2002-2003 I was honored to be elected President of that group.

I am happily married to a great woman, Lori Frances Hadley, and we have three wonderful, athletic children, Christopher (15), Jack (8), and Mollie (5).

Coach Jordan reinforced in me the merits of dedication, training, preparation, sacrifice, and a positive work ethic. He asked us to believe in ourselves, in our team, and our coaches. He taught me that the whole, the team, is bigger than the parts, the individuals. He reinforced the concepts of team achievement and the value of every member's contribution, no matter how small. He celebrated our wins and taught us how to lose with dignity, although never to be comfortable with losing. He taught us never to rest on our laurels but to consistently prepare to do our best - because on any given day the mighty might be defeated by the lesser known. He helped us set our sights and goals and showed us how to achieve them. He helped me translate my athleticism and the lessons learned in the athletic arena into my scholastic and personal life...and ultimately into my professional life. Coach Jordan was (and is) much, much more than a world-class athlete and track coach.

James Lofton

James Lofton's athletic accomplishments quite simply are so extensive, they warrant no further explanation. So, this author has chosen simply to list them below.

Athletics

- NCAA champion in the long jump, 1978 and two-time Pac-8 champion, 1977 and 78.
- Pac-8 athlete of the year, 1977, track and field.
- USA junior team member, 1975.
- USA track team member, 1977.
- World's longest long jump in 1978, 26' 11-3/4".
- Four-time All-American.
- Academic All-American, football, 1977.
- All Pac-8, football, 1977.
- All-American second team, football, 1977.
- Stanford Hall of Fame
- Green Bay Packers Hall of Fame, 1999.
- Pro Football Hall of Fame, 2003.
- Stanford All-Century Team, football.
- Eight-time NFL Pro Bowler
- NFC Rookie of the Year, 1978.
- Senior Bowl MVP, 1978.
- Senior Bowl Hall of Fame, 1977.

Reflections on Jordan

The most meaningful time I had with Coach Jordan was in March of 1978. Coach Jordan and I traveled to Detroit for the NCAA Indoor Championships. I had just finished my senior season of football and played in the Senior Bowl and our Stanford team had won the Sun Bowl. I was getting ready for an NFL career. It was just the two of us traveling. Coach Jordan talked about my upcoming NFL career and what life would be like as a pro athlete. He instructed me on continuing to train like a champion and conduct myself like a champion. We had a sign above the door of the locker room that said, "Champions should be gracious and humble." To me that is the essence of Coach Jordan.

Post-Stanford
- Played in the NFL from 1978 - 1993; five different teams.
- Married to Beverly for 23 years.
- Three kids: David a sophomore at Stanford; Daniel a high school sophomore; and Rachel a seventh grader.
- Coaching with the San Diego Chargers 2002- present
- Worked in Sports Broadcasting for 8 years: 1994-2002 CNNSI, FOX SPORTSNET, NBC, and CBS Radio.

1979

Clay Bullwinkel

I was neither a famous athlete nor even a main point scorer in my time. The recollections of many who were, rightfully will dominate this book. In my case, though, I had an extraordinary experience with Coach Jordan, which bears inclusion. As a backdrop to that I first provide a few images.

1976 - a Stanford teammate had just lost his father. This teammate had spent a long time with Coach Jordan before practice. Ole Coach regularly made counseling gestures and comments to us athletes. Some who did not have fathers or who were far away from their families took more to this side of him than I did. I had a father to whom I was close. That was good enough for me.

1977 - Mexico City. With his 1968 Olympics connections, Coach Jordan arranged for the Stanford team to be invited there to compete against the Mexican national team. The local track officials greeted him with full regalia and honors. We had a blast. Coach Jordan could have visited his friends without us, and not have taken the trouble to haul us along. But he did.

1976-1979 - the end-of-year team banquets. Alumni showed up out of their regard for Coach Jordan and to see their former teammates. I was jolted when I received the Maree Rodebaugh Award my senior year. Coach thought I deserved it.

1979 - Coach Jordan wrote a recommendation for me in my application to Stanford's Graduate School of Business. He can sure pour it on thick. He did, and with great care.

1992 - Stanford Athletic Department Hall of Fame Induction Gala. Coach Jordan was a cutting figure in his white tux, commanding from the podium in his typical presidential manner. Marge and daughters were beaming. James Lofton and Ken Margerum were inducted in the same ceremony. Master of ceremonies, Gary Cavalli, told us that a dozen or so of Coach Jordan's former athletes had named their sons and daughters after him.

2002 - U.S. Track and Field Championships. A pre-meet formal reception honoring Coach Jordan with many 1968 Olympians present. For everyone's entertainment, Ole Coach reenacted in a vaudevillian manner how he recruited Mexican security personnel at the 1968 Olympics to bodily haul off reporter Howard Cosell as Cosell attempted to drum up scandals.

Now back to the most special experience. It was April 1998. I had spoken with Coach Jordan a couple times already on the phone about raising money for Stanford track and field. He had sent me several letters and reference materials for ideas. I met Coach Jordan at Stickney's, the old restaurant located in Town & Country near the edge of campus, which has since been replaced by Scott's Seafood.

I had been working for months trying to pull together a new, broader fund raising tactic for Stanford's track and field program. A jealous fund raising manager in the athletic department was trying to downsize our designs despite clear precedents in the tennis program. On the phone and through the mail Coach Jordan had already provided me inspiration to stick with it. Over two decades since his retirement he had often helped the track program. What a gracious guy, I thought.

We ordered and waited for our food. Whether sitting or standing, Coach Jordan comes across as energized and spry. I could not help but start thinking of my loss of my father four months earlier. I mentioned dad. Coach Jordan said a few things that showed he remembered him well. Ole Coach could read my face all the way. He showed complete acknowledgement when he nodded a few times. Nothing more on that topic needed to be said. A feeling came over me as if I was with a close relative. But who? Not a grandfather. An uncle? A much (much!) older brother?

I thought about all those athletes naming their son Payton. Then it dawned on me. I sat up in the booth smiling ear to ear at Coach Jordan. We returned to the topic of fund raising. It took me 19 years, and a dear loss, but I finally understood him, and he understood me. This fellow was not only an athlete, a coach, a teacher, a mentor. His greatest mission, his foremost gift, is to be there when a person needs something a bit more heavy duty. Fatherliness can incur risks. Kindness is not always returned. Yet he does it readily, repeatedly, and graciously.

Thank you, Coach Jordan, for your patience and understanding. Thank you for your inspiration for the Tributes Among the Greats fund raising program. All is being passed on.

Roy Kissin

Pre-Stanford

I grew up in Spokane, Washington, where distance running phenoms Gerry Lindgren and Rick Reilly were local heroes (Rick's brother Tim was grade school friend), but I never imagined I would become a runner until after we moved to Danville, California, in 1969. One fateful day, I departed from my custom of jogging my laps in junior high school P.E. and for the heck of it decided to see how fast I could run. I finished way ahead of everyone and was promptly informed by my teacher and first coach, Warren Conrad, that henceforward I would be spending my lunch hour running with him. Coach Conrad was in his late 20s, an ex-Cal Poly SLO football player turned distance runner well before the time such a transformation became fashionable. By the time I finished 8th grade, I had run a 2:11 half mile and a 5:05 mile and the die was cast.

Bob Vincent became my coach at San Ramon Valley High School. Coach Vincent had been coaching at San Ramon for about 30 years by the time I got there, and he was known for fielding tough and competitive track and cross country teams, yet I've met very few people as kind, soft-spoken, or committed to kids as he was. My freshman year, I worked my way up to become third man on the Varsity cross country team that placed third at North Coast Section (unfortunately, California held no state championship in cross country at the time). On the track, I ran bests of 4:37.4 for the mile, 9:47.2 for two miles, and set an age 14 10,000-meter record of 33:06. The latter mark resulted in a mention in *Sports Illustrated's* "Faces in the Crowd" feature.

That summer, my parents took me to the 1972 Olympic Trials in Eugene, which many observers recall as one of the best meets ever held on U.S. soil. I will always be grateful for the kindness and inspiration I received from several ex-Stanford runners, Don Kardong, Duncan Macdonald, and Greg Brock, who were nice enough to let me and a couple of my wide-eyed adolescent friends hang out with them during the meet. They were smart and funny and tough competitors, and I knew then and there that I wanted to follow in their Stanford footsteps.

My sophomore year I progressed rapidly, placing second to my teammate Mike Dayton, a 9:11 two miler, in just about every cross country meet and invitational. At the league meet, I finally found the wherewithal to challenge his sprint and won going away. He never beat me again. I finished second at the North Coast Section meet to Rich Kimball, who was to become a 4:02 miler the double State Champion in the mile and two mile. On the track, I ran 9:17.3 to make the State Meet and finished 14th.

Junior year, our cross country team won North Coast Section after placing well in the two previous years, while individually I again finished second to Kimball. On the track, I improved to 9:08.0 and 8th place at State.

My senior year, everything seemed to gel. I went undefeated in cross country against high school competition, up to and including the AAU National Junior Championships, where I finished third (behind two college freshman). Hitting the last barrier with 200 meters to go, I shot past two very tough rivals, Eric Hulst and Ralph Serna, and can still clearly recall seeing Coaches Jordan and Clark cheering me into the finish chute.

That finish not only sealed my scholarship to Stanford, but earned me a trip to the IAAF World Cross Country Championships in Rabat, Morocco, in March 1975, where I finished eighth as a member of the first place U.S. Junior team. In the build-up to the race, I won the high school two mile at the Sunkist Invitational in Los Angeles and the Examiner Indoor Games in San Francisco, the latter in 9:07.2, the third fastest time in meet history behind the great Marty Liquori and my childhood idol, Gerry Lindgren. On the track, I ran 8:56.2 at State to finish third in the two mile behind Hulst and Serna in one of the deepest fields ever (five runners under 9:00). Foregoing my high school graduation ceremony, I took second at the International Prep Invitational in Chicago in a photo finish with Carey Pinkowski, now Executive Director of the Chicago Marathon.

Stanford

I was looking forward to bigger and better things, but as it turned out, my first two years at Stanford were undistinguished and somewhat anti-climactic following the notoriety and heady success of high school. A decent cross country season ended badly when I blew up and finished well back at the Pac-10 Cross Country Championships (run on the Stanford Golf Course). Nothing like this had ever happened to me before and I was crushed.

That evening, I took a walk around campus and saw a light on in the coaches' office. Coaches Jordan and Clark reassured me that everything was OK; they knew I'd worked hard and done my best, but that adjusting to college life and the higher level of competition would take time. I bounced back in time to make a return trip to the World Cross Country meet along with Tony Sandoval and alum Don Kardong, but unlike the previous year, didn't run particularly well. On the track, I ran about the same times I ran in high school, and did manage to break Tony's freshman two mile record with an 8:58.8 mark.

That summer, I tried to bust out of the plateau I was on by training harder, but succeeded only in tearing a tendon in my knee. This caused me to miss my sophomore cross country season, but even after months of rest the injury was no better. It was a real low point, spending dreary afternoons in the training room icing and heating an injured knee instead of running with my teammates. I'd hang out at the track office, and to cheer me up Coach Jordan would often treat me to a malt at Peninsula Creamery. He always tried to keep me in a positive frame of mind, assuring me I'd work through my travails, never letting me give up on myself.

Finally, the trainers figured out that the injured tendon had atrophied. They put me on a strenuous twice a day rehabilitation program and by the start of track I was back on my feet, but far from fit. I labored through an abbreviated season, running only dual meets and foregoing the Conference Championship, but there was one big highlight. Thanks to Coach Jordan's Olympic connections, our whole team was invited to compete against a Mexican Olympic Development team at a meet in Mexico City over spring break. What an adventure! On the way down, the plane landed at every two-mule town between Sonora and Estado de Mexico. On one especially memorable landing, the pilot actually bounced the plane in the dirt just short of the runway. We arrived safely and checked into Olympic Village where we received emphatic and repeated warnings not to drink the water. That night we were serenaded by the strains of discus hurler Doug Greenwood's hurling (he drank the water). After the meet, Coach Kenny Kring led a delegation for a memorable meal at CafÈ de Tacuba near the Zocalo. High jumper John "Juan Muchachito" Littleboy was the life of the party, towering over the diminutive natives who shrieked with amazement every time he complied with their requests to stand up at the table. The only negative aspect of the trip was having to run our races at 7200' altitude!

The summer before junior year, I moved to Tahoe to train at altitude and attempt to get my running career back on track. By this time Coaches Jordan and Clark must have been as frustrated with me as I was with myself, but they were never anything but supportive. I kept them informed of my progress and received encouraging letters in reply. Cross country season that fall was pretty solid but I fell short of my goal of making the NCAA meet. It wasn't until track season that my patience finally paid off.

The breakthrough came unexpectedly during a 10,000-meter race at UCLA. I trailed my friend and frequent training partner Duncan Macdonald by a straightaway at the halfway point, but then started to chip away at his lead. No one, including Duncan, the American Record holder in the 5,000 at the time, was more surprised than I was when I passed him and went on to finish in just over 29:00, knocking a minute and a half off my PR and qualifying for the NCAA Championships, where I was the 6th American finisher and 14th overall.

Success carried over to my senior year as I finally ran consistently well in cross country and qualified for the NCAA Championships as an individual (unfortunately I have no record or memory of how I finished). On the track, I placed third in the Conference 10,000 meters, finishing strongly behind Alberto Salazar and another Oregon runner. When I finished, Coach Jordan came out of the stands to embrace me along with my teammates. It was a great moment. I went on to the NCAA meet and earned my only All-American certificate as the fourth American finisher and eighth overall. But in retrospect, what turned out to be perhaps my proudest collegiate accomplishment was winning the 1979 Big Meet 5,000 meters in a meet record that stood for 19 years.

Post-Stanford

The 1980 Olympic boycott took the wind out of my sails. I didn't see any point in training for a "Marathon Trial" that was destined to become a dead end. In addition, adjusting to post collegiate life and finding my way in the workaday world took its toll and I didn't train hard or compete again for two years. In 1982, I fell in with a group of runners living in San Francisco and decided to give it one more shot. By 1984 I achieved a modest breakthrough on the national level, running PR's of 13:42.2 and 28:19.5 for 5,000 meters and 10,000 meters. Unfortunately, a week before the 1984 Olympic Trials I badly sprained an ankle and hobbled through the heats. However, spending the summer racing on the European circuit as a sponsored athlete provided considerable consolation. I pressed on for another two years, running close to but never exceeding my 1984 PRs, before hanging 'em up. Approaching 30, I ultimately concluded that the marginal improvements I was likely to see couldn't justify further sacrifices in my personal life. My career was just beginning to take off and I had met the woman I was to marry a few years later.

So I became a guy with a wife, kids, job, mortgage, and lawn... not that there's anything wrong with that! I didn't run for a decade, but started up again when I was about to turn 40 and we moved to Marin County with its open spaces and trails. On one of my infrequent jogs around the neighborhood, an old running buddy I hadn't seen in 20 years drove by, rolled down his window and said, "You're fat, Kissin." These days, on 25 miles a week and my slimmed down frame, I can break 5:00 for the mile - or at least I could last year at age 46.

Fortune has smiled on us. I'm well into my second career as an investment advisor, following 15 years in motion picture production. My wife BZ and I have two wonderful children, Peter, 13, and Sonia, 11. Both run on the middle school cross country team I coach, but their main athletic interest is baseball. I'm tremendously proud of Sonia, who is one of two girls among 120 boys playing in our league. BZ went to Cal, but the kids are being raised Stanford.

Looking back through the haze of memory, it's hard to imagine the career I've outlined was actually mine — it almost seems like I've been describing someone else's life, and a charmed one at that. What stands out in solid relief are the men like Coaches Jordan and Clark, who provided guidance and support through ups and downs and opened the doors of possibility to me. To all of them, I am boundlessly grateful.

Coach? I owe you a malt.

Mark Stillman

I was a highly-touted high school miler but was disappointing at Stanford. Payton was energetic, professional and believed in each one of us. But, I had used up much of my emotional drive by the time I won the California State high school mile championship.

1980

Gordon Banks

A native of South Central Los Angeles, Gordon grew up without his father, who died a month before his birth due to a work related accident. As an All-American in high school, he began taking the first steps toward fulfilling his childhood dream of playing pro football. While at Stanford University, he was a four-year letterman in both track and football, graduating with a 3.4 grade point average in political science. Upon graduation, his dreams were realized when he was signed by the New Orleans Saints as a wide receiver. He later became a popular wide receiver for the Oakland Invaders (USFL) and the Dallas Cowboys from 1980 through 1988 and was Chaplain for the Cowboys from 1989 through 1992. He was the only receiver in USFL history to catch a pass in every game! (54 straight)

Today, Gordon is a highly visible business and family man who is well respected among his peers and community at large. He has used his football experiences as a springboard to appeal to both young and old alike. As a motivational speaker, his appeal transcends all social, economic and racial barriers. He has spoken to many schools, conventions, major corporations, non-profit organizations and churches.

At the age of forty-five, this successful entrepreneur, television personality, and Associate Pastor of the 8,000 member Covenant Church in prominent North Dallas, has a reputation for having great wisdom and insight.

1981

Darrin Nelson

Athletics
- Long jumped 25 feet and ran 10.3 100m my first two years
- Track improved my speed for football between freshman and sophomore years
- Participated on school record 4x100 meter relay team
- Competed for Jordan two years; Brooks Johnson two years
- Made NCAA finals in 100m in 80.
- #1 draft pick by Minnesota Vikings in 1982; played for Vikings and Chargers until 92. "Running track definitely made the difference."
- Also worked for Piper, Jeffrey financial services during off seasons
- Currently an Assistant Athletic Director at Stanford

Stanford Track
Coach Jordan taught me how to run. I was very quick and had the potential to be very fast. After my freshman year of football I was instructed by Coach Walsh to run track. I was not allowed to participate in spring football. Turns out, Bill and Payton spoke and about half way through my freshman football season they decided I would run track. Coach Walsh assumed running track would help me in football in the long run; he was right.

I was long jumping at UCLA during my sophomore year. It was a great day and I jumped 25 feet plus on my first jump. Coach didn't think anyone could beat that distance, so he advised me to stop and concentrate on the 100 meters. I was undefeated at the time and was preparing to go up against some good UCLA sprinters. I was stubborn and decided to jump. On that next jump I ruptured a tendon in my leg. My track season and next football season were over. I recovered and was fine but my long jumping career was over. Coach Jordan, "Next time I'm listening to you."

1982

Robert Maiocco

High School
Freshman year - in my first meet I ran a 50.8 for the 440-yard dash. I was consistent in that range and ended up winning the California North Coast Section Frosh / Soph. 440 in 50.5 and finished the year undefeated.

Sophomore year - I qualified for the California State meet, but did not make it to the finals. In the summer I became the AAU National Champion (14 & 15 year olds) in the 440 by running a 48.89 in Xenia, Ohio. A couple of weeks prior to that, I placed 1st at the California AAU age group championships for both the 220 and 440.

Junior year - the first significant injury of what was to become an injury prone career occurred a couple of weeks before the state meet when I tore the tendon attachment to my plantaris. With muscle relaxants and ibuprophen, I was able to qualify for State, but did not make the finals. Later that summer I ran a 48.2 to take second at the AAU age group nationals. My best split for the year was 47.5.

Senior Year - the best run of my life occurred in late March of 1978 at the San Jose relays when I split a 46.6 (one watch even had me at 46.2). (My primary motivation for the run was to impress the then Joy Upshaw, who I think later married the Stanford football legend and track teammate Kenny Margerum). After running through a few minor injuries, I severely tore my hamstring during my final workout prior to the State meet.

Stanford
I only ran for Coach Jordan for one year, but what I remember most is his love for the sport and his dedication to training and discipline. I couldn't believe his foot speed...his turnover appeared as good as any sprinter's on our team, it was just that his stride was shorter...i.e., the reflexes and muscle twitch were still there, just the strength and elasticity had deteriorated.

Sophomore year - on a cold day at the Pac-10s in Washington I ran a personal best of 47.84 for the 400 meters but did not advance to the finals. I won the "Most Improved Award" and the "110% Award," neither of which was that difficult when you loved the sport, and were coming off an injury year.

Junior year - I was team co-captain and ran a couple of 800's for the first time. I also was on what was then a school record setting indoor Distance Medley relay. At a dual meet at Oregon or Oregon State, I ran around a 1:52 flat in the 800, which became my personal best.

Senior Year - again co-captain. Didn't do much...tore muscles in my calf while warming up at the Milrose Games at Madison Square Gardens (in late Feb. or early March), which negatively affected my outdoor season.

Post-Stanford
My first 15 post-Stanford years were spent getting an MBA, putting it to use, meeting and marrying someone who makes me extremely happy, and moving from city to city as we both pursued our careers. We have been in Florida now for about 7 ½ years and will probably stay longer as we have both passed up job opportunities that would have taken us elsewhere. Central Florida is not California, but we've gotten used to it.

We have one daughter, Claire, who is five years old. As usual, we believe that she is extremely cute, smart, and athletic. A year ago, she was diagnosed with Type 1 "Juvenile" Diabetes. As anyone with a child with health issues knows, this really causes one to look at life a little differently and to reassess one's priorities.

I've spent all of my career in finance of one sort or another. For the last seven plus years, I've been running my own small investment management firm that specializes in high quality, fixed income investments. Kathy currently is EVP of Sales and Marketing for Creditek.

Garry Schumway

Pre-Stanford
Growing up in Los Angeles, some of my earliest memories of track & field are the grainy television images of Coach Jordan's legendary 1968 Olympic squad. However, I did not really begin to catch the track bug until I was ten years old and my father took me to the 1971 USC-UCLA dual meet in Westwood. That meet was a battle of dual meet titans, where a USC squad led by Willie Deckard edged a UCLA team, featuring quarter milers John Smith and Wayne Collett.

I later attended prep school at Deerfield Academy in Massachusetts. After my baseball career came to an end due to arm problems in my junior year, I decided to try out for the track team. I competed in the sprints, jumps and hurdles, but my career took off senior year when the prep school league replaced the 180 low hurdles with the 330 intermediates. I won the New England Prep School Championship in the 330 IH (40.7), placed second in the 120 HH, fifth in the long jump, and ran a leg on the winning 4x110 relay team. Nevertheless, New England was hardly a track & field hotbed, so I was basically unrecruited. Although I was accepted at Dartmouth and Bowdoin, the urge to return to California was strong, and I was also curious to see if I just might be able to compete at the Pac-10 level. So, Stanford was my choice.

Stanford
When I arrived on campus in September of 1978, I stopped in to meet Coach Jordan. I was most impressed by the man, and he seemed genuinely excited that I wished to try

out as a walk on in the 400m hurdles. Of course, he failed to mention that my recruiting class (which was his last) already featured three strong 400 hurdlers, including (1) Kurt Roessler, an outstanding hurdler/jumper from Pennsylvania, (2) Greg Muhonen, an all-stater from Idaho, and (3) Sean Winterer, a high jumper from Australia who had put up some strong 400 IH times as a schoolboy.

I worked out with the team during the fall and winter and, in addition to the recruits listed above, I became friends with fellow freshmen Robert Maiocco (400/800), Gary Bruner (javelin/decathlon), John Schaer (800/1500), Art Varnado (400) and Rod Berry (distances), among others. I also came to know numerous upper classmen who were generous with their time, advice and friendship, including Clay Bullwinkel (triple jump), Harold Celms (steeplechase) and Dave Thomson (hammer/discus). At practice, the entertainment and competition levels increased dramatically once football season ended, as Gordon Banks, Rick Gervais, Darrin Nelson and Ken Margerum arrived. Each of these guys would become relay teammates and friends over the next few years. Also, James Lofton, then just one year out of school, returned to the track in the spring to work out with us, demonstrating a work ethic equal to his unparalleled talent level.

About one week before the first meet of the outdoor season, Coach Jordan arranged a time trial for Roessler, Muhonen, Winterer and me. I finished a comfortable third, and Coach informed me that I would be on the team for the first meet. My early performances were nothing special, but under Coach's tutelage I quickly improved. By mid-April, I had emerged as our top 400 hurdler, and I eventually set the frosh record for the 400IH (53.04). Moreover, after running a 48.3 relay split in my first ever 400m attempt, I became a fixture on the 4x400m relay for the next four years.

Coach Jordan retired at the end of my freshman year. I don't think there was any connection between my arrival and his departure. Anyhow, using the lessons that I learned from him, as well as his successor Brooks Johnson, I went on to have a reasonably successful track career, highlighted by stints as one of our team captains in 1981 and 1982, a ranking at graduation as Stanford's no. 4 (now no. 5) all-time 400 hurdler, and a semifinal birth in the 400IH at the TAC National Championships in 1984 (50.72 PR) while attending Stanford Law School.

Memorable Experiences
My most memorable experiences are not only the big races, but the moments with coaches and teammates on the practice track, working out, trading stories, telling jokes, and perfecting technique (or trying to). That said, a few experiences with Coach Jordan stand out:

1. Being informed by Coach that I was on the team following the time trial freshman year.

2. Attending my first Pac-10 Championship meet as a freshman, and being informed by Coach that due to injuries, I would run the lead-off leg on the 4x100m relay.

3. Seeing Coach absolutely DESTROY an outstanding senior 100m field at the California Relays in Modesto during the early 1980s.

Memorable Thing Coach Jordan Said to Me
I have vivid recollections of Coach Jordan exhorting each of us to "act like a champion" and "run like a champion," two things that he did unfailingly.

Post-Stanford
After college, I worked in Denver for a year before attending Stanford Law School. I received my law degree in 1986, and I then worked for a law firm in San Diego for the next five years.

I married my Stanford classmate Sarah (Cook) Shumway in 1987. In 1991, I landed an in-house counsel job with Aon Corporation in Chicago, so we packed up and moved to Winnetka, a town about 15 miles north of Chicago on Lake Michigan, where we remain today. We have two children. Kate, 13, is the athlete in the family. She plays soccer and is an excellent swimmer, and she is eager to get to high school so that she can join the track squad. Jack, 9, prefers Legos and video games. Both, in my unbiased opinion, are all-around great kids.

I continue to work at Aon, which is the second largest insurance brokerage operation in the world. In the last few years, I have moved out of the law department and into a series of executive jobs, most recently as Sr. VP of our reinsurance brokerage operation and Managing Director of our securities broker-dealer.

Coach Jordan's Influence
Although I only competed for Coach Jordan for one year before he retired, his influence has been lasting. He always set a great example with his demeanor, attitude and enthusiasm. But for me, the key to his personality was his ability to say something that would leave me feeling good, even after a trying race or practice.

A few years ago, I ran into Coach Jordan and his wife Marge in Chuck Taylor Grove during my reunion. I had not seen him in many years, but we had no trouble striking up a conversation in which we discussed our lives over the years, reminisced about old times and teammates, and looked forward to more reunions in the future. True to form, when we finally parted, I left with a great feeling, as I always did with the Ole Coach.

Deceased Teammates

Sadly, as we researched the Stanford Alumni Association directory for information on former teammates, we found a number now reported as deceased. They always will be part of "our" team, so we wish to recognize them, here.

Stanford Class	Name
1957	Fred Peters
1958	Warren Wood
1959	Dick Hughes
1960	Norm Lloyd
1960	Dean Smith
1961	Bob Atlkinson

1962	Jack Hunter
1963	Jack Scott
1964	Steve Cortright
1964	Jim Sisler
1964	Gary Walker
1965	Rick Scherer
1966	Jack Chapple
1969	Tom Kommers
1969	Rick Sturm
1970	Leonard Mogno
1970	Pete Still
1973	Melvin Ho
1976	Vernell Jackson
1977	Roger Greer
1977	Scott Wingo
1978	Jeff Norton
1980	Rick Buss
1981	Rich Raftery